Contemp

Edited by Justus Nieland and Jennifer Fay

The Contemporary Film Directors series provides concise, well-written introductions to directors from around the world and from every level of the film industry. Its chief aims are to broaden our awareness of important artists, to give serious critical attention to their work, and to illustrate the variety and vitality of contemporary cinema. Contributors to the series include an array of internationally respected critics and academics. Each volume contains an incisive critical commentary, an informative interview with the director, and a detailed filmography.

A list of books in the series
appears at the end of this book.

Emir Kusturica

Giorgio Bertellini

**UNIVERSITY
OF
ILLINOIS
PRESS**
URBANA,
CHICAGO,
AND
SPRINGFIELD

Frontispiece: Emir Kusturica in *Maradona by Kusturica* (2008). Courtesy of
Photofest.

Library of Congress Cataloging-in-Publication Data
Bertellini, Giorgio, 1967–
Emir Kusturica / by Giorgio Bertellini.
pages   cm — (Contemporary film directors)
Includes bibliographical references and index.
ISBN 978-0-252-03889-1 (hardback) —
ISBN 978-0-252-08044-9 (paperback) —
ISBN 978-0-252-09685-3 (e-book)
1. Kusturica, Emir—Criticism and interpretation. I. Title.
PN1998.3.K88B4525   2014
791.4302'33092—dc23   2014025160

For Argia and Giovanni

Contents

Acknowledgments | xi

THE ART OF A ROMANTIC TRICKSTER | 1

Dissention   13

Beginnings: A Yugoslav Auteur from Prague   13

Historical-Romantic Cinema   23

A Yugoslav in America   63

Disconnection   73

Once upon a Time There Was a Country   73

Dissonance   97

Cats and Birds   98

Super 8 Music   108

Life Is a Miracle—He Promises   114

Kindred Spirits   136

Bridges on the Balkans   143

INTERVIEWS WITH EMIR KUSTURICA:

A MONTAGE | 151

Filmography | 157

Bibliography | 167

Index | 177

Acknowledgments |

This volume grew out of earlier Italian editions, published by Editrice Il Castoro (Milan) first in 1996 and, in a revised and doubly expanded edition, in 2011. I wish to thank Renata Gorgani, Andreina Speciale, and Alessandro Zontini of Editrice Il Castoro for their work on those earlier editions and for agreeing, in cooperation with Daniel M. Nasset, on an English version for the University of Illinois Press and its Contemporary Film Directors series. I am very grateful to Daniel, for his feedback and for shepherding the book to completion; to James Naremore, Justus Nieland, and Jennifer Fay, for welcoming the volume into their series; and to Louis Kibler, for his tremendous help in preparing this monograph for the English-speaking reader.

My work on Kusturica results from long-standing debts to a number of scholars, journalists, librarians, festival organizers, and friends. I wish to thank Richard Peña, program director of the Film Society of Lincoln Center and the director of the New York Film Festival, for a fundamental course on Eastern European cinemas taught at New York University back in 1995 and for the discussions that followed; Nancy Friedland of Columbia University Libraries, then at NYU/Bobst Library, for teaching me how to get ahold of all sorts of materials preserved in U.S. libraries; Mark Thompson of Article 19 for his intense critical feedback; Steve Erickson and Pavle Levi for their precious suggestions and many passionate conversations. I also wish to thank Denise Breton, UGC Hachette, and the now-defunct CIBY 2000, particularly Huw Morgan, for sending me press kits and copies of the films discussed in earlier versions of this volume.

I received great help and support also from Italy. I thank my friend Tina Guiducci, who sent me hard-to-find materials; Antonio Maraldi, who mailed me a copy of his work on Kusturica; Sabino Martiradonna, for sharing the materials of the conference "Ti ricordi di Sarajevo?" (Do you remember Sarajevo?), held in Rome in the fall of 1993, in addition to press clippings that I had overlooked; and Gianfranco Miro Gori of *RiminiCinema*, for much critical information. Since the first Italian edition of this study, I have incurred numerous personal and scholarly debts, particularly with Pamela Ballinger, Herb Eagle, Victor Fanucchi, C. Paul Sellors, and, once again, Dina Iordanova and Pavle Levi. I wish to acknowledge their scholarly work and friendly suggestions: they have taught me new things and made me understand better what I thought I knew already. I am grateful to Cecilia Sayad for accepting my paper proposal on Kusturica for her panel on New Paradigms in Audiovisual Authorship at the 2013 Society for Cinema and Media Studies Conference, and her work on the subject. I am also indebted to Karla Mallette and Joshua H. Cole, in their role as past and present directors of the Center for European Studies at the University of Michigan, for inviting me to give a talk on Kusturica and thus for giving me an opportunity to test, and receive precious feedback on, my argument. The Center for European Studies also generously provided the funds for the purchase of the illustrations.

To write a book sometimes means to be lucky enough to find evidence in the most disparate places and receive help from colleagues and individuals one has never met. I am gratetul to Nicoletta Romeo of Alpe Adria Cinema (Trieste) for the promptness and kindness with which she has sent me the catalogs of the exhibitions on the Yugoslav Black Wave, held in 1998 and 1999; Phil Hallman, the film-studies field librarian at the University of Michigan, for locating DVDs from around the world; Aleksandar Saša Erdeljanović, of the National Film Archive of the Republic of Serbia (Jugoslovenska Kinoteka), for kindly answering my queries; Andrea Gambetta of Solares Fondazione delle Arti (Parma), for his willingness to share information on the making of *Super 8 Stories* and for various suggestions; Lorenzo Codelli for his support; and Matthieu Dhennin for his generosity in fielding my questions and for the extraordinary work he does with his Web site, kustu.com. I am particularly grateful to the superbly constructive feedback that I received from Daniel Goulding and, especially, Justus Nieland and Jennifer Fay. Their suggestions have improved tremendously my argument and my prose. Needless to say, I take full responsibility for the views expressed in this monograph. For permissions to reproduce sections of previously published interviews in the final section, I am grateful to Luisa Ceretto and Paola Cristalli (*Quaderni del Cinema* and *Cineteca di Bologna*), Matthieu Dhennin (kustu.com), Luisa Fava (*La Stampa*), Brenda Fernandes (*Sight and Sound*), Adriano Piccardi (*Cineforum*), and Christian Viviani (*Positif*).

For their patient observations on accents, as well as linguistic and cultural differences within the former Yugoslavia, I am grateful to Aleksandra Nikolić and, in particular, Romana Capek-Habeković, who with great affection keeps correcting my spelling and pronunciation of Serbo-Croatian names. A special thank you also to Marco Müller for his precious help early on. Lastly, I wish to thank my father, Enzo Bertellini, who for years has collected precious clippings from newspapers and periodicals, as well as Benedetta Bertellini, Pierluigi Ercole, Margherita Sacchi, and Gilberto Zacché, for their help, patience, and support. This volume is once again dedicated to Argia Lavagnini and Giovanni Cocconi, without whom I would not have started.

Emir Kusturica |

The Art of a Romantic Trickster |

Quand je pense à la Yougoslavie, c'est la Bosnie
qui est dans mon coeur.
—Emir Kusturica, "L'acacia de Saraevo"

The end of the cold war and of the dichotomous framework of East versus West radically altered the geopolitical landscape of Europe. This change resonated vigorously east of the Iron Curtain. Facing enormous institutional and civic challenges, former Communist regimes began to transition to democratic and quasi-democratic statehood, while cultural productions, including art and popular cinema, had to articulate new categories of aesthetic legitimacy and relevance.

Before 1989, several Eastern European filmmakers had gained fame and appreciation at home, abroad, and then back again at home, in the context of what in the West were known as New Waves. The expressions conveyed radical and self-reflexive poetic revisions in the context of a new aesthetic commitment. The application of the New Wave category to the East added an overt political dimension, one relying on ideas of opposition, freedom of expression, and personal vision, which often translated into anti-authoritarian dissidence—whether in the form of biting Czech humor, Polish moral commitment, or Hungarian artistic ambition. In the 1990s, as film production in Eastern Europe declined sharply, this aesthetic charter became obsolete. In the last two decades, not only have new kinds of films emerged, but their selective circulation in the West has also promoted a fresh critical platform. For instance, a whole new generation of filmmakers from Romania (Christi Puiu, Christian Mungiu, and Radu Muntean) and the Czech Republic (Jan Hrebejk, Jan Sverak, and David Ondricek) have become known for their uncompromising revisionist narratives and the blunt realism of their treatment of daily life, amid the vicious inertia of state corruption, new criminal violence, and the devastating effects of an imported neoliberal economy. If the cinema of the Second World had been characterized by acrobatic moves between ideological officialdom and personal expression—regularly admired and romanticized in the West by the likes of the *Cahiers du Cinéma, Sight and Sound,* and *Cineforum,* among others—post-1989 cinema in Eastern Europe has often revealed the emergence of a new palette of aesthetic colors, ranging from realist aesthetics to irreverent Balkan poetics, to cite two polar opposites. The same new palette implies different authorial positions.

If a poetics of realism often postulates the notion of the engaged author—namely, that of the responsible and visionary chronicler of modern social ills—the Balkan mantle is far more complicated and perhaps not easily, or solely, conducive to the idea of personal expression. It impinges upon notions of geopolitical and anthropological alterity that the West has endorsed and cultivated for decades before World War II (and even before the emergence of motion pictures) and that reemerged with dramatic and renewed cogency during the Balkan wars of the 1990s. Absorbed and processed within the Balkan borders, over the years such alterity has found translation into a range of (self-)othering audiovisual and narrative strategies whose radical and even experimental fabric has hovered over that of individual, spontaneous authorship.

Generationally and critically, Emir Kusturica (b. 1954) is the most renowned filmmaker associated both with the old cold war's divide and its post-1989 aftermath. His work emerged out of a context that proved to be resiliently unlike any other within the Eastern European bloc. For decades during the cold war, the Yugoslav Federation held a sort of progressive primacy in the eyes of eastern and western observers due to its peculiar history of anti-Stalinism and loose travel policy, unique among

Communist countries. In the 1990s, the Yugoslav exception turned horrific with the country's explosive disintegration, prompting the return of the term "balkanization" from the political vocabulary of the early twentieth century, and, most dramatically, with the campaigns of ethnic cleansing—unprecedented since World War II.

As one of few directors capable of thriving before and after 1989 (and between East and West), Kusturica appears to have adjusted his poetic pitch multiple times—from romantic revisionist to daring satirist and, finally, "obscene" and sentimental jester—just as critics on both sides of the Iron Curtain have felt compelled to reassess their judgment about his work. In reality, as this volume seeks to show, his productions and activities have revolved around a poetic core that, in a dialogue with pressing historical occurrences, has undergone an expansion in terms of public political engagement and intermedial reach without altering itself. His poetic imprints reveal what I would term an *untimeliness* or *unmodernity*—a penchant for characters eloquently out of sync and out of place with their native cultural environment and with western modernity, operating against the dogmas of historical determinism, and in intimate relationship with nature and themselves. Formally, Kusturica has articulated such poetics of existential dissidence and exile, beginning with his professional upbringing *away from home* at the FAMU film school in Prague, through a constant engagement with rather experimental, and originally subversive, aesthetic models, drawn from his reception of Hollywood and European art cinema, Yugoslav nihilistic filmmaking (Black or Novi cinema), and a distinctly Bosnian performative tradition that, while indebted to avant-garde practices, also pervaded popular music shows as well as radio and television broadcasting. The result has been a proclivity for provocative political revisionism, a resilient ambivalence toward western modernity, and a devotion to the condition of the cultural expatriate, infused with romanticism and Bakhtinian humor, but also a good dose of poetic solipsism.

Within this critical hypothesis, I would concede that history has certainly affected Kusturica's cinema and more broadly his multidimensional authorship in terms of thematic concerns and audiovisual approach—particularly in terms of his use of slapstick comedy, Balkan music, and surreal lyrics. Yet, I would also emphasize the productive critical stance of reading changes as stemming from, and thus readable through, his poetic imprint and not directly caused by historical occurrences. The result is that his oeuvre speaks to resilient questions of art and popular cinema in an epoch of massive geopolitical transitions and related critical recastings.

The obvious test of any broad interpretation of Kusturica's work is the controversial film *Underground* (1995), released during the Bosnian war. In the polarizing context of the Balkan conflicts, Kusturica's stunning and inflammatory take on Yugoslav history since World War II provoked a poisonous domestic and international controversy, particularly after the film received the Palme d'Or at the Cannes Film Festival. Infuriated detractors alleged that in its perverse historiographical interpretation, the film irresponsibly disconnected the cause of the recent Yugoslav wars from Slobodan Milosević's actual actions while shielding them underneath the critical discourse of "Balkanism." A well-known geopolitical and cultural concept, Balkanism consists of a deviously antihistorical intellectual tradition that before and after the cold war has projected violent instincts, primitivism, joie de vivre, and political irresponsibility onto the Balkan Peninsula and its populations.[1]

In very different ways, the film's boorish and hypereroticized protagonists, a manipulative Serbian and a big-hearted Montenegrin, continue to fight an imaginary Nazi occupation long after the end of World War II—indeed, until the end of the cold war. Marko, the Serbian, does so through vulgar propaganda while holding high office in the party. Blacky continues his fight while hiding underground from what he is led to believe is a prolonged and atrocious German occupation. What they share is a cartoonish and satirized anachronism, which points to the backward-looking foundations of Yugoslavia's post–World War II national ideology, which lasted for forty years until ethnic divisions erupted. Beyond diegetic illusions and manipulations, the film stirred intense divisions and controversies due to its treatment of Bosnians and Croatians and created an irreparable wedge between the director and his native Sarajevo.

I would argue that the trope of Balkanism, which explained the fascination and horror for the film's primitive violence and passions, may also apply to the rest of Kusturica's work. It may cast a light on his earlier films' appeal, in terms of their ethnic exoticism and Balkanic unmodernity, as well as on his later works and activities, as a conduit for his off-screen performances and engagement with geopolitical questions. Over the course of three decades, and in conjunction with dramatic historical changes, Kusturica's Balkanist poetics has undergone tonal changes, expanded its reach, and elicited very different types of reception. Yet, I would argue that it has changed more fate than form.

In this volume I thus divide Kusturica's career into three stages, which I term Dissention, Disconnection, and Dissonance. His unmodernity first appeared suggestive and inspirational as *subversive dissention* when associated with the fictional lives of defiant children and adolescents raised in Communist Yugoslavia (*Do You Remember Dolly Bell?* [1981]; *When Father Was Away on Business* [1985]), of unruly Gypsies attached to their myths and lifestyles (*Time of the Gypsies* [1989]), and of melancholy Americans refusing to grow up and at odds with the American dream (*Arizona Dream* [1992]). In the mid-1990s, with the release of *Underground* during the Yugoslav wars, the hard-to-presume innocence of the Balkanist untimeliness revealed to many an *obscene disconnection* from reality. Was the film a historical allegory, pointing to and unmasking the manipulations that were at the core of Yugoslav nationalism? Or was it skillful Serbian propaganda, operating through an overidentification with proud Balkan primitivism that supported the Serbian-as-Yugoslav political manipulations? In brief, was the film subversive of nationalism or deviously nationalistic? If with his previous works Kusturica had appeared as a skilled dissenter, for many with *Underground* he became a defector.

In the third, post-*Underground* phase of his film career, Kusturica has continued to show exceptional cinematic imagination, but he also has become many other things—musician and city planner, to name a few—mostly by fully embracing the dissonant poetics of *Homo Balkanicus*. This, in retrospect, has defied his own claim of having allegorically deployed a Balkanist aesthetic in *Underground* against his detractors' charge of overidentification with it. In his later productions he naturalizes his Balkanist poetics by presenting ethnicized narratives, musical motifs, and costumes as if their representation were situated outside any political sphere and perspective. He has begun what I would term a "Balkanist drift" by furthering two interrelated cinematic strategies already deployed in his earlier works: broad comedy and ethnic music. His post-1995 feature-length films, *Black Cat, White Cat* (1998), *Life*

Is a Miracle (2004), and *Promise Me This* (2007), as well as his shorter works *Super 8 Stories* (2001) and *Maradona by Kusturica* (2008), have made ample and irreverent use of slapstick humor and horseplay, including mockery and tricksterism, and a wide range of both original and rearranged Balkan songs. His films have continued to win awards but, with one exception, not the most prestigious ones. *Black Cat, White Cat* won, among other prizes, a Silver Lion at the Venice Film Festival, but his other films have not garnered awards comparable to the ones collected until the mid-1990s. Kusturica has expanded his presence in the media beyond film production, however: he has increased his acting roles, especially in Italian, Russian, and French films; he has entered into film production and city planning; and, most succesfully, he has begun a musical career as a performer and, at times, even a songwriter.[2]

The director's Balkan poetics has even assumed demiurgic traits. One of Kusturica's most important enterprises has been the planning and construction of a village known as Drvengrad (Wooden Village) or Küstendorf (Coastal Village), which was erected almost from nothing on the hills of Mokra Gora in Mećavnik, Western Serbia, near the border with Bosnia. The village emerged out of the set of *Life Is a Miracle*, which tells the story of an idealistic engineer who is building a railroad that will link Bosnia with Serbia and is often seen playing with a scale model of the local countryside that he obviously adores. As a brick-and-mortar reification of the film's fictional universe and, more broadly, of Kusturica's poetic stance, Küstendorf tells of an authorial expansion so conflating of art and life that in 2005, in a long profile in the *New York Times Magazine*, Kusturica described the village as "the best film he has ever made."[3] From Küstendorf have originated a series of holistic initiatives (preservation of artisanal, culinary, and musical traditions) and diverse manifestations with didactic and promotional aims, including a film school and an international film and music festival.

When read through Hans Georg Gadamer's notion of the "history of effects" (Wirkungsgeschichte), according to which the cultural density of the present determines the perception of past phenomena, these later developments may stimulate us to revise, without disproving, earlier readings of Kusturica's work.[4] Particularly cogent is the question of Kusturica's expanded authorship, beginning with his complex relationship with music and music performance, which paradoxically brings us back to the beginning, to the dissenting culture of 1980s Sarajevo.

Music, and sound in general, is not an addendum to Kusturica's film poetics and, more broadly, authorial cipher. Rather than mere accompaniment, music and music performances have informed the texture of the films themselves, and later they have extended the life of his cinema onto actual stages. As a continuation of his films by other, often more daring means, music has actually defined his poetics—locally, nationally (until Yugoslavia existed), and internationally, to the point that it is possible to tell the story of his career by focusing on the score he has chosen and the musicians that he has elected to surround himself with.

Up until *Underground,* Kusturica had collaborated with the Sarajevo-born musician Goran Bregović, the former leader of one of the most celebrated Yugoslav groups, the Bijelo Dugme (White Button), widely known for his unique talent in blending Bosnian ballads (*sevdah*) with Macedonian and Hungarian melodies, Gypsy music, and techno-rock. Popularized by Kusturica's films, a few of these songs became soccer anthems and thus acquired unyielding ethnic and national currency. After a public falling-out with Bregović in 1995, Kusturica became much more invested in the scoring of his films and joined the Belgrade-based band the No Smoking Orchestra (originally from Sarajevo) as a guitarist. Not only has Kusturica worked with the No Smoking Orchestra on the soundtrack of all his post-1995 films, he has led the band on world tours (*Side Effects* in 1999; *Collateral Damages* in 2000; *Life Is a Miracle Tour* in 2004) and played in more than a hundred concerts, which he later documented in the film *Super 8 Stories* and in the DVD *Live Is a Miracle in Buenos Aires* (2005). In 2007 he staged the opera *Time of the Gypsies* at the Opéra Bastille in Paris, with the No Smoking Orchestra providing the music.

His affiliation with the No Smoking Orchestra has affected his poetics and revealed *ex post facto* the appeal of his earlier films. The fact that the band achieved a most visible prominence in his cinema after *Underground* should not be taken as a sign of a later influence. Kusturica's poetics of unmodernity and untimeliness is markedly indebted to a group of vanguard artists called New Primitives from which the No Smoking Orchestra originated.

After the death of Tito in 1980, certain sectors of the Bosnian youth culture developed a poetics of ironic rebellion, alteratively juvenile and eloquent; they also adopted a primitivism of customs and street language as a preferred performative strategy. All this was done in an inventive way, mixing familiar avant-garde experimentations with the multicultural localism of Sarajevo and the Bosnian dialect (both of which had for decades been regarded in Yugoslavia as signs of backwardness and provincialism), used as a vehicle of Balkan irreverence. From this environment emerged a movement of artists, playwrights, singers, performers, and musicians known as the New Primitives (also spelled "Primitivs"). Initially interested in experimental narration and in a derisory automystification through rock music, the "primitives" also turned to poetry and to video art. The New Primitives and Kusturica shared the same artistic sensibility. The youthful, anti-ideological, and rock-music rebellion of *Do You Remember Dolly Bell?* became a sort of manifesto of this Sarajevan climate, but it also and quickly spread to all of Yugoslavia. For years it defined Kusturica's national popularity within the boundaries of the former Yugoslavia.

A constant point of reference of the New Primitives was a cult radio program broadcast from Sarajevo in the early 1980s called *The Surrealists' Top Chart* (*Top lista nadrealista*), which later became a television variety show—a kind of Yugoslav response to the American *Saturday Night Live*. What is striking today about this show, local in its cultural resonances but national in its popularity, is the fact that the regime did not suppress it right away, as it did with so many other groups considered subversive. Recently, Pavle Levi has lucidly explained that the insubordination and the sarcastic surrealism of the program's authors and of their fans were not necessarily ideological or anticommunist in content: their rebellion was formal, libertarian, and anti-institutional.[5] The program derided the jargon and action of power through an impudently Balkan taste for paradox and irrationality. The transition from the Communist regime to an ultranationalist one did not cause this surrealist inclination to disappear; instead, it mixed its budding anticonformist subversion with the excesses of ethnic pride.

One of the most striking examples of primitivism's continuity between the Communist and nationalistic period is the destiny of Sarajevo's cult musical group, ironically named Zabranjeno Pušenje (No Smoking), whose members played a key role in *The Surrealists' Top Chart*. Founded by one of Kusturica's childhood friends, the explosive Nenad Janković, also known as "Doktor Nele Karajlić," Zabranjeno Pušenje achieved great fame in the 1980s because of its irreverence toward local and national customs. In the mid-1990s the Bosnian conflict caused the band to split up: one group kept the name Zabranjeno Pušenje and moved to Zagreb before returning to Sarajevo, but it never progressed beyond regional fame. The other group, based in Belgrade, was renamed the No Smoking Orchestra by Janković and added a now-permanent member, Kusturica, who had already collaborated with the band in the late 1980s by co-authoring songs and joining them on stage. The addition of Kusturica's famous name to the band launched the group on international stages and circuits.

From the beginning, the group maintained strong ties with the real world, given that one of its distinctive traits was the demystification of the shibboleths of Communist ideology, but also with cinema's fictional universe, particularly with the veritable national genre of the partisan film. It should come as no surprise that the Bosnian New Primitives singled out one of the regime's most iconic partisan films as the chief target for their satire: *Walter Defends Sarajevo* (*Valter brani Sarajevo*, 1972), by Hajrudin Krvavac—a close friend of Kusturica's father and the director's early mentor. Intertwining personal experiences with poetic inclinations, the New Primitives turned the film's narrative determinism and ideological excesses into subversive *jouissance* and facile caricature. The first album of the original Zabranjeno Pušenje came out in 1981 (the same year as *Do You Remember Dolly Bell?*) with the title *This Is Walter* (*Das ist Walter*), after the protagonist of Krvavac's film.

The links between cinema and the band's music intensify when Kusturica joins them in concert. Regularly introduced by the Soviet national anthem, the shows of the No Smoking Orchestra cum Kusturica are spectacles of unruly dissonance and exotic backwardness, featuring nostalgic Yugoslav tunes, melodic homages to Spaghetti Western films, and Gypsy ballads with English lyrics extolling a proud Balkan unmodernity and a performative overidentification with violence. This effect recalls the strategies of other Yugoslav avant-garde practices from the 1980s, particularly the Slovenian experimental art collective known as Neue Slowenische Kunst, because of the complicated history of Slovenia with Austrian and German culture. Like its affiliated punk-rock band Laibach (the name for Nazi-occupied Ljubljana), Neue Slowenische Kunst targeted the ideology of past and present totalitarian regimes through a provocative overidentification with their rituals, slogans, and idioms—a tactic that also informed the workings of *Underground*.

Different from other film directors who have written scores for their own films (such as Charlie Chaplin or Clint Eastwood), Kusturica has expanded the notion of film authorship through his public role as a musician and his skills in using his concerts to promote his films (and vice versa). Ultimately, Emir Kusturica's self-reflexive and intermedial career trajectory raises timely questions of protean authorial status, from committed Second World visionary to master of media ceremonies regularly on world tours that celebrate an intra-European primitive difference for eastern and western audiences alike.

This volume seeks to untangle these various dimensions of his work (influence from foreign and national cinemas, Balkanism, music and experimental performances) and reconstruct their intertwining. As such, it has greatly benefited but also differs from two of the most productive monographs on Kusturica's work, Goran Gocić's and Dina Iordanova's, which appeared in 2001 and 2002, respectively. Written still in the shadow of earlier controversies and only a few years after his first post-*Underground* film, these works could not account for the latest on- and off-screen expansions of his authorship and their critical effects on earlier works.[6] The Kusturica that emerges from their profiles is largely that of a film auteur. Gocić astutely privileges a reading of his work as a postmodern champion of "ethno and Third Worldism," with a corollary of foreseeable effects (and western projections), ranging from nostalgia, intertextuality, openness, and antidogmatism, to eclecticism. In his assessment of Kusturica's antihegemonic stance against communism, fascism, capitalism, and other sinister conformisms, Gocić identifies a wealth of cinematic references that the filmmaker edits with the skill of a bricoleur enamoured of Balkanist (and Nietzschean) jouissance. While Gocić recognizes the traumatic effect of *Underground* in the context of Kusturica's aesthetic continuities, he cannot bestow sufficient critical weight to the filmmaker's thenstill-underdeveloped music career, nor to his New Primitive imprint of experimental irreverence and dissention.

In her work, Iordanova has extensively addressed the issue of film authorship in the context of Eastern Europe by adopting the critical notion of Balkanism as a set of recurring themes and stylistic registers that unify authors of very different national and cultural backgrounds. In her treatment of Kusturica's "artistry," she has detailed narrative and cinematic traits (such as camera work, light, color, and music) and a staggering range of cinematic references (Yugoslav, European, and American). Given the period of her writing, however, she too could not elevate Kusturica's music performances to the level of key onscreen (and off-screen) poetic determinants. Still, her analysis, when making explicit reference to Jean-François Lyotard's *Postmodern Condition* (1979), has identified a poetic stance that one could adopt for avant-garde or performance artists. Kusturica, she writes, "defies prescribed procedures for the sake of an increased 'being and jubilation,' and for the sake of exchanging energy with his audiences."[7] Even though the strategy of unsettling audiences with experiences of transporting enjoyment gets superseded in her analysis by the broader cultural trope of Balkanism, it is indicative that Iordanova detected it as a somewhat shaping trope.

Differently from Iordanova's and Gocić's approaches, and with the advantage of writing more than a decade later, I find that the issues of audiovisual jouissance, Balkanism, and antidogmatism ought to be viewed *together* to grasp the different forms and destinies of his expanded authorship. And to do so, one must reconnect the present to the origins, to all the earlier strains of his poetic trajectory. Namely, one must begin with the fact that Kusturica debuted as a specific kind of "Yugoslav film *auteur*" and, specifically, as a Sarajevo-born filmmaker trained in Prague.

Kusturica has never hidden his debt to the directors who received their training at FAMU, the prestigious film school based in the Bohemian capital, and who preceded him there by less than a decade. It is not by chance that his first and most faithful collaborators, from the composer Zoran Simjanović to his director of photography Vilko Filač (who died at an untimely young age in 2008) have worked constantly with the "Praguists" and were even, in the case of Filač, older classmates. Moreover, the stories that Kusturica has told so successfully hark back to a poetic atmosphere halfway between a realistic dimension (youthful, political, and historical) and a fantastic one (ludic and magical at one and the same time) without ever becoming *purely* surreal. It was his exposure to the Czech absurdist and sarcastic humor that provided him with an antidote against the bleaker and more nihilistic confrontations of the Yugoslav Black Cinema of the 1960s and fed his attraction for the New Primitives' entertainment talent.

As for his card-carrying Yugoslavism, while it was both natural and expected at the beginning of his career, with *Underground* it became a choice, and a controversial one at that. Until then, Kusturica was able to proclaim his professional loyalty to a group of collaborators few in number but coming from the entire former national territory (the director of photography was Slovenian, the set designer Croatian, the writers Bosnian and Serbs, the musicians Serbs from Sarajevo). As I have often been reminded, these ethnic distinctions had no dramatic meaning in the 1980s, the period of Kusturica's artistic coming of age. After 1995, however, his repeated declarations of Yugoslavism seem filled with a perverse innocence and nostalgia, especially because they echo the recriminations of a single ethnic group that once was dominant.

Today, whether explicitly or not, when Kusturica says that he has remained a "Yugoslav auteur," he is referring polemically to a disruption—the war—rather than to a continuous biographical and cultural bond to a nation that no longer exists. His Yugoslavism today seems like the driving force of a poetics of exile, a "Balkan" poetics, in the increasingly westernized international psyche. If the risk of this exilic position is a tendency toward a pure aestheticizing nostalgia somewhat akin to the current shabby merchandising of Soviet uniforms and gadgets to be found in Prague, the antidote is an attachment to a real or a re-created Sarajevo. Multiethnic and cosmopolitan more than any other city in the former Yugoslavia, the Bosnian capital was and remains for Kusturica the most deep-rooted geographic and cultural matrix, the most credible source of inspiration for family and political dramas both microhistorical and national.

For Kusturica, Sarajevo is ultimately an inescapable narrative, visual, and musical cosmogony, even, or perhaps especially, after his professional and political exile. After all, the city never disappeared from the director's aesthetics nor even from his personal life—his project of creating a village all his own, Küstendorf, was publicly described as the reconstruction (and restitution) of his lost native city. The magic of Sarajevo runs through many of Kusturica's recent films: it is visible in the biographical and aesthetic origins of the musicians in the orchestra, as language, humor, or poetic reference, whether diegetically mentioned or not. In *Life Is a Miracle,* for example, the mayor looks into the camera and with a sort of nostalgic irony describes Sarajevo as "a magical city." This remains true even though in his recently published autobiography, *Smrt je neprovjerena glasina* (Death is an unverified rumor), which remains untranslated into English, the director has stated that the only time he dreamed about Sarajevo, it was in a nightmare.[8] Furthermore, if we consider the fact that Kusturica's characters have never ceased hovering above the earth like Chagallian figures, we cannot help but call to mind the soothing and sad verses of the Bosnian writer Dževad Karahasan (he, too, in exile). In his beautiful *Sarajevo, Exodus of a City* (1993), Karahasan imagines the entire city rising and moving off: "Behind lowered eyelashes I saw Sarajevo, so much ruined and so much loved—loved as never before—rising up from the earth, taking off and flying away, somewhere beyond, where everything is gentle and tranquil."[9]

And it is in Sarajevo that Kusturica's story began.

Dissention

Beginnings: A Yugoslav Auteur from Prague

Emir Kusturica was born in Sarajevo in 1954, the only child of a family whose ancestral origins were Serbian but who had converted to Islam during the Turkish domination of Bosnia. Although his paternal grandfather was deeply religious, the future director grew up under the influence of his father, Murat, a confirmed atheist and socialist who spoke good English, loved Russian songs, and had served as a partisan with Tito before becoming head of the Secretary of Information for the Socialist Republic of Bosnia and Herzegovina. Kusturica often described his father as akin to character out of a Čechov novella, enamored of looking at politics and history from the perspective of the ordinary man.

Growing up in Gorica on the outskirts of Sarajevo, Kusturica experienced an almost Felliniesque childhood among the many *haustorćad,* his friends in the courtyards and corridors of his apartment building—the communal histories, lots of soccer, frequent fights, and the smells of the Muslim festival Bairam.

Before his 2011 autobiography, which has appeared in Serbian (*Smrt je neprovjerena glasina*, French (*Où suis-je dans cette histoire?*), Italian (*Dove sono in questa storia*), and other languages, there was only scant information on the adolescent Kusturica. We now know that he had no special talents, marked inclinations, or ambitions except for a great attraction to Gorica's lively street life, the *jalija*. Luckily for him, his family's pressures and connections prevented him from losing himself in his friends' juvenile adventures or their friends' less-than-honest enterprises. A facile comparison with a figure like Martin Scorsese does not work well: on the small side and nonviolent, the young Scorsese defended himself from the Lower East Side gangs of Manhattan by telling funny stories and by developing a narrative vocation at an early age. By contrast, the young and tall Bosnian was a keen observer of and an active participant in his buddies' neighborhood exploits without being inclined either to initiate or to further them to dangerous ends. The only common denominator with the American director is perhaps the emotional sensitivity that they share, which in Kusturica's case became a poetic advantage and, for some, a political liability.

Despite past interviews in which he declared that he discovered the cinema rather late, Kusturica has peppered his autobiography with frequent references to the influential films he watched while growing up, from Charlie Chaplin's *The Great Dictator* (1940) and Jean Vigo's *L'Atalante* (1934) to Jean Negulescu's *Titanic* (1953) and Alfred Hitchcock's *The Birds* (1963). Personal circumstances were also favorable. A regular presence in his home life was the film director Hajrudin "Šiba" Krvavac, one of his father's closest friends, whom Kusturica describes in his autobiography as "Uncle Šiba." It was Krvavac who, by way of frequent metaphors that mixed filmmaking and romantic life, instilled in the young Kusturica the notion that he too could be a filmmaker. His were not just words of encouragement; Krvavac offered him a tiny speaking part in his *Walter Defends Sarajevo* (*Valter brani Sarajevo*, 1972), the popular partisan film that told the story of Tito's wartime battles (Walter was one of Tito's *noms de guerre*). It was a brief but decisive film experience.

When Kusturica saw in the window of a shop in Sarajevo that year what in his autobiography he describes as a photographic camera, a Russian Zorki model, he begged his parents to buy it for him. Uncle Šiba mediated the purchase, since the camera belonged to one of his assistant cameramen, a certain Uherka. The still camera signaled the beginning of his film career. Soon, he had written a script, complete with photographs of many scenes, and showed to Krvavac. He then persuaded Uherka to serve as cameramen for his first amateur film: it would become *Part of the Truth* (*Dio istine*, 1972). Taking its inspiration from a story by Ivo Andrić, the film focuses on a day in the life of a Sarajevo man who wakes up one morning to the sound of bells coming from three different places of worship: a Roman Catholic church, a Serbian Christian one, and a mosque. The man whiles away his day in bars, daydreaming of an ideal life. Then he notices a woman going into the stage door of a theater: she is a dancer. He follows her and falls madly in love. She is the sister of one of his old classmates. When the classmate learns about his feeling for his sister, a fight erupts.

Years later, Kusturica would dismiss it, together with his second film, *Autumn* (*Jesen,* 1972), as "a very superficial social drama."[10] Still, *Part of the Truth* was a formative experience, poetically and practically. It was extremely important for him as "an exercise of 'how close and how far,'" as he put it in the same interview, with reference to the themes of proximity and distance. The film also represented a necessary passage because, while shot basically at home, it taught Kusturica to impose his ideas against his cameraman and whoever felt the need to offer advice. As for learning the taste of success, the film eventually won the first prize at the Amateur Film Festival of Zenica (Bosnia).

Kusturica often likes to recall that after he finished secondary school, his father urged him to lay plans for his future. Had he stayed in Sarajevo, he would have probably had a career as a small-time criminal, since his ambitions as as footballer were dashed early on by a bad ankle injury. Still, as he has often acknowledged, a familiarity with a world of Gypsies and small-time outlaws turned out to be a major personal and professional resource. The opportunity to leave his corner in Sarajevo came from thinking outside the box, beyond the limiting borders not only of his native city but also of the former Yugoslavia. Once more his extended family was instrumental. His father's sister, Biba Kusturica, enabled the young Emir to experience life outside Sarajevo. In 1963 he traveled for the first time outside the former Yugoslavia, while visiting her in Warsaw. She was living there with her second husband, who worked as a foreign correspondent for Tanjug (the "Telegraphic Agency of New Yugoslavia"). A decade later, again with the help of his Aunt Biba (who had moved with her husband to the former Czechoslovakia), and with financial aid from his family, he enrolled in the Film and TV School (FAMU) of Prague's prestigious Academy of Performing Arts. On his way to Prague for his oral examination, he was accompanied by three family figures: his father, Uncle Omerica, and Krvavac.

FAMU was a special place: masters such as Otakar Vávra and Jiří Menzel were working there, while influential former teachers included Ivan Passer, Miloš Forman, and even Milan Kundera, who taught at FAMU from 1958 until the Soviet invasion of 1968. Several generations of Yugoslav directors had studied cinema in Prague before and during Kusturica's time there. The Bohemian capital offered indisputable opportunities not only because of the high quality of its technical preparation (unavailable in the former Yugoslavia), but also for the possibility of professional exchanges with other Eastern European directors young and old, including many from other Yugoslav republics. In addition, the demonstrations in Prague's streets a few years earlier were poetically stimulating to authors and artists attracted by socialism's promise of justice and equality, but terrified—and awakened—by the images of Soviet tanks parading in Wenceslas Square.

In this highly politicized and cinematically dynamic atmosphere, Kusturica completed his education under the guidance of Otakar Vávra and in the wake of several young Yugoslav *cinéastes* only a few years his senior and already of some notoriety. Indeed, as early as 1976, the year of the twenty-sixth Pula Film Festival, critics had somewhat begun to identify them as the new representatives of the young Yugoslav cinema. Shortly after, a range of shared biographical and poetic traits came into focus and soon appeared to link such different works as Goran Marković's *Special Education (Specijalno vaspitanje,* 1977), Rajko Grlić's *Whichever Way the Ball Bounces (Kud puklo da puklo,* 1974), Goran Paskaljević's *Beach Guard in Winter (Čuvar plaže u zimskom periodu,* 1976) and *The Dog That Liked Trains (Pas koji je voleo vozove,* 1977), Srđan Karanović's

Fragrance of Wild Flowers (*Miris poljskog cveća,* 1977), and Lordan Zafranović's *Chronicle of a Crime* (*Kronika jednog zločina,* 1973) and *Occupation in 26 Pictures* (*Okupacija u 26 slika,* 1978). For one, this group of filmmakers had all been educated at FAMU around the time of the turbulent Prague Spring: they became known as the Prague Group. Secondly, they were creating simple films that the general public could understand and that were far removed from the obscure thematic and formal sarcasm of the intense Yugoslav cinema of the sixties.

To understand these relationships, it is useful to recall that the production structure of Yugoslav cinema—like that of other media (radio, the press, and television)—was split among the six former republics (Slovenia, Croatia, Bosnia and Herzegovina, Serbia, Macedonia, and Montenegro). Even though they were controlled by the central League of Communists of Yugoslavia, which determined programs of national interest and distribution (news, propaganda, sports), individual entities could still maintain some degree of control over cultural programs and other productions. The same was true of the cinema, with one important difference: the language and culture of the medium often allowed for initiatives of extraregional and even extranational character.

At the beginning, in the 1960s, Yugoslav cinema as a whole developed narratives of protest and subversion comparable to the kind of stories produced in the West. Yet, each republic contributed to this overall trajectory with its own artistic style and inclinations. In particular, 1960–61 was a season of sudden and extraordinary breaks from the poetic conformity of past productions that regularly glorified the figure of the patriotic partisan. Several excellent works gained wider visibility. From 1962 on, after the presentation at Cannes of Aleksandar Petrović's *And Love Has Vanished* (*Dvoje,* 1961), western critics began to look closely at a group of other Yugoslav films of the period, all from 1961, and hail them as representative of a new era: Bostjian Hladnik's *Dancing in the Rain* (*Ples v dezju*), Veljko Bulajić's *Boom Town* (*Uzavreli grad*), Ante Babaja's *The King's New Clothes* (*Carevo novo ruho*), and Mladomir "Purisa" Djordjević's *The First Citizen of the Small Town* (*Prvi gradjanin male varosi*).

The first coherent and recognizable movement of a new Yugoslav cinematic poetics was christened "Black Cinema" or "Novi Cinema" (literally, "new cinema"), because its novel, dark satirical and surrealistic tones subverted and demythologized traditional narratives and film poetics. Against empty and worn-out ideological proclamations, its antidogmatic directors explored unusual stories and dramas centering on individuals no longer captivated by socialism, nor by the patriarchal jargon of the so-called founding partisans. Black Cinema introduced, for the first time in Yugoslav cinema, an aesthetic that was ideologically ungrateful, pervaded by an ironic and excessive nihilism. No democratic and libertarian hero was to replace the shopworn nationalist hero. In his place instead were morally ambiguous and solipsistic figures, inept and apathetic. For Tito's cultural functionaries, this trend could only appear destabilizing and decadent. After all, these "black auteurs" had proclaimed the obsolescence of the partisan-national genre—that is, of the historico-mythic legitimacy of power so essential to Tito's internal propaganda.

Authors of these disturbing first full-length films were former amateur and experimental filmmakers, including Dušan Makavejev, Bostjian Hladnik, Živojin Pavlović, and Lordan Zafranović, who came from the creative and autarchical experiences of Belgrade, Zagreb, and Ljubljana;[11] provocative documentary filmmakers from the Serbian or Croatian contexts, including Aleksandar Petrović, Purisa Djordjević, and Ante Babaja; and "oneiric" animation directors, including Dušan Vukotić and Vatroslav Mimica, who worked at the Zagreb School, the widely admired Croatian animation film studio established in the mid-1950s. The ideological and cultural break with the past (and the resulting attack on the political foundation of the present) was embodied in a poetic gesture as noble as it was isolated. Most of the Yugoslav public did not appreciate their daring and uncompromising approach, a striking contrast with the warm reception reserved a few years later for the exponents of the Prague Group. A generation younger than the members of the Black Wave, the FAMU-trained Marković, Paskaljević, and Zafranović, among others, wisely maintained a middle road between the social realism familiar to the average filmgoer and the satirical and imaginative freedom admired in the older, aforementioned directors. The result was a series of exhilarating and romantic comedies as well as so-called naturalist melodramas that succeeded in establishing with the Yugoslav public, which had for years been somewhat indifferent toward its national cinema, a rapport based on ironic and critical complicity. In the works of the filmmakers of the Prague Group, everything was carried off with technical professionalism and an easy-to-grasp, realistic narrative rhythm. Significantly, however, they did not sacrifice the ironic and radical properties of Black Wave experimentalism. The Prague Group's commercial success gave rise to various trends and tendencies, among which were popular comedies in the style of Mića Milošević, bizarre imitations of film noir or American road movies, and even softcore pornography. The poetics of the early Kusturica, in fact, belongs in part to this current of popular entertainment. As critics have pointed out, it is not by chance that two of the main actors of *Do You Remember Dolly Bell?*—Slavko Štimac (Dino) and Pavle Vujisić (the grandfather)—bore increasingly heavy acting loads in the innumerable Serbian comedies of those years.

Although he was not biographically part of it, many consider Kusturica to be the last representative of the Prague Group because of his prized combination of formal irreverence, comedy, and romanticism. The only Bosnian in the Prague company, his critical and popular international reputation quickly made him a rising, and increasingly isolated, figure.

His critical successes came quickly. As part of the graduation requirements at FAMU, Kusturica adapted a Gogolian story by Anton Isaković into the short film *Guernica* (1978). The story had already inspired Petrović's masterpiece *Three* (*Tri*, 1965). Kusturica's twenty-five-minute entry carried off the top prize as the best student film at the 1978 Karlovy Vary International Film Festival in the former Czechoslovakia.

Set in Paris during the Nazi regime (although some critics maintain that the action takes place in 1941 in an unidentified village in Central Europe), *Guernica* tells the story of a Jewish boy whose parents have told him that the authorities intend to determine the family's racial identity on the basis of an anthropological examination. Performed by the local doctor, the examination focuses on measuring "typical" physical traits—especially the length of the nose. Concerned, the boy begins to cut out all the pictures of noses from the family's photo albums, reassembling them in a collage that recalls Picasso's *Guernica,* a reproduction of which he had seen for the first time with his father. At the end of the film he changes his mind and tries to put everything back in place, thus accepting the political reality and the allegedly suspect outer signs, including the most offensive ones, of his identity. When looking backward, Kusturica has not restricted his fascination with noses to *Guernica*'s main character. The same fixation reappears in the mimetic acts of one of the protagonists of *Underground,* and it was to be part of the aborted project *The Nose,* which, based on an idea of Dušan Kovačević, focused on the life of a stage actor who plays the role of Cyrano de Bergerac and who comes up against New York's Russian Mafia.

After receiving his diploma, Kusturica returned to Sarajevo, where he had no immediate prospects for making films. The production situation in Bosnia was precarious, far worse than in the other Yugoslav republics. He began to work in television, where he acquired an apprenticeship that proved quite useful later on, particularly since a few of his works were eventually expanded and edited as television series. His first production was a stylistically daring TV movie, *The Brides Are Coming* (*Nevjeste dolaze,* 1978), based on a controversial script by Ivica Matić, a much-admired young auteur who died shortly after directing his iconic film, *Woman with a Landscape* (*Zena s krasolikon,* 1975). *The Brides Are Coming* focused on many delicate and controversial themes, from incest to sexual violence. Many critical sources claim that *The Brides Are Coming* was censored and never shown on television; others maintain that it was exhibited in a movie theater in Sarajevo.

The film recounts the story of a strange family consisting of a mother, her two sons, and the wife of one of them who run an isolated bar-restaurant in the mountains surrounding Sarajevo. The establishment is called "Jelena's" (Gostiona Jelena), after the dominant and controlling mother who sleeps with the younger son and incites the older one to beat his wife because, in her view, she has failed to give him an heir. When the young woman dies, her place is taken by a newcomer, and although things initially seem to change for the better, in reality nothing does: the mother intrudes into the bed of the new couple, sleeping right between them. When Jelena urges the new bride to sing "Parlami d'amore, Mariù" (Speak to me of love, Maria), the song that popularized Mario Camerini's *Gli uomini che mascalzoni!* (What scoundrels men are!, 1932), the customers sing along until one of them tries to rape the young woman. The husband intervenes, but he is killed. The day after, the new bride-turned-widow escapes alone from the inn; after a long walk in the countryside, she comes upon the younger son, also on the run, and joins her destiny to his.

Constructed as a synthesis of Greek tragedies, *The Brides Are Coming* constitutes an important stage in Kusturica's poetics: it initiates themes and formal choices that will reappear in future years: the figures of dominating matriarchal characters and vulnerable wives, the pressing role of family and clan factors in provoking violence and exile, the repetition of convivial scenes that are filled with hidden tensions, and the dramatic relation of characters to a landscape that is both admired and feared. The repeated stylistic traits include the spatial tension between the high and the low present in the shifting positions of the bar's sign, the tendency to create framing effects by filming through doorways and windows, the many slow, Tarkovskian panoramic shots, and the inclusion of music as both counterpoint and intensifying force. Kusturica's use of an exotic Italian melody, associated with a famous film, recalls the orchestration of the Italian partisan song "Bella ciao" in Hajrudin Krvavac's *Savage Bridge* (*Most*, 1969) and anticipates Kusturica's later adoption of this strategy in his feature-length films, beginning with *Dolly Bell*. Other filmmakers used it too: Ademir Kenović's 1989 *Kuduz,* for example, uses Bobby Solo's popular 1964 hit "Una lacrima sul viso" (A tear on your face). In addition to a cameo by the director in the role of a supplier to the inn, the film also includes many shots of solitary fishes in fishbowls, a foreshadowing of future ichthyic references, mostly in *Arizona Dream. The Brides Are Coming* marked also the beginning of a long-standing collaboration between Kusturica and the Slovenian cinematographer Vilko Filač, whom he met at the student dorms at FAMU—a collaboration that lasted until *Underground.*

The following year, Kusturica directed *Buffet Titanic* (*Bife "Titanic,"* 1979), adapting Ivo Andrić's eponymous 1950 novel in collaboration with the Czech screenwriter Ján Beran. The TV movie tells the story of two characters who lead a solitary and exilic life: Mento Papo, an atheistic Sephardic Jew who runs the bar of the title, is obsessed with the famous transatlantic liner and rejected by the local Jewish community for his drinking habits; and the drifter Stjepan, the exceedingly shy son of an abusive Muslim bourgeois, who is constantly bullied by strangers. When news of Nazi Germany's military invasion reaches the city, Stjepan becomes an Ustasha, a Nazi collaborator, whose mandate is to kill Mento. While most of the film is in black and white, the scenes of

Stjepan in uniform interrogating and then shooting Mento are in color, as they reveal the yellow Star of David on the Jewish man's shirt. The film ends with Mento dying in a dreamy ecstasy as he imagines himself to be aboard the sinking *Titanic*.

For its focus on real and symbolic encounters between people of diverse ethnic backgrounds who share similar fates of racism and exile, critics hailed *Buffet Titanic* as a courageous work, awarding it the first prize at the Yugoslav Television Film Festival in Portorož (Slovenia). Others have stressed its foreshadowing of the poetics of the director, ever attentive to the process of human development (or regression) from adolescence to adulthood, and to Andrić's familiar geopolitical analysis. For Kusturica's literary hero, in fact, it is often the pressure of outside forces that fosters nationalism, ethnic hatred, and local fights in the Balkan Peninsula. Other, less admiring critics have discerned in the film the first emergence of an anti-Croatian dimension that would reappear in *Underground*.

In addition to recurring themes, the hypothesis of a continuity in Kusturica's oeuvre pertains also to visual strategies, from the inclusion in his mise-en-scène of highly symbolic objects (religious icons, naïve artwork, signs, and illustrations) and the use of windows, grillwork, and thresholds to frame his images to a predilection for 360-degree panoramic shots. From a thematic viewpoint, in addition to concerns about racial conflicts and their irrational causes, early on Kusturica showed a tendency to end his films with images of characters either departing for a journey or just wandering, even with their imagination, seeking to separate themselves from past relationships and achieve a new sense of freedom.

The critical literature on these films is rather limited, however. For years *Guernica, The Brides Are Coming,* and *Buffet Titanic* were unavailable or accessible only in the former Yugoslavia on a limited basis. After the release of *Underground,* however, the director himself tried to promote their distribution, particularly in Italy. Between the end of 1998 and the summer of 1999, a touring retrospective brought his early films to a dozen Italian cities. Provided with a tongue-in-cheek Balkanized title (*Emir Kusturica: Visioni gitane di un acrobata/Gypsy Visions of an Acrobat*) and together with a photographic exhibition ("From the Sets of *Underground* and *Black Cat, White Cat*") as well as a concert of Gypsy music by the Slobodan Saljevic Orchestra, the retrospective brought to light the common features of Kusturica's first three films. All three of them deal with the dangerous consequences of racial prejudices unleashed by external events, or else they examine the violence latent within close family groups.

Historical-Romantic Cinema

Of the score of new Yugoslav filmmakers who debuted in the 1980s, Kusturica was, along with Slobodan Šijan, among the most fortunate. Šijan's first work, *Who's Singin' over There?* (*Ko to tamo peva,* 1980), won the 1981 Georges Sadoul Prize for the best first film in the foreign category. In that same year, Kusturica's first feature-length film, *Do You Remember Dolly Bell?,* received thirteen awards, including the Golden Lion Award at Venice for the best first work and the FIPRESCI (International Federation of Film Critics) awards. These debut films have much in common. With a tone that is both ironic and bitter, each film explores in an original way crucial moments in Yugoslavia's history: the unexpected Nazi air raid on Belgrade in April 1941, and the Yugoslav economic and cultural boom of the early 1960s. In addition, Kusturica was the first Bosnian director to debut in fifteen years: his film received the financial backing of the local production company Sutjeska Film and was made possible by the tenacity of the director of artistic and cultural programming for Sarajevo television, Vesna Dugonjić.[12]

The narrative recounts a Sarajevan adolescent's search for his personal and social identity in the "libertarian" Yugoslavia of the early sixties. It is a story of the city's outskirts, of cramped spaces, and of heated domestic quarrels between a party-faithful Communist father who is often drunk and an idealistic son fascinated by rock music and hypnosis. Kusturica's first film to be exhibited in movie theaters brought to the screen an Oedipal journey with deep sociological insights.

The film is set in Sarajevo in the early 1960s, when Yugoslavia is experiencing something of a cultural thaw: the free circulation of pop music and daring films from the West disrupt the dreary life of young Bosnians and color their dreams. Rather than risk an increase in criminal activity, the local Communist leadership wishes to tame their juvenile energy and channel it into constructive initiatives, including the formation of a music band. The protagonist, Dino, played by Slavko Štimac (who will return in *Underground* and *Life is a Miracle*) is a sensible and introverted sixteen-year-old who lives on the outskirts of Sarajevo, thus at the margins of a city viewed nationally as provincial. Fond of hypnosis and chess games, he has a group of singular friends, all of them little rebels who drink and smoke precociously. They include the homely beanpole Bilia, also known as "Kliker," who is a gifted singer of poignant melodies and a terrible narrator of imaginary sexual conquests; a cute blond boy who limps but can play the harmonica; and the smallest boy, who always wears a bandage wrapped around his cheeks and ears because of an unexplained gunshot wound. With the approval of a local cultural official (Boro Stjepanović, who had played Mento in *Buffet Titanic*), their band, with Dino as lead singer, constantly plays a popular Italian song of the time, Adriano Celentano's "24 mila baci" (Twenty-four thousand kisses), which will become one of the film's refrains.

At home, Dino is far more articulate than his two brothers and his young sister. He is the only one who engages in serious conversations with the father, Mustafa, played by the gifted Montenegrin actor Slobodan Aligrudić. A Muslim Communist who drinks too much, the father turns family dinners into party meetings, regularly speaking about productivity and progress by combining in a surreal manner references to Marxist scientific materialism and Yugoslav alcoholic drinks.

Dino spends a lot of his free time in a barn reading about hypnosis and testing his ability on himself, rabbits, and his friend Kliker, until one day the local criminal boss asks him to hide for a while his beautiful

In *Do You Remember Dolly Bell?* Dino (Slavko Štimac) learns how to kiss from Dolly Bell (Ljiljana Blagojević).

girlfriend (Ljiljana Blagojević, who would reappear in *Promise Me This*). Though originally from the countryside, she is in age and life experience much more mature than Dino: she calls herself "Dolly Bell," after one of the dancers in Alessandro Blasetti's *European Nights* (*Europa di notte*, 1959), the first nude woman to appear on Yugoslav movie screens. The two become close: he tells her of his dream of flying over Sarajevo, and she teaches him how to kiss. As he falls in love, he also realizes the cruelty of the criminal boss who wants to turn her into a prostitute. He tries to protect her, and, although he is soundly beaten, he gains in maturity. His bildungsroman is completed as his father dies while dreaming of a better Communist society. The film closes with Dino playing with his band the usual Italian tune, while a new Sarajevo, still under construction, emerges on the horizon.

The ironic and sometimes surreal fabric of *Do You Remember Dolly Bell?* reveals Kusturica's Prague training. His attention to minor and marginal characters, whether they are timid and naïve adolescents or vulnerable young women or petty criminals in a working-class suburb, recalls—as the director himself has often recognized—the literature of Jaroslav Hašek and Bohumil Hrabal, which is full of antiheroes who lead unfortunate lives filled with irony and paradoxes. But the ingredients of Kusturica's cinema, particularly those visible in his early works, are also linked to local events and customs. *Dolly Bell* was both a symptom and a catalyst of the cultural (and subcultural) scene of the Sarajevo of the early 1980s, with its ironic takes on local music and culture, caught between ethnic tunes, political rhetoric, and foreign influences. Still, the film is not all irony and derision. It conveys a profoundly romantic attachment to folkloric and unmodern customs, which was more profound than any Communist rhetoric but deeply intertwined with it, particularly for western foreigners. This is apparent in the director's fondness for local and regional painting, particularly of naïve style, and in the film's unique deployment, in contrast to other Bosnian films of the period, of street speech. This is a conscious poetic choice: during his experience teaching in Sarajevo's Academy of Performing Arts, Kusturica proposed the use of local slang even in classical productions and in the absence of ethnographic aims. The exposure of a vernacular register, with its connotation of backwardness and primitivism, never had a documentary aim, but rather a seductive one: its mixture of self-deprecating irony and romanticism found great appeal among locals, non-Sarajevans, and foreign audiences alike.

While his film admirably conveys Kusturica's ironic and affectionate take on local culture, it was also the result of fortunate encounters. *Do You Remember Dolly Bell?* marks the beginning of a relation that is still very controversial, between Kusturica and another artistic figure closely identified with Sarajevo, the poet and novelist Abdulah Sidran. Born in 1944 and Muslim by education and culture, by the early 1980s Sidran was a well-known figure in the cafés and cultural circles of the city. The original subject of *Do You Remember Dolly Bell?* was his creation. At the beginning of the 1970s he wrote it as a four-page story; it was then written for the screen in 1979–80 and finally published as a "stand-alone" novel in 1982.

The screenplay was actually the result of a joint effort, a two-person collaboration that sometimes assumed the form of a conflict. As Sidran writes with no ill will in his splendid memoir, *Romanzo Balcanico (Balkan Novel,* 2009), not only did Kusturica reverse the chronological order of his tetralogy (still uncompleted) by filming *Do You Remember Dolly Bell?* before *While Father Was Away on Business,* but he even had the father figure die in the first film. He did so in spite of the protests of Sidran, who wanted to maintain a biographical continuity between the two narratives.[13] Even though Sidran had recounted stories and events that he had experienced first-hand, Kusturica's decision was an effective one, diegetically and poetically: the death of Dino's father strengthens the first film's dramatic coherence and separates Kusturica's cinematic destiny from that of his talented and celebrated collaborator.

Another episode in the script that provoked a heated discussion between the two, and which reveals their poetic difference, was the fight between the protagonist Dino and his older brother during an open-air banquet at the uncle's house and in front of the entire family gathering. The fight had never been part of the scenario outlined by Sidran, nor would it have occurred in reality: Muslim customs and ethics dictate respect for seniority among siblings, and the rule is commonly obeyed. Kusturica in the end prevailed, and the episode marks their differences: the writer saw the tone of his tale as serious and perhaps even austere; the director envisioned his as ironic and derisory. Still, Kusturica needed

Sidran, for no one could outdo the writer in capturing Sarajevans' voices and authentic local expressions.

Do You Remember Dolly Bell? opens with an ironic scene, as usual in Kusturica's cinema. There is the classic call to order: "Comrades!" exclaims an old and bespectacled party functionary, who begins each sentence with an air of exaggerated seriousness. Then, using the gestures and expressions of an official party meeting, he first complains about the setbacks of socialist society as far as the local youth is concerned; he stands before a municipal map, which he punctuates with a magnetic marker as he sets forth his "pro-youth" proposal. The functionary maintains that creating a musical band will distract young people from crime and boredom, and that once that problem is solved, similar measures can be taken to attract them to the local cultural club and turn Sarajevo into a major music center. The meeting's participants accept unanimously the proposal, and the film begins.

In this opening sequence, we already witness a thematic distillation of Kusturica's early films: the presence of marginal characters; the theme of their youth, with its display of primary emotions; the jargon and the gestures of adult Communists, all of whom appear as ludicrous provincial ideologues; and the popular entertainments, from rock and popular music to sex and alcohol, from cinema to soccer. Moreover, the director already seems particularly interested in that unformed but very fertile stage of adolescence: his characters are not yet adults, but in order to become so they are brutally confronted with dramas and decisions that require more maturity than their youth can muster. With Dino we witness a sentimental education that runs parallel with the westernizing (and modernizing) process of the culture and entertainments experienced by other Yugoslav youths. In the 1960s, Yugoslavia distinguished itself markedly from the other socialist countries not only in politico-strategic terms, but also in specifically cultural ways. It welcomed the cultural and emotional phenomenon of rock-and-roll, it adopted the expressions and customs of foreign countries, and in exchange—as Kusturica has repeated ironically in many interviews—it even became an international player in the boxing world. These processess stimulated more open confrontations with paternal, domestic, and ideological authority—which often resides in single figures, as in Dino's father, but is also foregrounded the provincialism and untimeliness of Yugoslav culture and, to a larger degree, that of Sarajevo. Kusturica translated these dynamics narratively and audiovisually with irony and nostalgia—two effects based on distance and separation—by grounding them in the protagonist's home, understood both spatially and emotionally.

Dino reacts to this flood of influences by expressing the powerful tensions between public and private life. Cooped up in a cramped apartment that leaks when it rains, the members of his family can find no personal space. Frequent fights erupt among the brothers. Dino, the middle son, hides away in a pigeon loft, where he practices his art of hypnotic enchantment on a rabbit, the companion of his dreams and his powers. Dino is thus the only one who tries to ensure for himself a space of personal development, even though it may be utopian. His existential mantra, provided by the French psychologist Émile Coué (1857–1926)—"Every day in every way I'm getting better and better," which he intones even before getting kissed by Dolly Bell—illustrates his unrealistic ambition to be a complete and mature human being in an environment where not even the family patriarch succeeds in controlling his own, exuberant emotions.

The contours of the young protagonist's bildungsroman are evident from the vivid representation of family scenes. The father—like Tito, a former partisan and now the manager of a self-service restaurant—applies to the family affairs an amateurish Communism fortified with alcohol, thus transforming ordinary dinner conversations into formal party meetings, ironically divided into "regular" and "emergency" sessions. As a counterforce, the housewife mother (Mira Banjac) is the patient mediator *super partes* of the ideological and domestic discussions of the little community. The parents are familiar figures in Kusturica's films. The father represents a muddled principle of pleasure and utopia. He is as epicurean and irresponsible in his behavior as he is serious and superficially involved in his ethical and political beliefs. He is often drunk and rough with his family, but a valiant defender and an unsurpassed interpreter of Marxist ideology (and rhetoric)—subjects upon which he does not like to be contradicted but at which one cannot help but smile. The mother, however, represents the silent but indispensable principle of reality, all alone in the keeping of the house but with no voice in the aforementioned "family sessions" because she is too busy doing the dishes.

Unlike Dino, his friends do not seem to have a personal intellectual life. They don't play chess but cards; they hang out all day, sometimes in the club, sometimes at open-air fairs, sharing cheap beer and cigarettes and often recounting splendidly inventive erotic tales that are rarely if ever brought to term. They resemble a circus company, varicolored and multiform. Naturally, this is the band chosen by the director of the People's Cultural Club because of their "evident" tendency toward crime; their erotic obsession is described as savage lasciviousness to be corrected through music for the good of the entire community.

Dino's maturation emerges out of his encounter with "Dolly Bell" and his experience of his father's death. The relationship with the young woman enables him to realize for the first time his adolescent erotic dreams and provokes his head-on clash with the local underworld boss. Even though by the end of the film Kusturica does not offer much of a narrative follow-up on their love, the intensity of the encounter, coupled with the loss of his father, has changed him for good. We can only imagine that Dino will continue to "get a little better" in the new apartment assigned to them by the paternalistic socialist system. Even more powerfully, the death of the father signifies the end of his adolescence and forces him to explore new personal horizons, since the father's life and speeches were much more than those of a parent. They represent the patriarchal socialist drabness that Dino, with his longing for inner perfection, seeks to defy in order for Communism to fulfill itself more completely in Yugoslav society. With him gone, Dino's political engagement could no longer be just a family affair. The film conveys this conclusion thanks to the skillfull ways in which Kusturica intertwines family and political subjects. One particular sequence is worth examining closely.

One evening, for no immediately apparent reason, the father brings home gifts for his wife and children. Then he reveals the secret reason for his happiness: the long-awaited assignment of a larger apartment has finally arrived. Kusturica accompanies the family's joy with a shot of apartment blocks under construction in Sarajevo and illuminated by the sunset. This is not the only time he will use such a scene. This brief picture-postcard shot provides not only a visual transition—the scene continues, but with a new organization of visual planes and points of view—but it places the narrative in a different spatial and geographical

After dinner, Dino's father, Mustafà (Slobodan Aligrudić), teaches Dino about the inevitability of Communism in *Do You Remember Dolly Bell?*

context. It opens up a new future for Dino and his family in what modern Sarajevo promises to become.

After telling his sons to set out the best liquor and to turn on some music, the father asks the mother to dance. As in many of Kusturica's domestic scenes shot without cuts, the camera remains at a distance, shooting different family scenes along an oblique line. In the foreground, the old couple dances and talks loudly enough that we can hear their every line; then, a bit farther back, we catch sight of the little group of children: the smallest are dancing out of step, while the other two sit at the table and silently watch their parents' rare exhibition of tenderness. The dialogue is important in the construction of the scene: it combines private vices and public virtues, family and history.

> FATHER: Communism must arrive by the year 2000.
> MOTHER: Don't drink! You'll not make better Communism.
> FATHER: You think there'll be no alcohol under Communism? No chance. From each according to his abilities, to everyone according to his needs.
> MOTHER: If you quit drinking, with Communism it'll be easier.

Frustrated by his wife's attitude, the father sits down at the table with Dino and continues the conversation, defiantly throwing out at him: "With Communism, all dilemmas will turn out to be false. What do you think?" The shot of the sunset over Sarajevo returns and introduces the final scene. Father and son argue over the differences between

Communism and hypnosis, while behind Dino the mother can be seen putting the young daughter to bed. The dialogue is symptomatic, both serious and surreal; the conversation is interrupted only by the common sense of the mother who, seeing how late it is, tells them all to go to bed.

FATHER: Must I repeat that Communism is a science? It regards the liberation of the proletariat. There are no individual cases here. All you think about is that hypnotism crap [. . .]
DINO: Everyone needs to create Communism in himself. Then it'll be easy externally.
FATHER: That means that Communism needs a good hypnotist?
DINO: If that's how you put it. I don't know. It's different.
FATHER: Don't play tricks. Your crap resembles the classic German idealism. Marx sorted that out.
DINO: I've got nothing against Marx. Why does hypnotism bother you?
FATHER: It's idealism, reaction. Communism is forged in factories, my boy. Fuck all the rest. Clear?
MOTHER: It's clear. And it couldn't be clearer. Let him sleep.

This brief sequence fuses into a single amalgam Communist jargon and utopia with the family's domestic tensions, as well as the unrealistic desire for a perfect future society with Dino's search for a complete personal identity. In so doing, it reveals a recurring element of Kusturica's narratives: the divisive effects of a regime's ideologies and deceptions on ordinary families. Without a complex shooting script, the director establishes dynamic relationships between the profilmic spaces and their filmic rendering. In the family kitchen, under the single ceiling light, Kusturica concentrates the tension between individuals, whether incompetent or alienated, and the physical and mental place in which they find themselves living. Through a few panoramic views of Sarajevo, the Bosnian capital and, by extension, Yugoslavia becomes a meeting ground both loved and hated, in which some characters blindly seize upon the party idiolects and utopias, while others, uncomfortable and confused, rebel, affirming their right to individuality. The ages of the protagonists and their family roles eventually seem to assume an almost metaphoric value: they become spiritual ages of individuals torn between adaptation and resistance.

Kusturica has often stated that he has never been interested in creating a historical portrait that is faithful to the past (in the historicist meaning typical of socialist historiography). On the contrary, he has aimed at staging films with the purpose of achieving more intense dramatic tensions. Following the example of Dušan Makavejev, who added the subtitle "Love Story" to his film *Innocence Unprotected* (*Nevinost bez zaštite*, 1968), Kusturica wanted to add to his first full-length film the subtitle "Historical Love Story" (which he succeeded in doing four years later with *When Father Was Away on Business*). His was an attempt at rebuking "historical" films, objective and superficial, that do not capture the spirit of an epoch but only useless details about customs and milieux. In this realistic effort, one should add, Kusturica always displays an ironic affection for his protagonists, which recalls not only the treatment of heroes and heroines in the Czech *nova vlnà* or in Italian neorealism but also the poignant portraits and the imaginative reconstructions of the films by Ermanno Olmi and Federico Fellini, respectively.

Even the title of the film can be read as an homage to Fellinian memory, an *amarcord,* a personal evocation of the past but also a reflective examination of popular collective history. In a republic that did not produce films with the same frequency as Serbia and Croatia, *Dolly Bell* appeared as a singular appeal, thoughtful and ironic, to recall a not-too-distant Bosnian past that had neither been represented in Black Wave films nor in the successful bittersweet comedies of the 1970s. At the same time, the phrase "do you remember?" as Lodovico Stefanoni noted twenty years ago, was a "Yugoslavian graffiti" addressed to the entire nation. The film, in fact, plays upon a number of shared traits of the nation's traditional and present history, including family relations, sexual discovery and freedom, the violent initiation into street life, and rock music. And yet, even though these were elements common to other neighborhoods of the former Yugoslavia, it was the first time they circulated with the vernacular Sarajevo inflections. The romantic tale of a juvenile rebellion against the drabness of socialist bureacracy had, in and of itself, a broad appeal on both sides of the Iron Curtain. In *Dolly Bell,* however, that appeal doubled, for it did not look at the shortcomings of the Marxist society from the perspective of a protagonist who uncritically adopts modern, western culture. Instead, the film, even in its references to the world outside Yugoslavia, appeared to reach back to an unmodern, somewhat more elementary core of local values. Its provincial dissonance, coupled with the youthful innocence of its protagonists, lent *Dolly Bell* a charming and ironic authenticity.

The choices made by Kusturica and his director of photography, Vilko Filač, were inspired by stylistic determinants rather than by philological accuracy or archival research. Kusturica had internal and external walls painted beige, brown, and even blue to achieve a distinct photographic effect. Similarly, the "do you remember?" of the title justified the use of a coarse-grained film so that focusing would result in imprecise and amateur images, as it happens for vivid but distant memories, thereby suggesting authenticity and representative verisimilitude. Many of the cinematic solutions that appeared unprofessional, including the poor sound quality in the diegetic sound reproduction of Celentano's "24 mila baci," were adopted precisely to encourage the audience to recognize and even appreciate the low-keyed dreams of freedom held by young Yugoslavs in the early 1960s. The character of Dino, in particular, according to Kusturica, was constructed by keeping in mind the stylistic lesson of Forman's *Loves of a Blonde* (1965), in which the young and innocent protagonist Andula becomes the model of the socialist (anti) heroine, who inspires affection and aloofness, smiles and irony.

Thus, *Do You Remember Dolly Bell?* did not affirm any ideology preestablished by the regime or the director, whether realist or engagé. Rather, it trips lightly along, playing a nostalgic and free game, leading the audience to a collective lightheartedness, imaginary and fascinating. Behind the camera was no auteur-ideologue, no creator of heroes and men made of marble, nor even a nihilistic artist awash in suggestive collages and incomprehensible games. Instead, there was an ambiguous and engaging narrator of true, provincial stories—not just "realistic" ones—to whom, at least in these early films, it was extremely difficult to deny complicity.

More than thirty years later, this film reminds us, like a sort of docudrama, what Sarajevo was like and how close and yet distant it was from the West. The many images of the city, caught up in perennial construction, photographed in its ancient quarters and inner courtyards, and reflected in the colors and the signs of the downtown hotels (Hotel Europa, Hotel Nacional, Hotel Central), are all testimony to the affection of Kusturica and Sidran for their hometown and a reminder of a vanished past and a place that are no longer.

When Father Was Away on Business, subtitled *An Historical Love Film*, continues Kusturica's historiographical exploration into the political and, especially, the cultural past of the former Yugoslavia. It also signals the continuation of his collaboration with Abdulah Sidran. The film examines a delicate historical period, the late 1940s and the early 1950s, which witnessed the traumatic consolidation of Titoism. It was an epoch marked by the political and ideological break with Stalin's Soviet Union and the affirmation of an independent diplomatic path (and a unique economic opportunity) for Yugoslavia as compared with other socialist countries. The break with Stalin also caused Yugoslavia's expulsion from the Cominform, the Communist Information Bureau that coordinated communication between the various Communist parties and the workers. Resulting from these new international relations was a political system predisposed to nationalism and capable of profoundly impacting the popular culture of a nation that had been morally and economically destroyed by the Second World War.

Sarajevo, June 1950, at the height of the tension between Tito and Stalin: an older man plays Mexican songs on his guitar, accompanied by two young boys. They are Malik, the protagonist, and his best friend Joza. Through voice-over Malik introduces himself, his family (the older man is his Uncle Franjo), and his friends. In the meantime, on a train from Zagreb Malik's father, Meša (Miki Manojlović), makes negative remarks about an anti-Stalinist cartoon published in a national newspaper. His jealous girlfriend, Ankica, who is impatient for Meša to leave his wife, listens attentively. Later, when she realizes that her lover has no intention of ending his marriage, she will report his pro-Stalinist reaction to his brother-in-law, the police inspector Zijo, who will interrogate and arrest Meša despite his sister's attempts to save her husband.

For a long time, Malik and his brother, the shy cinephile Mirza (Davor Dujmović, who will return as the protagonist of *Time of the Gypsies*), ignore the true fate of their father, now a political prisoner confined in Lipnica in western Bosnia. For them he is "away on business." As Meša's wife, Sena (Mirjana Karanović), works hard to keep the family together, Mirza plays the accordion, and Malik articulates his protest by starting to sleepwalk. When news about the father finally reaches them, they join him in Zvornik. There, Malik falls in love with a sweet but gravely ill Russian child, Masha, and embarrasses his father: while making a public address at a political ceremony, Malik inadvertently states that Tito *follows* the party's vision instead of the more orthodox reverse. By 1952, Meša's ordeal is over. Back in Sarajevo, at the wedding of Sena's younger brother, the extended family is reunited. Everything is forgiven, but nothing is forgotten, as Meša makes clear to a mortified Zijo. Meša asks his wife to forgive her brother, but not before he avenges himself by making violent love to Ankica, who has become Zijo's partner and who subsequently tries, in vain, to committ suicide. All this occurs in the context of the 1952 Olympic games, as the radio broadcasts an historic soccer match between Yugoslavia and the USSR, which Yugoslavia wins.

The final scene shows Malik, who has once again witnessed his father's infidelities, finding refuge in his sleepwalking. As he walks alone in the evening away from the camera, he suddenly turns directly to it, opens his eyes, and smiles.

Scripted and repeatedly scrutinized by Sutjeska Film's Artistic Commission two years before production started, Kusturica's second full-length work belongs polemically to the "revisionist" cultural climate (and its inevitable pushback) following Tito's death. The film developed a story that was quite "unpopular among Tito's heirs, because they had founded their political glory on the mythologized separation between Tito and the Russians."[14] Up to that time, Yugoslav historiography and literature had been forcibly reticent about reports of Titoist purges after the country's expulsion from the Cominform on June 18, 1948. Although the information never appeared in print, people knew about concentration camps, modeled on the Soviet gulags, that had been built on some deserted islands in the North Adriatic. One of these, Goli Otok (literally "Bare Island"), furnished the basis of Antonije Isaković's 1982 novel *Moment 2* (*Tren 2*), which collected astonishing interviews from some of the survivors. Written in 1979, a few months before Tito's death, the novel was published three years later and became an immediate national bestseller. In the same period, Dušan Jovanović's play *Karamazovs* met with comparable enthusiastic reception. Staged for the first time in Slovenia in 1980 and then in Zagreb in 1982, it also achieved great success as it was later performed throughout Yugoslavia.

Already in 1982–83, however, heated opposition was flaring up. The politicians, journalists, and intellectuals who defended and justified Tito's methods and punishments maintained that, without at least *some* gulags, the entire nation would have been subjected to Stalin's direct power and would have become one big concentration camp. They also accused those journalists and intellectuals who had begun to criticize Tito's actions of fomenting a cynical and subversive skepticism toward Yugoslavia's socialist past. In short, they denounced Tito's detractors as traitors to their own country, ready to sell it to whoever came to power.

In the mid-1980s, three films stood out for their groundbreaking reexamination of that precarious historical period. In addition to Kusturica's film, there was the caustic and surreal *Balkan Spy* (*Balkanski špijun*, 1984) by Dušan Kovačević (the future screenwriter for *Underground*) and Božidar Nikolić, and the much more dramatic *Happy New Year* (*Srećna nova '49*, 1986). Directed by Stole Popov and written by Gordan Mihić (a Belgrade writer and scenarist who would collaborate with Kusturica on *Time of the Gypsies, Black Cat, White Cat,* and *Life Is a Miracle*), *Happy New Year* was regarded by many as the most audacious of all. Before the 1980s, one should also consider the "accursed" *Holy Sand* (*Sveti pesak*, 1968) by the poet Miroslav Antić, a banned film in which Goli Otok became less a prison or forced-labor camp and more a site of dramatic moral choices and conflicts.[15] Of the three titles cited above, however, *When Father Was Away on Business* is perhaps the one that, while no less provocative and *engagé,* surpasses the others with its biting irony and black humor. While the film is not set in the harsh Goli Otok work camp, where Sidran's father spent two years, but in the more humane one at Lipnica, to which Sidran senior was eventually transferred, it nonetheless makes clear how little it takes to be sent off to an internment camp. Kusturica's film became the most famous of the three thanks to the decision of the Cannes jury, led by Miloš Forman, which awarded the film a Palme d'Or in 1985. The film also collected a FIPRESCI award at the Cannes Film Festival, a Golden Arena Prize at the Pula Festival, and was nominated for an Academy Award as Best Foreign Film in 1986. After these recognitions, beginning with the one at Cannes, film journals and periodicals began discussing the work and artistic personality of Kusturica, a name largely unknown previously.

Set between the two summers of 1950 and 1952, *When Father Was Away on Business* does not pretend to be a treatise on political history;

its ambitions and its limitations are clear from its subtitle, *An Historical Love Film*. Narrated from the point of view of a six-year-old boy who is certainly not the most historically lucid and objective of witnesses, the film recounts the private and public vicissitudes of a Muslim family caught up in the ideological hysteria of early Titoism. It achieves its aim by presenting a gamut of community archetypes. There are the sad and humorous stories of the neighbors who interact with the principal family: chubby Joza is Malik's best friend; Joza's father is arrested because he has a photograph of Stalin in his house (a foreshadowing of the coming political misfortunes of Meša); Nataša, a local Christian girl, ends up as the wife of the Muslim Fahro, Malik's "good" uncle. There are also the false funerals polemically staged as a protest against the functionaries of the regime who refuse to give any information on Joza's father, Vlado Petrović, even months after his arrest. Finally, the audience also witnesses long-awaited weddings, like the one between Nataša and Fahro, or the circumcisions of Malik and Mirza, with their inevitable banquets, drunkenness, and emotional ballads sung to the accompaniment of guitars, accordions, and *šljivovica*.

History, however, does not vanish in these domestic settings. It appears not only in powerful narrative events such as arrests and interrogations, but also in the details of everyday living, in the most innocent conversations, in frequent fatherly advice suffused with ideology, or in the sports programs broadcast by the radio, often heard in the background, which align political tensions with national soccer matches. It is a surreal history, though, lyrical and even humorous. Take, for example, the scene in which father and son attend a patriotic exhibition of gliders, and Meša gives Malik some practical advice about how to walk in public:

MEŠA: Don't swing your arms when you walk. You can tell if someone's clever by the way he walks.
MALIK: How, Dad?
MEŠA: The feet should be parallel. Whoever twists them this way is a fool.
MALIK: I don't understand, Dad.
MEŠA: You will when you grow up. Communists have an inborn aesthetic sense.

It is significant, but also grotesque, that the father is not at all joking. Although his words make clear the superficial substance of his ideological convictions, he is nonetheless sentenced for a banal comment first to forced labor and then to an internment camp. One cannot help but wonder what would have happened to a more serious and fully articulated dissident.

While less obvious to an international audience, there is no lack of detailed references to the tense political climate of those years. The origin of the film's narrative dynamics and of Meša's political woes is a vignette that shows Karl Marx busily writing in his study, while on the wall behind him hangs a prominent portrait of Stalin: this historical and ideological anachronism provides ample material for the regime's media to mock the Soviet leader's arrogance. Notice that this narrative device permits Kusturica to create a near paradox: instead of introducing a political rebel who satirizes the solemn seriousness of political propaganda (demonstrating his alienation from the regime by laughing at the powers that be), the director shows the official power satirizing a different regime and expecting that everyone will laugh. Anyone who does not appreciate the irony gets into real trouble. Thus in the film, mockery curiously becomes the language of orthodoxy and not of protest, while seriousness is a sign of rebellion and heresy.

Kusturica is also particularly subtle in displaying the vehicles of power and coercion. Putting into cinematic practice Marshall McLuhan's well-known formula "the medium is the message," he implies that it is also important to know *where* the satirical vignette was published. While the drawing is clearly "aligned" with the emerging Titoism of the times, it significantly appears in *Politika,* the historical daily founded in Belgrade in 1904. One of the few nationally distributed newspapers after the formation of the Kingdom of Yugoslavia in 1918, *Politika* was forcibly integrated into the regime's journalistic system in the years following the Second World War. And it was still read by the entire nation, including Meša, in spite of the fragmentation of the Yugoslav press along the lines of the various republics.

In his exposition, Kusturica does not offer us just the humorous little details of a "clash of Titans" that only in the West would seem serious and even ideological. Given the later history of *Politika,* which before and after Tito's death had tirelessly sought journalistic independence, the director reveals the authoritarian and Titoist past of a newspaper that in the mid-1980s the entire nation was reading and—with good reason—appreciating. Until the recent Serbian nationalistic appropriations, in fact, *Politika* was considered a kind of political and cultural equivalent of *The Economist,* despite its being part of a mammoth "independent" publishing conglomerate, the Politika Group, which controlled over twenty publications, including two dailies, a radio station, and a television channel.[16]

Another precise journalistic referent is offered by a single shot that Kusturica inserts into the sequence in which Sena visits her brother Zijo to ask for the release of her husband, or at least get some news of him. On a chair lies an unfolded copy of a newspaper, never read, on which Zijo has placed the tools of his trade: a pistol, his watch, and some medicine bottles. The newspaper is *Borba,* the tedious daily informational organ of the League of Communists of Yugoslavia; as a member of the party police, Zijo has to make a public show of reading it. *Borba* printed about 650,000 copies in 1949, many of which were never sold. Even in a brief insert that lasts only a few seconds, Kusturica succeeds in countering little dramas and microstories with the vast and sinister scenarios of the administration of power and information in the Yugoslavia of the early 1950s. Despite these details, *When Father Was Away on Business,* like all of Kusturica's cinema, never becomes an organically political film like those, for example, of Andrzej Wajda. There is instead a sensitive affinity with the grotesque and bantering tones of the "Black" Yugoslav films, of modern Czech cinema, and of Fellini. Makavejev's *Innocence Unprotected* (1968) comes to mind, evoked by the ironic image of a half-nude Joza standing on a chair in the courtyard and heroically striving to break a chain tied around his chest, like Zampanò in Federico Fellini's *La Strada* (1954). There is also an obvious reference to Miloš Forman's *Loves of a Blond* when Malik and his family gather on the parents' bed to eat and play music after a furious argument between Meša and Sena.

Thus the expressive means and the narrative orientation often leave aside the broader political and ideological plots in order to search out everyday and seemingly secondary episodes. As in an Ivo Andrić novel, Kusturica's second feature film is a bittersweet picture populated by many quixotic figures—Communists, ex-partisans, drunks, village idiots—as well as by ordinary people. As in a neorealist film, the overall vision, instead of getting lost in opaque or just plain insipid minimalism, gains in richness and significance by lingering on the emblematic details of everyday life. Kusturica effectively uses music and soccer to construct little scenes of popular culture. In his work, including this film, music translates as *live* performance—that is, as a genuine indicator of history, of the present and the past—while soccer emerges as radio broadcasts, which represent a key indicator of the linkage between daily life and political affiliations.

In the first sequence, Uncle Franjo plays exotic but neutral Mexican songs because, as he says, "nowadays it's the safest." In his opinion, many old or foreign tunes, even if they are Slavicized, are risky because they are identified too closely with this or that nation or ideology. It is therefore better to play Latin American ballads that are free of any political connection. Furthermore, throughout the film there are strange melodies that begin with a more or less diegetic accordion and end with the musical timbre of a Viennese waltz, complete with a background orchestra and violins. These transitions arise from a typically Bosnian type of melody, the anonymously composed *sevdalinka,* that appeared at the time of the Muslim conquest of Bosnia. Thematically and musically, the *sevdalinka* gives substance to *sevdah,* which in the Turkish language denotes "love" as "amorous yearning," but in a Bosnian context takes on the connotation of dark and deep melancholy. An example of the *sevdah* appeared in *Do You Remember Dolly Bell?* Entitled "Braća Morići" and sung at the final wedding banquet, it recounts the tragic fate of two Bosnian soldiers captured and condemned to death. The *sevdalinka* is the result of a musical stratification: while it includes many elements of Turkish origin, evident in the use of the saz (the large, guitar-like instrument played by the fattest uncle in *Do You Remember Dolly Bell?*), it also exhibits a Spanish influence, traceable to the immigration of Sephardic Jews. Furthermore, after the Austrian conquest of the second half of the nineteenth century, the introduction of the accordion and the inclusion of Viennese lyrics and rhythms added new dimensions. It is said that many *sevdalinkas* were composed in Vienna with German and Austrian lyrics and then exported to Bosnia through the Habsburg occupation. Bosnians are very fond of them, even though they know that they are not "real" folk songs but imported ones that often have an urban origin. Despite all this, Bosnians do not consider them any less authentic, just as the architectonic cityscape of Sarajevo is (or rather, was) considered completely Bosnian even if—or perhaps even because—it was the product of a melting pot of Central European, Muslim, and Yugoslav styles.

As for soccer, understood as an intrusion of politics into everyday life, this is not the sport played in a stadium or reported in the newspapers. It is soccer as it is heard on the radio, a genuine "tribal tom-tom," as one critic has called it. In the narrative of a film dealing with the cultural and political crisis of the early 1950s, soccer is an important index of history and, specifically, of the public life of communities, families, and individuals. It is an arena where encounters between nations, ideologies, and especially city loyalties are played out. When a game is broadcast on the radio, whether inside a house or along narrow streets and main thoroughfares, everything stops: enthusiastic and almost hysterical children play with figurines of their heroes, the adults solemnly drink wine and brandy as they toast to the most exciting plays, casual passersby stand throughout the game and listen in a religious rapture so intense that a drunkard can finally tell his story to a captive audience, not the distracted and indifferent listeners who would under normal circumstances quickly pass him by. That same radio broadcast, heard in the background at various times during the film, also reports the economic progress of the nation with the usual socialist pride in collectivist work, thus contributing to a shared sense of social and historic knowledge.

One sequence is worth discussing for its intertwining of soccer and politics. The radio is broadcasting a soccer game: Yugoslavia is playing. In different ways, the entire family participates in the victory of the national team. Isolated in individual shots, Malik and Joza appear as glued to the radio set, listening intently, noisy and boisterous at the announcement of the fifth Yugoslav goal. Mirza is busily working on his filmstrips, but he too is aware of the soccer win. Sena comes hurrying out of the kitchen, busy as always but smiling. Sitting at a table, Meša and Franjo drink brandy as they follow the game; at the announcement of the umpteenth goal, they get up, drink a toast, shake hands, embrace, and congratulate each other. Suddenly, Joza takes Malik up on his shoulders and heads for the kitchen: a quick panoramic shot shows us that the members of the family have all been in the same room, very close to each other.

While Joza and Malik repeat one after the other the lineup of the Yugoslav team, the radio recaps the highlights of the game that has just ended. In the meantime, the camera from outside the apartment frames Meša and Franjo deep in conversation. Yet, given the position of the camera—which is also the visual and auditory perspective of the audience—all one can hear are the words of the radio announcer and the shouts of Malik and his friends who are playing in the courtyard, bursting with enthusiasm for the national team's win; the voices of Meša and Franjo cannot be heard. This isolation permits Kusturica to narrate in a single sequence various visual and auditory stories. Suddenly we realize that the telephone is ringing; Meša goes over near the window and answers it. We share only Meša's point of view as he looks down on the boys playing in the courtyard: otherwise, for the audience, he is akin to an actor in a silent film. The expression on his face in a medium close-up shot suddenly changes: he loses his serenity, and his face registers an obscure and prolonged anxiety that leads directly to the next episode, his interrogation at the central police station by his brother-in-law Zijo.

The sequence reveals the unity of the family gathered around their passion for soccer, which plays on their feelings of national pride. It is, however, Mesa's approach to national politics in reference to the vignette in *Politika*, which reveals him to be the opposite of a blind and zealous Titoist, that has gotten him into trouble and is about to separate him from his family. Kusturica skillfully uses the same emotional register to uplift his characters and then depress them: they hover between the joyful acceptance of patriotic pride and the critical disapproval of the regime's exploitations. Above all, Meša may not be a pure and idealistic rebel, but in his intellectual and ideological mediocrity he represents the average and almost anonymous victim of the regime's nationalist repressions. One did not have to be an articulate, lucid, and dangerous opponent to end up in an internment camp and to be forced to abandon one's family.

The one person not interested in the radio reports and the soccer action is Sena, Malik's mother, the only character who is not farcical but literally pathetic, expressing and embodying *pathos*; it is, after all, her perpetual physical and moral sacrifices that sustain the family. Originally the screenplay was to be centered on her, but Kusturica later decided to give ample space to Meša as well. The spectator's rapport with the stoic but fierce Sena, played by the excellent Mirjana Karanović (who will have a minor, yet comparable role as wife in *Underground*), is both intimate and compassionate. She is always seen busy cooking, ironing, and taking care of the men in the house, and at times even trying to moderate her brother's political exasperations, all while enduring the erotic flights of her husband. And yet her modest attempts to get away, whether for entertainment or for pure desire, are usually frustrated.

Consider two episodes. The first occurs when the father returns from a trip to Zagreb and brings home a simple cartoon filmstrip that they watch that same evening. It should be remembered that in the early 1950s, a tradition of animated film production was just getting started in Zagreb, and it would soon become a veritable school, famous worldwide for its fatalistic and tragicomic outlook on the limits and paradoxes of human life. Despite their simple, abstract aesthetics, the Zagreb School's animated films were often irresistible and a major source of national pride—Kusturica pays explicit homage to the genre in a scene in which the sympathetic Mirza writes on a film strip just as the Zagreb animators did. At a certain moment during the projection of an animated short, Sena bursts out laughing. Her husband immediately rebukes her with an icy look, as though it were ill-mannered for parents to laugh in front of their children. A second and even more demeaning humiliation awaits her when Sena and Malik go to visit Meša in Lipnica at the forced-labor camp where he is interned. In the evening, the wife and husband try to make love while Malik sleeps in the next room. The little boy, however, mischievously upsets their plans, and the mother finally takes him into the bed, placing him between her and her husband. Malik and Meša are soon sleeping with their arms around each other while Sena, all alone, sobs in frustration. No one sees or hears her, and only the audience understands fully her sacrifices and mortifications.

As Kusturica has often stated, he abandoned the idea of having the film constructed around Sena's character in order to give a broader narrative perspective that extends to the multigenerational family and to the community of relatives and neighbors. In fact, even though there is a privileged rapport between the audience and Malik, the film gives ample representation to the patriarchal Yugoslav society as a whole,

When Father Was Away on Business.
Sena (Mirjana Karanović) remains without
affection, as Malik (Moreno Debartoli) and
Meša (Miki Manojlović) sleep on.

including its rough, authoritarian, yet comic male figures (Meša, the grandfather, Zijo, Franjo) and its strong or seductive but eventually compliant women (Ankica especially).

Meša is the emblem of this society. An affectionate father and a libertine husband who does not perceive the irony of or feel any remorse at such contradiction, he is incorrigibly unfaithful and a liar, but bound to his family. Politically, he is often indifferent or opportunistic but also ingenuously instinctive and rebellious. The advice that he offers to his son is more illuminating than his heretical comments on the satirical vignette in *Politika*—to his mistress Ankica, in fact, he had only said that "they're going too far now," without adding anything more incriminating. Coaching Malik, however, who had been chosen to recite a little formal speech before the mayor of Zvornik, Meša reveals all his paternal ineptitude, giving his son completely irrelevant and even abstract suggestions: "The words should roll off your tongue. And don't start fidgeting. When you run up to him stand proudly. Don't be shy. Let your gestures suit your words." Not quite satisfied, he then adds, "But don't overdo it," destroying any hope that the boy will understand all his instructions.

As might be expected, Malik, tense and awkward, stumbles over the regime's hackneyed phrases and turns the speech topsy-turvy, placing Tito's authority below that of the party and getting his father into some temporary trouble. Meša is subsequently forced to undergo a brief interrogation by the local party functionary, the bon vivant Cekić (subtly

When Father Was Away on Business. Meša, between his son Mirza (Davor Dujmovic´) and his brother-in-law Fahro, at the banquet following Fahro's wedding to Nataša. Courtesy of Photofest.

interpreted by Slobodan Aligrudić, Dino's father in *Do You Remember Dolly Bell?*, who died soon after the film was finished). During the interrogation, Meša answers the question with an exhibition of prudent scholastic eloquence: "The Party teaches us . . . Tito is the Party, the Party is Tito, and Tito is all of us." It is a perfect example of provincial socialist synthesis positioning itself carefully between tautological orthodoxy and ideological fanaticism. This capacity for survival, for superficiality, and ultimately for ideological indifference permits Meša to preserve intact his ineffectual human integrity: when the storm is over, he will have a new position as a municipal functionary, innocent and irresponsible as always. His character is clearly opposed to the blind and excessive zeal of Zijo, who has sacrificed love and family loyalty to the party. At the end, Zijo falls ill, cannot sleep, and is excluded from the warmth and love of the family.

Meša was never a dissident. His only attachment, despite his sexual escapades, has been to his large family. The banquet scene for Fahro's wedding, a Fellinian narrative topos of Kusturica's cinema, is revealing of his political agnosticism and his common sense. A subtitle introduces the scene: "22 July 1952." Although political tensions have to a degree lessened, friction within the family remains high. The camera tracks along the tables, pauses on a couple of characters, and records their conversation before moving on to other exchanges. Then Kusturica recomposes everything, placing the camera at the center of the plentifully laid tables arranged in horseshoe form and filming with panoramic shots. The director then frames characters, two at a time, who have not yet resolved their past differences, Meša and Zijo, victim and executor of a typical political internment of those "difficult" years, and Zijo and Sena, brother and sister, alienated by that same exile. In both cases, the characters scarcely look into each other's eyes, and they exchange the briefest of remarks, pronounced with controlled anger and an undercurrent of tension. It is a verbal settling of accounts—not so much a duel as a family balance sheet. For instance, Meša asks the brother-in-law and his wife to try to reach a reconciliation. If it is Meša who sits down beside Zijo, it is the latter who opens their conversation:

> ZIJO: Have you forgiven me?
> MEŠA: I can forget . . . but forgive. . . .
> ZIJO: Why did you invite me then?
> MEŠA: To talk, like two adults. Do you still think the same?
> ZIJO: About what?
> MEŠA: That I was guilty?
> ZIJO: What I think doesn't matter anymore.
> MEŠA: It did then. Did you put me away for my words or my thoughts?
> ZIJO: I didn't put you away.
> MEŠA: So who did?
> ZIJO: Your own tongue.
> MEŠA: My own brother-in-law did.
> ZIJO: During that craziness, it was brother against brother.

Recalling *ex post facto* the later generational take of *Underground*, Kusturica depicts adults as pathetic and vindictive (Meša exacts his own revenge on Ankica, forcing her to a sexual climax that Malik sees by chance), with no plans for the future except cynical or desperate ones. For every Meša, who naïvely believes he is now in a genuine democracy where everything is permitted, there is a Zijo, whose acts committed during the paranoid years of the Tito/Stalin rupture prevent him from sleeping at night; in desperation, he smashes his forehead against a bottle of brandy in an attempt to arouse pity and understanding in his sister.

The young, the new generation of the patriarchal Yugoslav culture, pay for their parents' inadequacies before History by becoming sentimental dreamers lost in utopian desires. Their dissention from the present translates as a form of regression, not of growth; their untimeliness is elementary and provincial at once. If the adolescent Dino in *Do You Remember Dolly Bell?* expresses his confused sense of rebellion through his spasmodic attraction to the practice of hypnotism, here Malik reacts to his unstable and senseless present by being "afflicted" with sleepwalking—that is, by re-creating artificial conditions of satisfaction and fulfillment. Malik is indeed the main character, but this is so because his point of view becomes the emotional and stylistic mediator of many scenes, and even the occasion of cinematic references like the crane shots of the trees at the beginning and the end of the film, which recall Andrey Tarkovsky's *Ivan's Childhood* (*Ivanovo Detstvo*, 1962). Similarly, his solitary excursions in the middle of the night—in one of them he even leaves the apartment and enters the bed of his beloved Masha—acquire a lyrico-magical dimension of pure romanticism. From the moving confession of love for his Russian friend as she is being taken away in an ambulance to the many scenes of his dangerous nocturnal flights (often photographed as though they were blue surreal paintings by Chagall), this ideal dimension pervades a number of sequences, including the one that almost ends in tragedy until Meša embraces Malik as he stands on top of a cliff. His older brother, Mirza, expresses his alienation and his imaginative integrity through the personality of a lonely and bespectacled cinephile, always busy with film strips, movie magazines, and posters. At the same time, however, Mirza's playing on his accordion the same extradiegetic melodies of the film invites the spectators to immerse themselves in the succession of diegetic events and thus acquire an intimate knowledge of family and political history and its strange mixture of drama and nostalgia.

And at the center remains Sarajevo, among Muslim families, Orthodox neighbors, and many synagogues. Before us are the cultural and architectonic stratifications of a city (and of a cinema) faithful to its own marginal origins and to its characters as a crossroads for different ethnic groups and tastes. *When Father Was Away on Business* is the second of two of Kusturica's films associated with the Bosnian capital, whose native poets limn its richly phantasmal character, as in the stanzas of the film's most moving *sevdalinka*. "Is Sarajevo still where it used to be?" they sing in unison. This is the same question that Meša, during his exile, had asked Sena, both of them in love with and homesick for a space and a time that the new socialist regime was already changing. *When Father Was Away on Business* launched Kusturica's career in multiple directions, at home and abroad. From 1985 to 1988, Kusturica taught at the Academy of Performing Arts in Sarajevo. He also began playing the guitar in the "neoprimitive" Zabranjeno Pušenje. During this same period, he worked with other Yugoslav filmmakers; he collaborated, for example, on the script of *The Magpie Strategy* (*Strategija svrake*), directed by Zlatko Lavanić in 1987. In 1988, Miloš Forman, the legendary maestro of cinema and irony whom Kusturica had met through common friends at FAMU, asked Kusturica to teach courses in film direction as an adjunct professor at Columbia University's School of the Arts Film Division, which the Czech director had headed for many years.

In 1989, Kusturica released *Time of the Gypsies* (*Dom za vešanje*), his third feature film, which received the special award for best direction at the 1989 Cannes Film Festival. After directing two "historiographical" films, albeit told through an oblique, fictionalized, and sentimental perspective, Kusturica dedicated his third feature film to a population, the Romany, whom history, including the Yugoslav one, has regularly forgotten or marginalized. Familiar with Gypsies' stories, language, and culture after growing up near them in Gorica, Kusturica follows their lonely, dramatic, and despairing pilgrimages across national and international borders. The result is a ballad tinged with sentimental and picturesque tones, this time free of any revisionist aims, dedicated to the most unmodern European minority.

Produced with funds that included American capital, *Time of the Gypsies* is a film replete with folkloric and quasi-ethnographic details, featuring dialogues that are for the most part in Romany and therefore *always* subtitled. Through this cinematic choice, Eastern and Western spectators are thus made to enter into a nomadic culture that has often been regarded as lacking civil dignity, to say nothing of literary or cinematic standing. Still, unlike its Western counterparts, Eastern European cinema has dedicated several films to a population that has been persecuted for centuries and that has found in the Balkan states its most permanent home. Leaving aside the evocative cinema of the Hungarian Sándor Sára, Yugoslavia has produced excellent works by directors from the Novi Film movement and the Prague Group. In 1967 Aleksandar Petrović filmed *I Even Met Happy Gypsies (Skupljači perja)*, in which he blended realistic and fantastic dimensions into a narration that was both linear and grotesque. Twenty years later, Goran Paskaljević made the touching *Guardian Angel (Anđeo čuvar,* 1987), on the traffic and exploitation of Gypsy children in the suburbs of large European cities. Once again, Kusturica's work differs from most predecessors by having attained international commercial and critical success, and by a choppy and surreal narration that carries magic realism to new heights.

The film opens in a Gypsy camp somewhere in Yugoslavia: it is raining heavily, and a series of local characters loudly reproach God for their ill-fated lives. A new bride complains about her drunk husband, a man complains about having been the victim of medical experiments, and the thirty-year-old local playboy Merdzan bemoans his bad luck at dice. The refrain is the same: when God came down to earth and met the Gypsies, he immediately took the first flight back.

At Merdzan's home, the ruler is his mother, Baba (Ljubica Adžović), who has special magic gifts and who takes care of her two beloved grandchildren, Perhan and Daca, both adolescents. Perhan has exceptional telekinetic and hypnotic talents—usually applied to spoons and turkeys—and plays the accordion (as the same actor does in *When Father Was Away on Business*); the paralytic Danira, known as Daca, however, is mostly confined to her bed.

Perhan is madly in love with Azra, whom he impresses by moving soda cans from a distance. At the local open-air movie theater, they watch a love scene from Rajko Grlić's *The Melody Haunts My Memory* (1981), starring Miki Manojlović, and Perhan boasts that he could kiss her "for about twenty minutes," without interruption. And kiss her he

Perhan (Davor Dujmović) often plays the accordion for his sister Danira (Elvira Sali) in *Time of the Gypsies*. Courtesy of Photofest.

does. Although he would like to marry her, he cannot, not on account of his young age but because he lacks the kind of money that her mother demands. Desperate, he awkwardly attempts suicide by hanging himself from the bell rope of a small local church, only to be rescued by his grandmother's friend, Zabit. Luckily it is St. George's Day, one of Balkan Gypsies' most important holidays. The celebrations restore Perhan's morale: he plays the ballad "Talijanska" on his accordion and laughs at Merdzan's interpretations of Chaplin's slapstick routines. That night, he also dreams of a mythical rite of passage in a river, where he embraces Azra, surrounded by flowers, fires, and turkeys.

The celebrations also mark the return of the duplicitous local boss, Ahmed, greeted at the camp like a king as he throws a few notes to the begging children. That night, Merdzan loses all his money at Ahmed's. Drunk with rage and alcohol, he returns home and literally lifts the roof and the four walls of his mother's house by attaching a cable to his three-wheeled Apecar and pulling it over the electrical wires. His entire family is forced out into the rain. The scene explains the film's original title, *Dom za vešanje*, which means "Home for Hanging."

The next day, after Baba saves the life of Ahmed's son through her magical touch, the local boss consents to take Daca and Perhan to the hospital in Ljubljana and to pay for the girl's much-needed operation. Before departing, Ahmed's van collects livestock, newly born children to sell, and a number of poor kids whom he will exploit in Milan by turning them into crafty beggars and thieves. Once in Slovenia, and after learning the costs of the operation, Ahmed asks Perhan to make up the difference by leaving his sister at the hospital and accompanying him to Italy. Perhan accepts and within months becomes a skilled thief himself. When Ahmed falls ill, he becomes the interim boss. Upon his return home he feels entitled to marry Azra: now he has the money, the experience, and the respect of the locals. To his surprise, she is pregnant, and he does not believe he is the father of her baby. He marries her nonetheless, and takes her with him to Milan where, on a cold night, while giving birth to the child, she dies in his arms. Distraught, Perhan tries one more time to kill himself.

Four years later, he meets his sister by chance in Rome: she is still disabled, now works for Ahmed, and lives with his own son in his old boss's new camp. Perhan shows up at the older man's umpteenth wedding and, with his telekinetic powers, throws a fork into his neck. Like the bride at the film's opening, the gangster's new wife angrily bemoans her ruined wedding, then chases after Perhan and mortally wounds him. Before dying, he sees a flying turkey in the sky. Back home, at the funeral of Perhan senior, the young Perhan steals the coins that friends and relatives have customarily placed on his father's dead body. Then, hiding in an open cardboard box turned upside down, he dashes out into the rain, followed by a running Merdzan, who seems to mimic, one more time, Chaplin's antic gestures.

Filmed between September 1987 and May 1988 in Italy and Yugoslavia, and chiefly in Sutka, the Gypsy quarters on the outskirts of the Macedonian capital of Skopje, *Time of the Gypsies* is divided into two distinct parts. The first consists of stories and scenes of Gypsy life, featuring a range of original characters. In the second part, attention centers on the young protagonist Perhan, and on his tragic odyssey from adolescence to adulthood, ending with his violent death.

Kusturica had initially planned a project focusing on a Ukrainian minority living in Canada, the Dukhobors (also known as Dukhobortsy or Doukhobors, literally "spirit wrestlers")—following the Columbia producer Harry Saltzman's suggestion. The project was later abandoned. The director has often said that he changed his mind after reading an article published in 1985 in the Belgrade daily, *Express Politika,* that reported on a Romany family that had sold their newborn baby in Italy. Goran Paskaljević had based his *Guardian Angel* on a similar theme. Although Kusturica has said that he had not seen Paskaljević's film before filming *Time of the Gypsies,* he had one of his characters, Ahmed, refer to *Guardian Angel* in one of its scenes.

Conceptually, *Time of the Gypsies* is a strange film. Kusturica does not deal with a familiar historical and political theme but rather portrays a traditionally marginal community that, growing up in Gorica, he got to know better than most. Kusturica nurtured and amended different versions of the screenplay, developed in collaboration with the Mostar writer and screenwriter Gordan Mihić, on the basis of the stories collected during his first-hand research in Skopje. He spent a great deal of time in close contact with members of the local Gypsy community, made friends and played soccer with them, and urged them to tell him their stories and myths. Among so many possible subjects, he was particularly impressed by the story of a boy who lived alone with his grandmother and who recounted several episodes of his wanderings with no passport throughout northern Italy in search of a modest fortune.

During two months' residence in villages and quarters, Kusturica gathered 3,500 photographs of two thousand potential actors. Of these, he interviewed and made screen tests of 120. Ultimately, only about twenty remained, among them the grandmother Baba (Ljubica Adžović), Uncle Merdzan (Husnija Hasimović), and the neighbor Zabit (Zabit Memedov, who will also have the role of Zarije in *Black Cat, White Cat*). For the other roles, he chose professional actors, both young and established. For Ahmed, he chose Bora Todorović, a well-known actor in the theater, television, and cinema of the former Yugoslavia; for Perhan, he selected Davor Dujmović, whom Kusturica had earlier cast in the role of Mirza in *When Father Was Away on Business*; and for the part of Azra, he chose Sinolička Trpkova, who held a degree in acting from the Skopje Academy.

Kusturica has often said that this ambitious film would not have been possible without American financing. His good fortune was once again of Bohemian origin: Miloš Forman showed the fourth draft of the screenplay to David Puttnam, a producer at Columbia Pictures, who courageously decided to finance this unusual work, whose dialogue is almost entirely in Romany. Harry Salzman later assumed production of the film. The shooting was interminable: with many interruptions, it lasted about nine months. Although filming was done in the middle of Skopje's Gypsy quarters, the director had many locations entirely rebuilt in order to concentrate the architectural features, the alleys, and the most typical, intense colors within a very limited, workable space. Realism in Kusturica is a destination; it is never simply a point of departure.

The original screenplay anticipated a running time of slightly less than two hours, but with the many nonprofessional actors, and in such close contact with a Gypsy culture so rich in everyday and mythical stories, Kusturica and his crew shot many unplanned and not easily usable scenes. Between improvisations and new episodes, the available material grew inordinately. In particular, the additions frequently dealt with examples of Christian and Pagan syncretism in the Romany culture, from the ancient cosmogonic stories to the main characters' eccentric daily practices—above all, the relations of the protagonists, and particularly Perhan, with turkeys. We should remember that the oneiric dimension is an integral part of Romany daily life, as we learn early in the film from a monologue recited by a bald Gypsy man, the victim of experiments on his brain: "What will my spirit do without wings? My spirit flies. She cries, sings, or laughs, when she wants to. When God lived down here, he couldn't get along with us Gypsies, so he had to go up there. It's not my fault."

Taking into consideration the sheer quantity of film shot (approximately four hundred thousand feet), one of the film's producers, Sarajevo Television, decided to draw from it a six-part TV series, with each episode lasting about one hour. Kusturica apparently did not participate in this undertaking, but he did give his approval to the final product. Although it did not circulate in Western Europe and is now available only on a double DVD edition distributed in Russia, this adaptation was successful in the former Yugoslavia, where the folklore and lightheartedness of Gypsy life are not utterly extraneous to mainstream culture. Kusturica has also recently revisited the paradigmatic untimeliness of Gypsy life by writing an opera based on his film, with original music scored by the No

Smoking Orchestra. The work premiered in Paris at the Opéra Bastille in June 2007.

A few Anglo-American and Italian critics have expressed reservations about a film that only briefly hints at the characters' motivations and that presents vague narrative transitions. In particular, commentators zeroed in on the remarkable difference between the first and second parts, deploring false diegetic continuities that, in their view, bring together distant narrative and temporal periods in a rather arbitrary way. Others, more sympathetic toward the film, have pointed out that its stylistic architecture does not suffer unduly from these random ellipses. That the film eventually intensifies or even abandons its diverse narrative trajectories with great aplomb and freedom—they have claimed—does not disturb an equilibrium that the director had never sought.

Anthropology and magic realism regularly feature in Kusturica's films. To understand the poetics and the choices that the director has made, one must regard his films—and this one in particular—neither as thesis projects nor as traditional narratives with an appropriate message tacked on. Akin to an avant-garde work, *Time of the Gypsies* was conceived as a *cinematic experience,* consisting of a succession of emotions to live with for two and a half hours, where life and death, space and time, diverge from their usual Western configurations. The dead, for example, may return in the form of a wind-blown wedding veil, like the one associated with the mother of Perhan and Daca, who during the trip to Italy dreams of it though her eyes are wide open. Living persons, too, like Azra, are made to adopt a veil, symbolic of marriage and a new life, to foretell their imminent death, which is also anticipated by her levitation above the earth as she is giving birth to Perhan's son. Likewise, throughout his life Perhan regularly fantasizes about ancient rites of passage of a clearly pagan origin, and is endowed with amusing and superhuman powers of telekinesis.

Some of the film's characters entertain asynchronous relations with modern times and very detached ones with modern sites and spaces: grandmother Baba and the neighbor Zabit exhibit an abiding interior atemporality composed of primitive mythologies and of perennial rituals and ceremonies. There are characters with a passionate vitality who never stir from those three houses in the nomad quarters, such as Baba and Zabit, Azra's parents, and others. In contrast, Ahmed and his gang,

Time of the Gypsies. In one of his dreams, Perhan imagines his grandmother Baba (Ljubica Adžović) in Milan: her colorful image and playful temperament strikingly contrast against the grey and imposing backdrop of the city's Duomo. Courtesy of Photofest.

including Perhan, travel or have traveled far and wide in all of Europe for reasons of more or less honest trafficking, although they never appear to adjust to their new worlds. Uncle Merdzan himself spent a long time in Germany, which, in a moment of anger and discouragement, he remembers as his one and only true *Heimat*, even though nobody believes it to be the case.

Whether immobile or on the go, in fact, these characters "re-create" a home for themselves with surprising ease and naturalness, suspending external time in favor of an internal one and passing through modern Western cultures and foreign languages without being totally contaminated or captivated by them. They break into elegant apartments or into the unguarded automobiles of Milan's upper bourgeoisie, as the agile dwarf of the gang does, simply to rob money and valuables. Gypsies do not adapt, nor do they convert to any civilization that is not theirs, even when they may outwardly take on some of its superficial characteristics. Life away from their homeland does not do anything to alter their unique body temperature.[17] In comparison, the middle-class passersby in Piazza Duomo seem like hurried runners in a timed relay race that has no end in sight. Through the film's exoticizing modes of address, western spectators see themselves as extras in a comedy with foreign rhythms and tunes.

If in western societies one of the key indicators of modernity has been the emergence and refinement of individuals' private self, *Time of the Gypsies* reveals how elsewhere this distinction, as well as all the efforts spent in maintaining it, could be fruitless and artificial. "When the Gypsy is not celebrating or not participating in collective ceremonies," Kusturica noted in an interview, "it is as though he were not living."[18] In the obstinate defense of their culture, Gypsies fill all the available space with that social and shared dimension we call "myth." Every phenomenon, from rain to bringing up children, even the production of lime, is the result of a struggle or a negotiation between two or more mythic divinities before whom the human being is impotent and thus serene. Those ceremonies that offer the greatest synthesis of intimacy and sociality—weddings, for instance—preserve an absolutely sacred aura, not to be boycotted for any reason. This explains the deep anger of the two brides at the beginning and the end of the film, who lament not so much the state of their husbands (dead drunk or literally dead) but the ruination of the supreme ceremony of their youth.

Among all of the film's culturally "immobile" and most unmodern characters, only one figure is in transit—Perhan. He is the one who best reflects Kusturica's poetics: Perhan repeats the parabola of passing from adolescence to adulthood that we had already observed with Dino in *Do You Remember Dolly Bell?* Moreover, like the director's earlier heroes, Perhan has a singular autonomy of thought and of personal action. If Dino practices hypnotism as an exercise in inner growth, and if Malik realizes his deepest dreams in the movements of a somnambulist, Perhan communicates with turkeys, plays the accordion (as the same actor did in *When Father Was Away on Business*), and has visions of spectacular rites of passage, imbued with fluvial eroticism and primitive loveliness. Despite his itinerant life, however, Perhan too remains faithful to his own self and to his own history right up to the final vendetta. Although through his "voyage to Italy" he becomes a seasoned criminal, he never stops looking for his sister and dreaming of a return to the environment where he grew up, even if only to build a house and live there with his grandmother. His last wish, expressed as he lay dying in the open car of a freight train and gazing into the void, remains that of a fantastic and primitive freedom: a soaring white turkey outlined against a blue sky. One cannot help but recall the ramblings of the bald Gypsy who, at the beginning of the film, accuses "the world" with horror and irony for having almost chopped off his soul in a psychiatric hospital.

After completing the film, Kusturica has often stated that in the fashioning of his characters he sought to avoid the classical psychological or narrative dramaturgies of nineteenth-century European novels that Paskaljević had adopted effectively in his *Guardian Angel*. Kusturica has claimed that he restricted himself to Gypsy mythologies, with their unmodern sense of exuberant commonality and fatalism as well as with their sacred animals. In this universe, there is no such thing as marked individualism or stories' linear progression; characters do not generally seek personal security, stability, or closure. Gypsy daily life appears instead profoundly marked by cyclical or recurring social events, whether highly expected feast days or phylogenetic ceremonies (births, funerals, but especially weddings), and a distinct ethological scenography made mostly of geese and turkeys. In Gypsy legends the Romany emigrated from India by following a flock of geese; the same legends hail the turkey as a noble and sacred symbol of the community's past.

While in *Time of the Gypsies* geese are ubiquitous, the presence of one turkey accompanies and registers the stages of Perhan's existential procession by marking off his relations with power and destiny. As an early gift of the grandmother, the turkey is immediately trained, or "possessed." It is present when Perhan meets Azra for the first time at the beginning of the film; it follows them to the movies and sits next to them during their first kisses; its squawking saves Perhan's life because it alerts Zabit and directs him to the isolated little church where the youth is attempting a comical suicide. When Merdzan kills the turkey and puts it into a boiling pot, the narrative undergoes its first notable shift: Perhan and Daca leave home and set off for Italy. Here, in the camp on the outskirts of Milan, Perhan will again meet other turkeys, some in the daily mists of the Po Valley but especially in his dreams. Turkeys appear throughout, right up to the final mirage, with its mythic outline of a white turkey in flight and caught in slow motion; it is a cathartic and conciliatory image that reconnects Perhan with the beginning of his own story and restores him to the affection of his loved ones.

In *Time of the Gypsies,* Kusturica naturalizes his characters' unusual anthropological features through cinematic inventions that accustom the spectator to appreciate distant folkloric behaviors. One of these inventions is the transformations of human characters into puppets or marionettes that reveal their strange and "comic" alterity in moments of emotional intensity. The first example is the scene in which Azra's mother, Ruza, forcefully rejects Perhan's request to marry her daughter; in the woman's hysterical outburst she insults and beats her husband. He reacts by literally hanging her up on a hook outside the house, transforming the angry woman into a marionette with no strings; she seems to be frightened ("Help me neighbors! He wants to kill me!"), but in reality she is furious ("I'll pull out your eyes!"), paws at the air, and deforms her face like a figure in an Adriaen Brouwer painting. Mostly shot frontally and from a distance, with basically no close-ups, the scene reveals the intertwining gesticulations of the husband and wife, master and marionette, in a scene worthy of a *Punch and Judy* show.

A similar act is repeated in the next sequence. Overcome by grief and depressed after Ruza's denial, Perhan takes his turkey in his arms and decides to commit suicide by hanging himself in a nearby church. A frontal long shot reveals Perhan attached to the bell rope and moving up and down like a marionette, all the while shouting out his love for Azra. Standing in front of him is Zabit, whose hesitations and words ("Who are you, politician, to hang yourself?") drain tension from the scene, which immediately becomes comic and farcical. In fact, when Zabit tries to cut the rope, he dangles for a bit with Perhan, and then the pair falls on the scaffolding, causing it to crash down out of sight. Kusturica will resort to suicides later in his films, with different poetic goals. In *Arizona Dream,* when Grace tries to kill herself with a pair of pantyhose, the result is comic. There is only tragedy, instead, when, in *Underground,* a militiaman finds Ivan hanging lifeless in a bombed-out church.

To emphasize the special, magical character of the lives of his characters, Kusturica makes repeated use of certain props and actions, including wedding veils and dresses as well as levitations—all elements that will return in *Arizona Dream* and *Underground.* Daca had seen a wedding veil trailing behind the van carrying her to Ljubljana when she and Perhan were leaving their native village for the first time. She had associated it with her mother, who died young and whom Daca longs for even though she never saw her. When, later in the film, Perhan notices Azra's wind-blown veil, which twists and wraps itself around the lamps of the nomad encampment outside Milan, he intuitively perceives the impending tragedy. As he, together with Ahmed and his wife, is looking for his young bride, it is the whiteness of her dress that enables them to find her along railroad tracks in the darkness of the night. What they see is Azra levitating while still maintaining the horizontal childbearing position. When she returns to earth, her baby is born, but she dies in the arms of her inconsolable Perhan, as the wedding veil, suspended on the wind, again wafts through the camp, far away from the faint lights of the city.

These suggestive cinematic solutions should not imply that Kusturica constructed the entire film on the basis of an ethno-racial alterity (or a chromosomal one, as described by the off-screen voice of the BBC documentary that Merdzan is listening to as he shaves). *Time of the Gypsies* aims to create an epic work for a people whose epic is generally *not* known. The film is a certainly an opportunity for an ethnograpic celebration, but it is also infused with cinematic homages and media references. Without maintaining that all films ultimately refer to each other, one could argue that Kusturica developed his approach to Gypsy culture through his marked cinematic talent—fantastic and surreal, visual and musical—which apparently has little to do with Gypsy surrealism. Consider the reference to the Chaplin of *A Dog's Life* (1918)— impersonated by Merdzan during a domestic skit in which he shows an animal's tail sticking out of his pants—or to Orson Welles, whose face looks out from a poster, or even to Italian commercials, as Perhan practices an horizontal leap over a fence trying to replicate what the actor Nino Castelnuovo famously did in a corn-oil advertisement visible on a giant street poster by Ahmed's camp.

If the repeated use of a stubbornly stationary camera and the technique of filming emotional and affective states rather than narrative events recalls John Ford's *The Grapes of Wrath* (1940), the deeper cinematic influence on *Time of the Gypsies* seems to be Andrey Tarkovsky: from the telekinetic obsessions to the oneiric ones and even to flight, understood as total fulfillment and destiny but also as sacrifice and death, all of these are found in *Ivan's Childhood* (1962), *Andrei Rublev* (1966), and *The Mirror* (1974). Nor should one forget the images of the burning house, so similar to the main scene of *The Sacrifice* (1986). In various interviews Kusturica has recalled having profoundly admired the emotional attitude that Tarkovsky experimented with in *Ivan's Childhood*: his attempt to enter *visually* into the dreams of his characters. The Russian auteur, moreover, seems to have played a fundamental role in the choice of the visual details of Perhan's dreams and of the rituals for the feast of St. George, as well as for the idea of human flight as the complete offering of self. Recall Perhan's dream in which, holding the turkey, he floats above the Drina River adorned with crosses and fires glowing on the water; there is also Azra's levitation before she dies, the coincidence of gift of life and destiny of death. These debts, infusing a story about a marginal population, found a central role in the film's narrative and audiovisual organization.

Less restricted than in the past by precise historical and ideological articulations, Kusturica's third feature creates a flowing narrative style in which irregular currents speed up or slow down at will, alternating between unstable calms and unexpected whirlpools. The narrative structure is especially undisciplined in the first part, while in the second one that initial *panta rei,* or "everything flows," of the diegesis leads toward a more traditional exposure of the protagonist's odyssey. Addressing these narrative architectures, Kusturica has often encouraged the use of critical terms such as "magic realism," borrowed from South American novelists such as Gabriel García Márquez, Pablo Neruda, and Julio Cortázar, or references to the natural ontological "decantings" between reality and dream of such films as Tarkovsky's *The Mirror.* Within these magical perspectives, the special powers of Baba and Perhan are perfectly plausible, just as the most fantastic and archaic dreams become real. Even the costume design and the décor of the sets, tinted with the yellows and oranges of the palette of the Croatian Hlebine School, acquire tangible presence and truth. The colorful surrealism of many scenes takes on an astonishing pictorial concreteness, comparable to the physiognomic dramas of a Hieronymous Bosch (*Christ Carrying the Cross,* 1515–16) or a Pieter Bruegel the Elder (*The Peasant Wedding,* 1567). Furthermore, all these references are enriched by music.

The film's soundtrack was arranged by the well-known composer and performer Goran Bregović, a musician originally from Sarajevo, of mixed parentage (a Croatian father and a Serbian mother) and with a Muslim wife, and the leader of the celebrated band Bijelo Dugme (White Button). Originally a friend of Kusturica's from the streets of the Bosnian capital, Bregović became a recognized composer of soundtracks with *Time of the Gypsies*. To reproduce the primitive sounds of the Gypsy community, Bregović not only adopted local melodies, but he used ox horns and brass from the First World War—dirty and out-of-tune instruments. He arranged the music not with traditional dance rhythms in 3/4 time but instead following typical Gypsy patterns, the *aksak* asymmetric rhythms of 7/8, 11/8, 13/8, 9/16, and 10/16. Finally, he used mountaineer singers from Bosnia because, as he explained, "they sing in a most powerful way, as though they were accompanying very heavy physical work."[19] The soundtrack sold several thousand copies in the former Yugoslavia. A heart-rending piece, "Ederlezi," the song for St. George's Day (here performed by the Macedonian singer Vaska Jankovska), had a broad appeal. It is still widely played in the former Yugoslavia at weddings or funerals, or wherever there is an emotion-laden ceremony.[20] The piece, however, stirred controversy: Bregović has claimed that the text and the music were his creations, but others maintain that it was part of the repertoire of traditional Gypsy music. Other songs, from the film and from his broader repertoire, were used as national anthems and sung in political gatherings and at soccer matches. Their widespread popularity embarrassed Bregović, for he had tried to break down many nationalistic barriers; for example, in some of his concerts he sang in Albanian (something no Yugoslav rock singer had ever done), or he controversially mixed Serbian and Croatian anthems in a single song, which often caused violent turmoil at concerts. Bregović was—even if he is no longer—a key figure in Kusturica's career: their collaboration signaled the beginning of a much closer bond between music and images in the director's film poetics. Kusturica's subsequent career would embody new expressive syntheses through the inclusion of rock-and-roll.

One question still remains: Why Gypsies? Why the artistic interest in such a singular culture and civilization? Since the early twentieth century, there have been many precedents in European cinema; more recently, one may avail oneself of a conspicuous critical literature on their media representation.[21] A very early example was a film produced by Pathé: *En Serbie: Un mariage chez les Tziganes* (1911), which already featured the pivotal archetype of the wedding. Perhaps more than other regions, film production in Yugoslavia, before and after the recent wars, developed a special attention to Gypsy life, which included, as we have seen, Petrović's 1967 *I Even Met Happy Gypsies,* which was distributed in 140 countries, and Paskaljević's *Guardian Angel* from twenty years later. But neither Petrović's ethnographic current nor Paskaljević's sympathetic but external approach measured up to the popularization of the Dionysian spirit of Kusturica's work. The explanation must be sought elsewhere, even outside cinema. In this regard, it may be useful to consider the pervasive fortunes of "world music" following the fall of the Berlin Wall.

The post-1989 historical context featured a widespread acceptance of the inevitability of capitalism and its global liberal economy and, simultaneously, an intensified fascination for the rebellious or just spontaneously anticonformist diversity of peoples and cultures that were either not at all in tune with such mainstream modernity or skillfully operated at its margins. Attention to groups or people long considered peripheral, particularly minorities and immigrants, and above all the eternally ahistorical Gypsies, presented a combination of ethnography and aesthetics. Consider the fortunes of such musical groups as the Bulgarian Voices and the Romanian Taraf de Haïdouks. It was in this context that Bregović, as a *bricoleur* rather than just a composer of Gypsy *sevdah,* or folk music, managed to internationalize his early success with Bijelo Dugme by means of a Balkanizing use of choruses and brass—the first being Bulgarian, and the second Gypsy. His "Ederlezi" became an anthem for the Gypsies just as "Djelem, Djelem" had been twenty years earlier, thanks to Petrović's film. In the post-1989 environment, the success of Gypsy music was indeed geographically linked to the Balkan contexts, but more precisely to Balkanism, the exoticizing (and self-exoticizing) geopolitical framework that had identified an unmodern Orient within Europe. As the synesthetic and almost hypnotizing effect of Gypsy music reinforced geopolitical prejudices and nostalgic forms of ethno-nationalism, these in turn also revealed new opportunities, aesthetic as well as commercial.[22]

Consider the case of the Algiers-born Gypsy-French director Tony Gatlif. If in 1983 he devoted his *Les Princes* (not distributed in the United States) to a Gypsy community based outside Paris, after the late 1990s he regularly set his musical renderings about Gypsies, including the successful *The Crazy Stranger* (*Gadjo dilo*, 1997), in Eastern Europe, the cradle of Gypsy life. It is also no coincidence that Gatlif has since begun to receive important prizes, including a Cannes Festival award for best direction for *Exile* (*Exils*, 2004). Although another obvious "Balkan" comparison can be made with Theo Angelopoulos (and his collaboration with the composer Eleni Karaindrou), no one more than Kusturica has found in the Gypsy minority his own poetic homeland. In conjunction with an international context so favorable to romanticizing politically disadvantaged minorities, Kusturica's aesthetic proclivities, including his penchant for characters, narratives, and melodies that entertain a dissonant, asynchronous, and even carnivalesque relationship with modern life, have made his poetic association with the Gypsy world and its Dionysian fullness somehow to be expected.

To the rhythm and the melody of the soundtrack, however, must be added the expressive dimension of the Gypsy language, notoriously incomprehensible to most outsiders. It is perhaps not just by chance that a little-known language, Eskimo, is inserted at the beginning of Kusturica's next feature, *Arizona Dream*. Shot in a land far distant from his beloved Balkans, the Eskimo segments that open and close the film help him relocate his charmingly unfitting characters from the gray and misty winters of upper Macedonia and Milan to the sunny climate of the Arizona desert. There, in his most "American" production, Kusturica sought to adapt his poetics of untimeliness with a greater amount of difficulty.

A Yugoslav in America

Kusturica's fourth film, *Arizona Dream* (1993), immediately stood out as the most unusual in his short filmography. Even now, it retains that place in his oeuvre. The setting, language, and production values (i.e. stardom) reveal quite clearly the results of the director's encounter with the Hollywood system. Sometimes these results are highly expressive, sometimes less so.

Filmed in Alaska, Arizona, and New York, the film won the Silver Bear award and the top prize for Best Direction at the Berlin International

Film Festival. The story was originally written by the twenty-five-year-old David Atkins, whom Kusturica had met at Columbia University's Film School during the two years (1990–92) he taught screenwriting there. As a final result, however, *Arizona Dream* explores the American cultural universe and its related emotional economy through the wonderstruck and polemical eyes and ears of a European filmmaker. Although American scenarios present well-defined narrative sequences, informed by natural diegetic plausibility, the close collaboration of the young Atkins with the almost forty-year-old director led to the redeployment of two familiar Kusturician features: suicide, understood as the most direct confrontation between life and death, and dreams, as characters' epiphanies capable of revealing their most profound truths. From such extreme atmospheres, the film acquires a slightly morbid and obsessive tone, depending heavily on dialectal inflections, slang expressions, and linguistic references to classic Hollywood films.

The suggestive opening sequence, set in Greenland and centered on an Eskimo family's dangerous life of ice fishing, eventually proves to be a dream of the protagonist, Axel Blackmar (Johnny Depp), who is obsessed with the so-called arrow-fish, or arrow-toothed halibut. Axel works for the Department of Fish and Game of the City of New York, and his voice-over narration introduces us to the film's dreamy register. Upon waking up, he is visited by his friend Paul (Vincent Gallo), an adopted and proud New Yorker who is in love with old Hollywood cinema. Despite Axel's resistance, Paul manages to take him to Arizona, where Axel's Uncle Leo (Jerry Lewis) is about to marry Millie (Paulina Porizkova). The American landscape of strip malls and automobile dealerships depresses Axel, as do Leo's kitschy clothes and cheap cologne, and most remarkably, his American dream of material success, through which he will compare his younger wife to a new sports car. Filled with guilt for the death of Axel's parents in a car accident in which he was the driver, Leo wants his nephew to go into business with him as a car salesman. The ensuing meeting with a customer, the rich widow Elaine (Faye Dunaway) and her rebellious and suicide-prone stepdaughter, Grace (Lili Taylor), who hates her stepmother, will change Axel's life. At first he falls in love with the fearless Elaine, who listens to his Eskimo dream, has a talent for engines, and dreams of building a motorized hang glider. Axel's reaction equates love with flying ("I was not falling in love,

I was actually flying in love for the first time in my life!"). But soon after their attempt to build a reliable hang glider fails (as does their love), he begins to be drawn to the vulnerable and solitary Grace, who plays the accordion and seems to understand him better. In all these narrative developments, Paul is often alone disengaged from Axel's eventful life and busy trying out his monologues drawn from famous films ranging from *North by Northwest* (1959) to *The Godfather Part II* (1974).

Leo's sudden death from a heart attack and Axel's growing fondness for Grace persuade the young man to reveal to her his love. That night, however, eager to reincarnate herself in a turtle, Grace commits sucide. It is another epiphany for Axel, who is happy to be alive and returns to his dream of Eskimo life in the Arctic, this time featuring Leo, who in Eskimo language comments on the peculiar features of the arrow-toothed halibut: born with one eye on each side of its head like most fish, the halibut will overcome the nightmare of being born and will grow into an adult by shifting one of its eyes to the opposite side of its body. At that moment, Leo and Axel watch in amazement as their fish rises into the air and flies away.

Arizona Dream is a work about the aspirations and mirages of the American way of life, as its working titles ("American Dreamers" and "American Dream") confirm. The film opens with what we soon realize is the dream of the protagonist, who imagines a scene of primordial struggle and a miraculous rescue at the North Pole. An Eskimo saves his day's catch of fish from the dangers of melting ice but, exhausted, is on the point of giving in to the blizzard when his sled dog comes to his aid and, after hypnotizing him, takes the man to safety. Once at home, the Eskimo's young son and family observe (or perhaps conjure up) everything from inside the igloo, through a window pane made of ice that provides the only visual outlet to the arctic storm outside. Not only is this opening sequence Axel's dream, as we understand from the journey of the red balloon that flies from the Pole to Manhattan; it also marks the film's philosophic register. It points to the characters' difficulty in managing their balance between dream and reality, between a well-protected and intact inner life and an outside world that seems savage and full of dangers.

One cannot help but wonder whether Kusturica has made a European film about America or has simply continued to explore his earlier

poetic obsessions (i.e., the passage into adulthood, the relations between youth and ideology, dreams and rebellion, and the clash between
elementary and modern life) by simply transplanting them to North
American soil. To address this question, it may be useful to recall the
"American" films of directors like Michelangelo Antonioni, Louis Malle,
and Wim Wenders. Rather than fims about America, these filmmakers'
works perhaps inevitably are metaphoric and even somewhat "parasitic"
productions. Their satire, nostalgia, and lyricism are to be critically associated to the poetic perspectives of their authors. For Kusturica, the
same approach should apply. His America is one that is interpreted
liberally by a "Yugoslav from Sarajevo," enamored of the magic realism
of Gabriel García Márquez, Iggy Pop's rock music, the iconic faces of
Jerry Lewis and Faye Dunaway, the kitsch of the American hinterland
(the Southwest, in this case), flying objects and animals, and the ever-
present accordion.

   This is not to say that Kusturica remained culturally entrenched in
Sarajevo but, more simply, that his American transposition seems to
possess some of the characteristics of his most solipsistic characters.
Vladimir Mayakovsky's poem "Brooklyn Bridge" (1925) comes to mind,
and especially the unrealized film that Sergei Eisenstein so much wanted
to make in the late 1920s, *Glass House*. The story was entirely set in a
glass-walled American skyscraper—an architectonic image of America,
according to the Soviet obsession with a totally industrialized and vertical
United States. In the proposed film, the observer-narrator is protected
in the glass-and-steel tower (a mythic emblem of efficiency and modern
comfort) as he observes and derides the other America, the one "out
there," consisting of real, humble working people who walk about in
the streets and squares beneath him. That is to say, the journey inside
America's boundless diversity is ultimately an odyssey that one experiences within oneself, a voyage of the soul that becomes a personal stream
of consciousness, emblematically incarnated in the diegetic and visual
weight of dreams. In this sense, one may appreciate how Kusturica's
project articulates a desire for total and thus experimental cinema, free
from the Hollywood naturalism and the verisimilitude of genre cinema,
and closer instead to an existential cartoon.

   Arizona Dream was filmed with many interruptions during the outbreak of the war in the former Yugoslavia. The difficulties of filming

under American production schedules and pressures were compounded by personal distress—during the siege of Sarajevo, Kusturica lost first his family home and then his father, who had moved away from the Bosnian capital. Because the shooting was interrupted for three months, Kusturica ran into serious trouble with the original executive producer, later replaced, even though the funding for the film was mostly French, with backing from Constellation, UGC, and Hachette, and the participation of Canal+ and CNC. While the production problems did not weaken the incentives of making a film totally focused on the illusions and deformities of dreams (not only American), they without doubt darkened its tone.

The film's expressive quality remained as heterogeneous and inventive as his past works, yet *Arizona Dream* displays a pessimism foreign to Kusturica's "magical" poetics. Every character has an intimate aspiration that ultimately proves impossible to realize. Grace, for example, wishes to be reincarnated as a turtle; like his father, Leo dreams of reaching the moon by piling Cadillacs one on top of the other; Paul would like to break into films and perform like (or together with) Pacino, De Niro, and other stars. And it does not seem so much the real or logical impossibility of their desires that stymies the characters and makes them perpetually restless and dissatisfied; their failure instead seems due to the absence of an internal *force*, a seriousness, and sort of maturity that is also cynicism or resignation. What makes them not only solitary and solipsistic (like Dino, Malik, and Perhan) is not simply the unrealistic quality of their dreams. Rather, it is their imagination's inherent *lightness*, its (and their) state of being suspended between life and death, between reality and fiction. In their innumerable levitations and in the aerial acrobatics of their hang glider, Axel and Elaine are even literally suspended between earth and sky. Paul, who mimes the scenes and the dialogues of cinematic classics, is similarly suspended between life and the silver screen.

At one point, Axel recalls a common saying of his father: "If you ever wanted to look at someone's soul, you'd have to ask to look at their dreams." And the film consistently does exactly that: it interrogates its characters, exploring the ways in which they live with their most secret desires and the most genuine aspirations of their being. More prosaically, the film poses the problem of the ways in which dreams mediate between the private and public sphere—a cardinal element in Kusturica's film poetics. In *Arizona Dream,* however, we witness an off-kilter and schizophrenic relation between dream and reality. There is no preordered and sound myth for their synthesis, as there is for the Gypsies of the previous film. The initial disparity between the images of the clear Arctic atmosphere and the coarse-grained pictures of the bay around Manhattan, though tempered by the red balloon, is striking and traumatic. The conflict that the characters set up within themselves is no longer just a passage from adolescence to adulthood, but also an opposition between life and nothingness. The diversity of the American landscape embodied by the Arizona desert setting, the absence of the typical Yugoslav political and ideological references, but especially the lack of strong family ties—Axel is an orphan with an uncle who was once but is no longer his hero—all intensify the dark existential fabric of the film. These absences create a void around the characters, causing them to implode in a narrative sense: many of their actions seem inexplicable and even arbitrary.

Kusturica has often observed that the family represents the principal dramatic context of his films and the optic through which one perceives history. In *Arizona Dream,* the traditional family is almost nonexistent. As far as history is concerned, the director seems to be saying that there is no need to waste much time on it, since the setting is Arizona. By transferring his dramatic constants to American soil, Kusturica weakens his preferred narrative axis centered on the household. As a result, he makes his characters' dreams literally incredible, at other times vaguely metaphorical, and very often coarse. In one instance he is capable of combining all these qualities, as in the case of Uncle Leo—Jerry Lewis in a pink jacket, white undershorts, and snakeskin cowboy boots, obsessed by his materialistic ambitions.

Having found a quiet corner in his dream world, Axel has memories of his own family, but they are more contradictory—distant inner instincts rather than actual emotional reminiscences. Once taken forcibly "home," Axel loses for a certain time the capacity to articulate his own dreams; instead, he becomes fascinated with others' dreams. He tries to fly with Elaine, kill himself with Grace, and sell cars like Leo, until each of these characters dies to him, either mentally or physically. He then begins once more, in the company of the arrow-toothed halibut,

Leo Sweetie (Jerry Lewis) as the glorious image
of American materialism in *Arizona Dream*.
Courtesy of Photofest.

to reconstruct a new personal faith, just like Dino did with the rabbit
and Perhan with the turkey. He loves fish for their desire to be free and
for what he believes is their determination not to compromise. At the
beginning, in fact, he notes: "I've never caught a fish in a lie." And it is
indeed a fish that accompanies him in his lonely wanderings between
dream and reality. The arrow-toothed halibut becomes the magical representation of Axel's development and of his inner journey: it appears
to him, for example, when he makes love with Elaine for the first time.
It is a fish unique to its species, capable of revealing its physiological
maturation by changing the position of its eyes. Allegorically, the fish
changes its visual perspective: "You lose something, but you also gain
something," as we learn from the film's last words, spoken in Eskimo
by Jerry Lewis.

Axel will stop feeling like a "fish out of water" only after the death
of Grace in a scene that combines—without perhaps succeeding
perfectly—various *topoi* of Kusturica's cinema: these range from the
figure of a white-clothed woman dying in the middle of the night and
in tempestuous weather (wind or rain), to the "unrealistic" presence of
a soaring fire near to the house and the lifeless body of Grace, shot in a

spectacular long take. This unusual scene's imposing character is not often found in the director's stylistic register. Shot from a high position, we first see Axel run toward the flames, then, with a panoramic view that moves away from the fire's terrestrial light, a long shot reveals the arrow-toothed halibut that flits about in the sky and then heads off toward the moon. This same flight is repeated in several scenes, including the final one with Lewis and Depp dressed as two Eskimos intent on catching the arrow-toothed halibut, the metaphor of a personal growth never to be postoponed.

Arizona Dream presents other stylistic strategies rarely used before. One of these is the fade-in frequently adopted to mark progress in the construction (or destruction) of rickety flying contraptions. Especially in the first part, Kusturica alternates these scenes with marvelous images of desert sunsets, sometimes with backlit shots and with the presence and the yapping of a sled dog obviously out of place. The spectator may be left with an impression of gratuitousness, but also with a sense of authentic astonishment at the facile metaphor.

Another controversial element in this film with so many poetic intersections is the music. The unusual soundtrack is once again in the charge of Goran Bregović, then well on his way to an international career. Among his credits are collaborations with Nicolas Klotz (*La nuit sacrée*, 1993), Philomène Esposito (*Toxic Affair*, 1993), and a joint effort with Patrice Chéreau for the melodies of *Queen Margot* (*La reine Margot*, 1994), extraordinarily similar to the music of *Arizona Dream*. Bregović's function in *Arizona Dream* is fundamental: his music must create a bridge between Kusturica's personal universe and the world of America. Besides recruiting an old and glorious voice of American rock like Iggy Pop, who gives to the film a classic, if stereotypical, flavor, the Sarajevo-born composer included the curious Yugoslav-Mexican tunes already heard in the opening sequence of *When Father Was Away on Business* and, especially, the atmospheric Macedonian and Bulgarian melodies of pieces like *Old Home Movie*. Moreover, he retrieves the irregular tempos in 7/8 and 11/8, which he combines with the rhythms of Iggy Pop's American pieces.

Mexican music has an obvious narrative justification in a film set in Arizona—a band plays at the farm all day on Elaine's birthday—yet the Yugoslav-Mediterranean motifs are certainly more poetic, at least in their intentions, even though they may appear arbitrary. Appealingly, Kusturica makes audiovisual reference to his own work when, halfway through the film, we see and hear Grace play "Carnevale di Venezia" and a Kusturica mazurka on the accordion while Axel, wrapped in an enormous nightshirt, playfully mimics the movements and the sounds of a turkey (an obvious reference to *Time of the Gypsies*). Still, Paul's metacinematic performances, characterized by a solipsistic and heart-breaking mimesis, are unsurpassed.

Further, by employing two icons of American film like Faye Dunaway and Jerry Lewis, Kusturica seems to elevate his discourse on dreams and illusions to a metacinematic level, taking up a position on Holly-wood, the "dream factory." In Kusturica's Eurocentric vision, these two stars, nearly forgotten and even "tragic" in their post-fame existence, are seasoned icon-bodies, engulfed in the void and the nothingness on the fringes of the American imagination and rendered insane, fragile, and alone by their characters' strange utopias. Dunaway, after years of alleged personal difficulties with alcohol and tranquillizers, had left behind forever the role of femme fatale that launched her career in

Axel (Johnny Depp) and Elaine (Faye Dunaway)
try to realize their dreams of flying in *Arizona
Dream*. Courtesy of Photofest.

Arthur Penn's *Bonnie and Clyde* (1967) and glorified her in Roman Polanski's *Chinatown* (1974). Against the constraining fame of her past roles, Kusturica liberates her, within and without the film. Dunaway's Elaine (whose fictional surname is Stalker, like the title of Tarkovsky's film) personifies the slightly capricious, youthful, but for her never obsolete fascination with flight and personal freedom. As Axel explains at the end, "Elaine and Grace were really one person who were too big to really share life in one body."

Even more than for Dunaway, the roles for Lewis have been almost nonexistent. For years, before and after this film, he was seen only on charity telethons, and Americans grew fond of laughing at the French enthusiasm for him and for his once-popular films with Dean Martin. On the one hand, his character is a marginal figure, almost an outcast, like the protagonist of Jane Campion's *Sweetie* (1989), which in the film is his surname. On the other hand, however, he incarnates the most excessive and cloying picture of the humor of the provincial American dream. In their flamboyant obsolescence, Elaine and Leo demonstrate a simplicity of mind and language unrecognizable to the modern Axel and Grace. Their metaphoric discussion about love between individuals of strikingly different age, with examples from old and modern car models, is an old piece of Americana, as is the way their conversation concludes with with shotgun blasts.

By conveying a sense of "dead end," these metacinematic references contribute to the bleakness of a film that often lingers on the visual and narrative theme of suicide. Although suicide is an extreme and tragic example of the human encounter with death, Kusturica has often treated it comically. In *When Father Was Away on Business*, Ankica, after her subjection to Meša's violent and vindictive sexual assault, decides to hang herself with the cord of the lavatory tank, but succeeds only in flushing the toilet. Perhan's sole accomplishment in *Time of the Gypsies* is to ensnare himself and dangle up and down, ringing the country church bell in the middle of the night. In *Arizona Dream*, Grace's first public attempt at suicide resembles Perhan's awkward effort: she hangs like a marionette, becoming an existential caricature of herself. Her final scene is radically different; drowned out by the sound of thunder, the gunshot that Grace fires into her mouth signals definitively the end (or the new beginning) of her inner exile.

Thematically, Kusturica's next work, *Underground*, is connected to suicide, but this time the scale has changed. *Underground* explores the notion of suicide on the level of an entire nation: a cruel and much bigger battle of power and exploitation replaces the emotional injuries of characters' dreams and the precariousness of their existence. The various interpretative possibilities that focus on the director's political maturation or, simply, on a new poetic ambition remain to be discussed.

Disconnection

Once upon a Time There Was a Country

Twenty years before *Underground's* release, the Serbian playwright and screenwriter Dušan Kovačević (b. Sabac, 1948) wrote a play, *Spring in January (Proleće u januaru)*, about a man who holds people locked up in a cellar, making them believe that there is still a war going on outside. Actually, he had written two plays on this subject, *Spring in January* and *The Gathering Place (Sabirni centar)*, which together inspired one of the most politically controversial films of recent years and which, for a few months, seemed to signal the end of Kusturica's cinematic career. Eventually *Underground* came to represent Kusturica's most dramatic act of disconnection from Yugoslav and western culture—whichever way one assesses his allegorical constructions. The controversies around the film made the director persona non grata in his native Sarajevo and produced forms of exilic film poetics that spilled over real-life domains, including urban architecture and landscape design, and that overshadowed earlier cultural dissentions.

According to the film's pressbook, everything began in Germany. Karl Baumgarten, head of the production company Pandora Film, had acquired the rights to Kovačević's story and with Kusturica had begun to develop it as a film project. It immediately became clear that the dark and satirical tragicomedy they had in mind could not be produced with their initial budget of a few million dollars, even with the inclusion of Serbian financing. They sought and received help from the Paris-based production company Ciby 2000 (as well as from the Hungarian Novo Film), whose decisive contribution enabled the director to develop a much more ambitious—and ultimately more dangerous—project. It should be noted that Ciby 2000 has always denied any contribution from the Radio Television of Serbia (RTS, a.k.a. the Serbian Broadcasting Corporation), contrary to what the Centre de recherche Droit International 90 maintained. Admitting any form of Serbian financing would have constituted an infraction of the international embargo in force against Milošević's nation. For his part, Kusturica has often spoken only of Serbian logistical and technical support, not financial backing, in return for the rights to serialize the film on television at a later date—something that actually occurred in the late summer of 1995.

With French, German, Hungarian, and (debatably) Serbian financing, the filming of *Underground* grew in scale and ambitions. Eventually it took shape as a European-style *Apocalypse Now*, whereby the production and destruction of reality that are inherent in the practice of cinematic representation turned out to be more than fictional constructions or even artistic licenses. When considering the historical context, the plot, or even the film's final scene alone (which I will describe later), *Underground* dramatically surpasses the "fiction" of its own production to arrive at a perverse (and, given the demiurgic nature of cinema, perhaps inevitable) *re-creation* of reality. And that reality is one of military conflict, past and present, and of the cruelest of deceptions, all leading to the fratricide of civil war.

Filming began at the Barrondov Studios in Prague in October 1993 and ended at Belgrade in February 1995. The production designer, Miljen Kljaković, familiarly called "Kreka," had collaborated with Kusturica ever since the days of *Time of the Gypsies*; between underground areas, thirty-two subterranean passages, and exterior locations built from scratch, Kreka designed and built almost 320,000 square feet of sets. It was a kind of giant scaffolding, similar to the one appearing at the end of Fellini's *8½* (1963), with which the former boy from Sarajevo attempted to unravel, like a tangled ball of yarn (and *not* like a historical essay), the genealogy of the government's lies in Tito's former nation.

Of the original stage play, Kovačević has observed that Kusturica, as the film director, changed and appropriated many of the dramatic features of the original story. Differently from the source play, where the idea of an underground existence is mainly associated with a family, the director pushed for the story to involve a nation. In the end, this became a film about Yugoslavia, which lived under circumstances that were different from, say, those affecting life in Russia or Romania.[23] After a dedication ("to our fathers and their children") and a fairy-tale line ("Once upon a time there was a country . . . and its capital was Belgrade. April 6, 1941"), the film begins with the loud, diegetic tunes played by a Gypsy band. The piece is called "Kalashnikov," and the band is playing it while running behind a buggy carrying two drunk friends, Marko Dren (Miki Manojlović, from *When Father Was Away on Business*) and Petar "Blacky" Popara (Lazar Ristovski), who are returning home after a long night out. Boisterous and irreverent, the two friends empty their pistols into the air, throw bills and bottles at the musicians, pass by the city zoo that is the home of Marko's stuttering brother Ivan, and finally arrive at Blacky's house. Tired of waiting for her man, his wife Vera (Mirjana Karanović, also from *When Father Was Away on Business*) is furious at Marko for making her husband join the Communist party even after he promises he will always remain a free man despite his possessive wife. He could not be more mistaken.

Part 1: The War. In the early morning, German aircraft begin pounding Belgrade. The raining bombs destroy the zoo, freeing some animals and killing others, including Ivan's pet monkey. The invasion upsets Blacky only when a liberated elephant roaming in the streets below his apartment interrupts his meal. He then dresses up to the nines not only to fight the Nazis but to meet his lover, the actress Natalija (Mirjana Joković). The attack has also interrupted Marko, who was busy making love to a prostitute. But he is intrigued: business opportunities in time of war can be exceptional.

Before coming to Belgrade, and meeting its citizens' hostile reaction, the Nazis had invaded Slovenia and Croatia, where the local population, seen cheering in Kusturica's use of historical footage, welcomed their arrival. Still, in the Serbian capital, behind the occupation and the resistance, there are deals to be made. Natalija has found a loving protector in Lieutenant Franz, who promotes her stage career and supplies medicine for her paralytic brother (Bata). The most active under the Nazi rule is Marko, who, in addition to making money as an arms dealer, persuades a few trusted individuals to hide in a giant underground basement and to build weapons for the anti-Nazi resistance. Among them are Marko's brother Ivan, Blacky, and Vera, who soon dies while giving birth to their son Jovan. Initially, Blacky manages to exit the underground to try to meet Natalija. One night, after beating up some fellow black marketeers, a Croatian and a Bosnian, he and Marko kidnap Natalija from the theater where she is performing: Blacky wishes to marry her on a boat along the Danube. During the banquet, surrounded by the ubiquitous Gypsy band, Marko shows his most manipulative side: he describes his friend to Natalija as simply an electrician, or actually a "pole man," who owes him everything. When the Germans show up, Marko manages to escape. Blacky is not so quick and is imprisoned. After liberating him, Marko hides him in the underground basement, not for a little while, but for decades. As a result, Blacky loses contact with both Natalija and history, while Marko becomes a hero of the Communist resistance, a key member of Yugoslavia's top political circles, and Natalija's partner.

Part 2: The Cold War. Belgrade 1961: as Marko publicly celebrates the alleged sacrifice of the partisan Blacky by turning him into a "man of marble," Blacky remains underground, fed by Marko's lies about a soon-to-come decisive battle with the Nazis. The basement is now an

Marko overseeing the wedding between Blacky and Natalija; Gypsy musicians in the background in *Underground.* Courtesy of Photofest.

efficient weapons factory, always on alert against Nazi attacks, where even the passing of time is skillfully manipulated—twenty years become fifteen. Outside, in the real world, the events of the resistance have given rise to a film tradition consisting of countless productions that follow a rigid script of national celebration and sacrifice. If Marko is the effective patron, demiurge, and master-exploiter of these representations, Natalija has growing doubts that she cannot suppress during Jovan's underground wedding, when she meets Blacky after two decades of lies.

When Soni, Ivan's pet monkey, accidentally operates a tank and fires a cannon shot that opens a breach in the basement wall, Jovan and Blacky discover a maze of underground tunnels linking Belgrade with other European capitals. They surface right in the middle of a film set, where a resistance film is being shot. Firm in their belief in the continuing Nazi occupation, they kill the actors impersonating German officers and escape along the Danube. Jovan drowns in the river, but not before seeing beneath the water his bride whom he believed lost, just as Jean sees his wife Juliette in Jean Vigo's *L'Atalante* (1934). Meanwhile, Tito dies, and the lid that had contained Yugoslavia's latent interethnic conflicts is abruptly removed.

Part 3: The War. Looking for his inseparable Soni, Ivan surfaces in Berlin, only to be told that the war ended fifty years before, that Yugoslavia no longer exists, and that his brother Marko is on Interpol's most-wanted list as an arms dealer. After reentering the tunnels, he emerges in a section of the former Yugoslavia where he recognizes his aging brother, now in a wheelchair, negotiating a sale of arms to another trafficker (played by Kusturica himself). Once the quiet Abel, a furious Ivan kills Cain-Marko

Biblical justice in *Underground*: Ivan (Slavko Štimac) hits his brother Marko (Miki Manojlović) as a Chagallian inverted crucifix is visible in the background.

in the ominous presence of an upside-down crucifix before committing suicide.

Meanwhile, Blacky is now the commander of a small army at war with everybody—Chetniks, Ustashe, and U.N. soldiers—perennially seeking his long-gone son, whom he finally looks for by throwing himself down a well. The final scene shows all the protagonists, as young as they first appeared onscreen, seated at an open-air banquet for Jovan's wedding, surrounded by Gypsy musicians. They drink and celebrate life together, without forgiving each other's evil deeds. Ivan, looking straight into the camera, recites an homage to their fertile land. In closing, he tells us: "With pain, sadness, and with joy we will remind our children of our land when we will tell them stories that begin with, 'Once upon a time there was a country. . . . '" Happy and inebriated, they start dancing just as the piece of land they are standing on separates itself from the mainland and drifts along the Danube before a closing intertitle reads, "This story has no end."

The film discussed here is the version distributed to movie theaters, which runs about two hours and forty-six minutes, twenty-six minutes shorter than the one seen and awarded at Cannes (three hours and twelve minutes) and almost two hours shorter than the very first cut, which reached five hours and forty minutes of Gypsy frenzy. Despite the cuts (concentrated for the most part in the "central" scene of Jovan's and Jelena's marriage), so many things happen in *Underground*, as in Kusturica's other films, that it is as hard to recount them all as it is to explain all the film's visual and aural metaphors. The narrative plots, the visual stimuli, and the emotional impulses that had seemed to reach the height of chaos and complexity in *Time of the Gypsies* are here intensified to the extreme. And yet, in its poetics of extravagant staging, emphatic camera movements, and histrionic acting style, *Underground* succeeds as an imposing genealogical and eschatological representation of a nation that once was but now is no more.

Underground is undoubtedly Kusturica's most ambitious, visceral, and controversial film. Disguising himself as a Bakhtinian clown and as a Foucauldian historiographer, Kusturica dared to speak of the history of the former Yugoslavia as though it were a dark carnival in which Cain tries to be the demiurge, manipulating and standing guard over Abel for half a century; in which the state of war, whether true or fictitious, was never interrupted in order to control the Yugoslav people; and in which the surreal character of the regime's lies can, at times, become hilarious. *Underground*, among many other things, is a film about the reality and the spatiotemporal illusions of a nation. It is also, and perhaps inevitably, a film about the "spatiotemporal ideology" of its director. Nostalgically and rather provokingly, Kusturica had initially proclaimed himself a "Yugoslav from Bosnia," harking back to a time and to a geography that, in the opinion of many, was suspect and indefensible because it was solely endorsed by Serbians and, moreover, negated by the terrible reality of the Balkan wars.

In a country in which the recent and, in many ways, still-unfinished political and military battles had destroyed from within all traditional national, ethnic, and territorial relations, the irreverent and exaggerated exploration of the deceptions of communism, accompanied by the affectionate and contradictory memory of the former Yugoslav nation, seemed to many like the actions of someone who did not want to call the villains by their rightful name. On the contrary, Kusturica seemed to be repeating the Serbians' nostalgic cries for the reconstruction of a nation, *their* nation, that had now disintegrated.

The Palme d'Or at the thirty-eighth Cannes Film Festival, where *Underground* won out over a very different Balkan epic, *Ulysses' Gaze* by Theo Angelopoulos, gave Kusturica a great deal of publicity and spurred infinite controversies. Other films in the 1990s could have caused similar reactions, including Boro Drasković's *Vukovar* (1994) and Srđjan Dragojević's *Pretty Village, Pretty Flame* (*Lepa sela lepo gore*, 1996); but timing and visibility, among other factors, were not on their side. The accusations of Serbian propaganda leveled at the two films were overshadowed by the glare from the Cannes spotlights reserved for *Underground*.

In May and June 1995, a virulent series of attacks was leveled at Kusturica. A number of intellectuals, newspapers editorialists, and professional *maîtres à penser,* from France but also from Italy, condemned in unison the newly awarded film as criminally endorsing a Fourth Reich, its director as an "irresponsible opportunist" and "traitor," and Cannes as a theater of hypocritical bourgeois operetta. What the *nouveaux philosophes* Alain Finkielkraut, Bernard-Henri Lévy (fresh from directing

Bosna! [1994]), and Pascal Bruckner had in common, in addition to a public aversion for the film and its director, whom they often compared to Céline, was the fact that they had not actually seen *Underground* and were unperturbed by this basic rule of intellectual integrity. And neither were their editors and publishers, from *Le Monde* to *Libération*. Later on, Finkielkraut, in reviewing the film for *Libération*, reiterated his accusations by finding the film packed with "oneiric propaganda."[24] In 1999, in his film, *Nothing about Robert (Rien sur Robert)*, the former *Cahiers du Cinéma*–editor-turned-director Pascal Bonitzer commented on this intellectual disonesty by having his protagonist-journalist rushing to judge a Bosnian film he has never seen as "pure fascist propaganda."

In Italy, the film did not fare much better. The usually respected journalist and alleged Balkan expert Enzo Bettiza did the same on the pages of *La Stampa,* and so did other intellectuals and editorialists writing for Italy's preeminent daily *Il Corriere della Sera*, including Giuliano Zincone, Enzo Siciliano, Sergio Quinzio, Erri De Luca, Pietro Melograni, and even the theologian Sergio Quinzio. European dailies, including *La Repubblica*, joined the fray by publishing an article by Zlatko Dizdarević (a writer and journalist for *Oslobodjenje,* the heroic newspaper published in a Sarajevo under siege) who criticized Kusturica's personal and public life, without ever discussing the film. Only a few critics, including Lietta Tornabuoni (*La Stampa*), Gianluigi Melega (*l'Unità*), and Roberto Silvestri (*Il manifesto*), denounced the gratuitous bias of those interventions. Similarly, Jacques Almaric of *Libération* praised the film as a work about manipulation and rejected its description as an artful piece of propaganda.[25] This shorter list of reviewers who actually saw the film would include, among others, Serge Regourd of *Le Monde* and Mr. Busy, the fictitious name of an editorialist for *Sight and Sound.*[26]

The echo of these polemics eventually reached the United States, thanks to the partial summary written by Adam Gopnik in the *New Yorker,* which focused more on the eternal in-fights among French intellectuals than Kusturica's political allegiances.[27] Still, American critics generally preferred to emphasize the boundless compositional and musical energy of the film, likening the complexity of the political and ethnic references to the chaos of the war in the Balkans. No one was overly surprised when CiBy2000 withdrew *Underground* from a pre-

Oscar screening, and thus from competition for Best Foreign Film, "on the grounds that they did not know which version was being shown, one being potentially libellious," as the above-mentioned editorial contribution to *Sight and Sound* reads. The film's nomination by the Academy of Arts and Sciences of Belgrade, however, was an admission that at least two of the three elements of the film (production, direction, screenplay) were Serbian—*contra* Kusturica's own public statements.

Among the unfavorable judgments, one of the most substantive was that of the Montenegrin journalist Stanko Cerović, the author of an informative article published June 12, 1995, in *Monitor* and at the time affiliated with the French public-service radio station RFI. Slightly expanded, the piece was reprinted in English translation in the British periodical *Bosnia Report* in 1995, but its distribution was limited to specialized circles. Cerović's article is rare for its critical cogency, which contrasted with the polemical smoke of the early Parisian and Roman reaction. While not a professional film critic or historian, Cerović brought to light aspects of the film's style and narrative construction that may not have been obvious to a non-Balkan audience and which instead were hurriedly identified as the features of a very personal and stylized poetics.

Cerović made some accurate observations. If Kusturica was not under the influence of a politically misguided aesthetics, why put at the head of the revolution a typical Belgrade pair of popular heroes, a Serb and a Montenegrin, who—according to the Serbian nationalist myth and pride—fight and make love better than anyone else? Why construct Marko and Blacky as two champions endowed with indefatigable genetic vitality who may indeed cause irreparable damage, but only because of their irrepressible generosity resulting in an "irresistible charm"? Why choose to represent the two corrupt traffickers, beaten as traitors, as a Muslim and a Croatian? And why, in his selection of archival clips, did he not also include, along with those that reveal the pro-German parades in Zagreb and Maribor, those showing the destruction of Vukovar or the triumphal sendoff that Belgrade gave the military tanks leaving for Slovenia and Croatia in the summer of 1991? And, if one moves outside the film, why did Kusturica speak in his interviews of the war in Bosnia as an "ethnic and social earthquake," when he knows it was prepared in detail by the generals in Belgrade? Finally, why at Cannes was he accompanied by and photographed with not only the minister of culture Nada Popović-Perišić but also with Milorad Vučelić, a majority whip in the Serbian Parliament and, most ominously, the director of the Radio Television of Serbia, which for years broadcast nationalist propaganda for the Milosević regime?

Another *philosophe*, André Glucksmann, did not condemn the film but reviewed it as a remarkable transnational allegory on the cold-war totalitarian regime, as an unholy alliance of Mafia and political authoritarian powers. The only author who sought to understand *Underground* on its own terms, in addition to Cerović, was the Paris-based Austrian playwright Peter Handke. Of Carinthian Slovene background, Handke replied to Glucksmann's macro analysis in the pages of the *Süddeutsche Zeitung* and the *Corriere della Sera* by pointing out that his alleged defense of the film has the same anti-Serbian prejudice of Finkielkraut and displays the same disregard for the plight endured by the Serbian people and disinterest for the place of the Balkans in the future of Europe. He reiterated his argument in the controversial reportage *A Journey to the Rivers: Justice for Serbia* (1996), where he also critiqued the European intellectuals' consistently hostile view of unknown populations.[28]

For months, following the victory at Cannes and the ensuing attacks, Kusturica remained quiet. Then, at the end of October 1995, *Le Monde* published a letter of his ("Mon imposture") in which he sarcastically attacked Finkielkraut. He wrote a fictional review of a journalist who has not seen the film but who discovers in Kusturica's basement the access to a network of underground tunnels linking Rouen (where the director was allegedly living) and Belgrade, and thus Milosević. Shortly after, in early December 1995, Kusturica announced in a brief statement published in *Libération* that he was abandoning filmmaking. Fortunately, he later reviewed his decision, but apparently he has not set foot in Sarajevo since the outbreak of the war.

The range and cogency of critical-political exegeses do not, however, exhaust the cinematic ones. A critic like Cerović, for example, did not touch upon the specifics of the film's historico-narrative architecture, intent as he was to explore the causes of the most recent conflict and to review the deceptions and perverse expedients of the post–World War II period. He did not discuss the now-familiar metaphor of Communism as a subterranean cavern, devoid of light and truth. Above all, he did not address what for many people was an element in Kusturica's favor—that is, the fact that the two principal characters are not exactly heroes. On the contrary, they are swindlers and womanizers, with no true love of their country, absolutely irresponsible, egoistic, and ultimately self-destructive. The carnivalesque and Bakhtinian folly of their revelry does not redeem them: the two madmen are morally indifferent or apathetic. If Blacky makes us smile when he bites the electric cord in order to repair a short circuit, or when he detonates a hand grenade between his legs while locked in a trunk, the best we can do is pity him as a father perpetually in search of his son, whom he inadvertently left in the water to drown thirty years earlier. In similar fashion, Marko is the perverse Bentham-type guardian of the underworld, but we laugh at him when, dressed in pajamas, he awkwardly cranks up the mechanism of the fake air-raid siren; when he plays his erotic, fetishistic, and masochistic games with Natalija's pointed-toe shoes; when he clumsily dances to the beat of Gypsy music at the abortive wedding of Blacky and Natalija; or when he savagely masturbates after the prostitute has run away in terror during the German bombing of Belgrade. To be sure, it is not that Blacky and Marko are comic and nothing more. Their clumsiness makes them frightening because of the power that they exercise, above and below ground, before and after Communism: Marko, as a party functionary and friend of Tito, and later as a trafficker in arms; Blacky, first as a national legend and then as an undisciplined and dangerous warlord.

Let's take things in order. The film is structured like a stage play: three acts, each of which centers on a conflict (the Second World War, the cold war, and the recent interethnic wars). The three parts are neither of equal length nor similar in tone; the first, introduced by a band of musicians running behind the carriage of Marko and Blacky, is certainly the longest and the most surreal, while the last one, the most recent, tries to minimize any aspirations toward journalistic accuracy with highly symbolic images (the Western European entrance to the underground located next to the Berlin Reichstag, the inverted crucifix, the half-destroyed church, fires everywhere). In each act, however, the narrative and visual mechanisms seem based on the superimposition or overlay of spaces, people, and interests.

On the surface, there is a nation oppressed by the enemy, a world war, and a militant state ideology—that of Tito's partisans. Yet, against this historical reality, captured by archival film footage, an establishment of manipulative party functionaries pretends to exercise their allegedly moral guidance while instead trafficking in arms and heroes. When Marko tells Vera, Blacky's wife, that he has enrolled her husband in the Communist party, what he is really telling her is not that Blacky has entered a group of people united by an ideology but rather that he has finally gained acceptance among a den of thieves and exploiters. Later, Marko will physically impose his own role as party functionary and arms dealer on the existence of at least two dozen people, imprisoning them in the immense basement of his house to manufacture weapons. This image of an underground world, obvious and heartrending at once, has illustrious literary precedents, including Dostoevsky's novella *Notes from Underground* and Kafka's unfinished short story "The Burrow," as well as cinematic ones, most memorably Fritz Lang's *Metropolis* (1927). With his good friend Blacky, Marko will go even further. After freeing him from Nazi torture, he will imprison him in the basement with the others, monitoring his behavior with an inverted periscope (i.e., one that points

Underground. The continuation of a lie: Blacky (Lazar Ristovski), Natalija (Mirjana Joković), and Marko at the underground wedding of Jovan and Jelena. Courtesy of Photofest.

downward!) and above all subjecting him to the regime's speeches and fables, according to which the Nazis (the "capitalist fascists") are still firmly in power, and Tito personally is waiting for Blacky to join in the final battle, but *not before*.

Moreover, together with Natalija, Marko adds his own voice—that of a hero and a national poet—to the official fate of Blacky and participates in his friend's mythic hagiography. Standing before the statue of his hero-friend, who has now become a perpetual walk-on film actor, Marko actually ends up being moved. It is the supreme and inevitable fascination of a deception drawn out for too long and eventually becoming a historical reality. That is to say, lies told and retold invariably acquire the value of truth. Whether this is a phenomenon or a process of manipulation, Kusturica ridicules and, ironically, exalts it in his film.

In *Underground*, superimposition identifies the form of its historical script and cinematic representation, as it is evident in what we may call "fictional doublings." For example, the insertions of Blacky and Marko in the historical footage (through CGI effects reminscent of *Forrest Gump*) enter and leave the fictional world of the tale. On the one hand, the historical reality of these insertions is *true* in the diegetic universe of the film; on the other hand, they themselves are proof of their contrived nature—they are colored and historically impossible. Or, consider Blacky's intrusions onto the set of the film dedicated to him (even the title is a parody: *Spring Is Coming on a White Horse*). The fraud that endured for twenty years (which in turn were "reduced" to fifteen) causes Blacky to mistake the fiction of the movie set as reality and, absorbing it completely as *lector in fabula,* prevents him from recognizing the improbable "naturalist" dramas of the genre directors. There is a gibe here at Veljko Bulajić, who studied in Italy during the neorealist period. He was an assistant to De Sica, and when he returned home he besieged Yugoslav cinema with "real" dramas, allegedly simple and popular, including *Atomic War Bride* (*Rat,* 1960), *Kozara* (1962), and *The Battle of Neretva* (*Bitka na Neretvi,* 1969). The joke unwittingly played by Blacky (the real one) becomes hilarious when he actually kills the actor playing the part of Franz and thus becomes the involuntary agent of the realistic aesthetics of the director who maintains that "the more natural cinema is, the more terrifying it is."

Similarly, when Marko and Natalija visit the set of a film about their life story, even though they are made to watch unrealistic scenes that are thought to be real but that never occurred, they end up almost believing the truth of those grotesque representations. Kusturica plays with both cinema and history: on the one hand, he uses perfect physical resemblances between the "real" and "fictional" Marko and Natalija, obviously obtained by casting the same actors; on the other hand, he employs unrealistic sets and solutions for the skirmishes between partisans and the Germans, as was typical of many Yugoslav films of the postwar period that were produced to celebrate the partisan resistance.

Not only is manipulation in *Underground* a political and cultural fact, it is also a constant measure of Hobbesian human relations. In Marko it becomes almost an anthropological trait: he does not hesitate a moment to deceive his best friend Blacky and his brother Ivan; he has no scruples in seducing Natalija with his amorous lies; he even deceives himself when he says that he does not know how to lie or, behaving like a whimpering bourgeois prig, that he can no longer live in a country of maniacs, liars, and criminals. In this situation, Marko and Natalija are Yugoslavia's most surreal and perverse heroic couple. By mastering the pretentious and ridiculous language of absolute power, its studied and rehearsed gestures, its deceptions and fictions, they produce and represent the regime's most effective and enticing dramas to keep the underground population in a state of fear. Erect before the couple, the subterranean prisoners sing songs and recite slogans in chorus and thank the two heroes humbly for protecting them from the outside enemy.

Natalija's scruples of conscience last as long as her drunkenness at Jovan's wedding. When Marko, lying, confesses that he arranged all the sham of the underground just for love of her, her vanity and personal pride prove stronger than any moral doubt ("Marko, you lie so beautifully," she tells him). When the monkey destroys the apparatus of their power, the couple, now inseparable accomplices, stage their final fiction: they blow up the underground, arrange their own disappearance from history, flee to Germany, and become what they already are: arms traffickers sought by Interpol. We are at the beginning of the 1960s. The audience is informed that at the loss of Marko (i.e., of the regime's perfect fiction), Tito "fell ill" and lingered for twenty years before dying. Eventually his death becomes a spectacle that the film helps us to interpret. Accompanied by the notes of "Lili Marleen," the television footage of Tito's funeral acquires the flavor of the ultimate hoax and political manipulation: what are those Yugoslavs doing there, sad and weeping, and those oh-so-serious heads of state from all over the world? To a western audience, *Underground* showcases above all its own cultural diversity: a derisory and unmodern paganism of actions and feelings, accompanied for three hours by the Dionysiac cadences of Gypsy music, amounting to a repertoire of sarcasm and excess, allegedly of a purely Sarajevan taste. The band's heady music, almost always diegetic, intoxicates characters and spectators alike within a larger-than-life elementary vitality, composed of never-ending banquets and celebrations, where the boundaries between opposing feelings such as joy and despair or euphoria and exhaustion are remarkably blurred, and artful ambiguity reigns supreme. Here a quick change of music can set aside even ideological differences: on the boat, the Gypsy orchestra at a certain moment begins playing the Chetnik anthem. Someone points out to them that Blacky is a member of Tito's partisans (who succesfully fought the Chetniks). Not a problem: with serene ease and in the twinkling of an eye, the musicians strike up the Communist anthem to satisfy their audience.

One of the most decisive differences between Blacky and Marko is the tumultuous emotional passion of the former (a stereotypical Montenegrin) compared to the superior and cynical self-control of the latter. It is true that Blacky is a partisan who steals for himself and for his amorous intrigues, but there is still in him a tension and an ideal loyalty, a Marxist illusion, foreign to Marko. Blacky appears as the Communist believer for whom there cannot exist conflict or radical expedients between an individual and the collectivity, between reality and the party, between will and imagination. As such, he is the perfect gang leader, coddled while he bathes surrounded by music, brandy, and tobacco; his companions (later his soldiers) love him for his sensitivity and emotional vulnerability (particularly visible in his never-ending search for his son), as well as his inexhaustible natural and professional generosity. Kusturica does not portray the two spirits of Balkan emotionalism, the swindled and the swindler, as distinct. He pairs them off in their partisan enterprises and in their erotic and bellicose instincts; he makes them rivals for love and power. Blacky is the lord of the underworld, but his cruel friend reigns over him. The dynamics of their rapport is Hegelian, the relation of slave to master, where both need each other to maintain their authority despite one seeming to be stronger than the other.

Marko is never simply the horrible and disagreeable tyrant, however; he is the great seducer, the fascinating swindler, perhaps even a little awkward and amateurish, whom everyone loves to hate. Kusturica has often declared that there would be no wars without such characters, and he notes that cinematic history is full of unpleasant people that we cannot help but love, beginning, paradoxically, with Chaplin's Hynkel in *The Great Dictator* (1940). It is perhaps in this sense that one of the most Felliniesque scenes of the film, the one near the beginning in which Marko enjoys the view of the plump posterior of a prostitute, or those in which his grimaces of pleasure accompany his fistfights, all contribute to making him a terribly ambiguous character and turns his spectators into his accomplices. In this completely masculine universe, Natalija remains a strange figure, uncertain and suspect, and treated almost like a sketch. She perhaps represents the protean resilience of power, in her codified fictions (she willingly performs as a stage actress under any political banner), in her "Soviet" moments (during the wedding banquet she begins speaking in Russian, claiming it is her "mother tongue"), in her unpredictable actions (drunk and rueful, she almost betrays Marko), in her perverse implications (she is the instigator of the sadomasochistic erotic games), and in her self-satisfied stubbornness (she will never abandon her treacherous but faithful companion). During the whole film, however, she always appears discreet and innocent, the victim of the misogynistic ardor of Franz, Blacky, and Marko; yet she exploits the affections of them all.

In sum, *Underground* is a film about the reality and the spatiotemporal illusions of a Balkan nation. The film itself presents a high degree of cultural, cinematic, and even Kusturician self-reflexivity. In addition to Fellini, present everywhere in the beginning of the film, there is Chaplin in the way Marko runs, Tarkovsky in the use of fire and water, Ophüls in Jelena's majestic entrance, Herzog in the little carts in flames, Gilliam in the laborious and premodern technology, Chagall in the flying brides, the inverted crucifixes, and in the colors, and Vigo in the amorous encounters of friends and the wedding couple under water. But there is also Kusturica, who makes references to his past films: the arrow-toothed halibut, the white bridal veils, the hypnotic obsessions with socialism, as well as the autohypnotic compulsion for solitude and diversity, his choice of actors (from Marko to Vera, from Golub the gang leader to Bata, from Ivan to the Gypsy bands), the attempts at suicide by hanging (by Ivan, Ankica, Perhan, and Grace), all the way to the almost autobiographical cameo role in which the director plays the part of an arms and drug smuggler, who upbraids Marko (actually he is poking fun at himself) for no longer understanding the Yugoslav language of war, because he has spent too much time abroad.

The author's self-reflexivity is strategic rather than simply narcissistic. *Underground* seems like an introspective and bitter "look back in anger," not without nostalgic dangers and strong temptations of self-deception. This is a constant in Kusturica's work, well personified by Bata, Natalija's paralytic and "abnormal" brother played by Davor Dujmović, the adolescent hero of *Time of the Gypsies*, who hypnotizes himself with a watch. From the casting to the music, from the cinematic references to the autocameo, from the characters' levitations to the flights of geese (barely viewable, though, in the version distributed to theaters), Kusturica speaks of *his* Yugoslavia and of *his* favorite cinema, but not because of a vain solipsism: the strong pressures exerted on him to take a certain nationalistic position led him—as he has often stated—to choose a very personal path, perhaps a controversial one, but a way that was at least his own.

Significantly, the only character in the film who is in some way positive is Ivan, the first alter ego of Kusturica in his debut feature film *Do You Remember Dolly Bell?* from fifteen years earlier. He is not positive in the classic sense of western narrative; that is, he is not someone who takes the initiative or performs concrete actions in the service of an ideal. Ivan does none of this. His positive character lies in his honesty and human vulnerability. When the Nazis bomb Belgrade at the beginning of the film and destroy the zoo in which he works, Ivan is *already* in despair. Seeing the effects of blind and incomprehensible violence reflected in the eyes of a dying monkey is, for him (but also for us), more terrifying and symbolic than the death of a human. Ivan is not at all a classic hero: he loves only animals and has been deceived for decades by his brother, whom he finally will beat to death at the end, beside an inverted crucifix (as in Andrzej Wajda's 1958 masterpiece, *Ashes and Diamonds*), neither believing nor accepting the self-destruction of his country. Then he will hang himself with the bell cord in a church almost identical to the little model given to Jovan as a wedding gift.

The afterlife on the river banks: the wedding of
Jovan and Jelena and the perpetual Gypsy band
in *Underground*. Courtesy of Photofest.

The height of the woeful but also farcical tone that has characterized the entire film is reached in the final scenes. The eternal return
of history is realized in the mythic replica of Jovan's wedding, this time
on the banks of a river (which symbolically can only be the Drina).
Once more seated at the same banquet table and accompanied by the
perennial Gypsy band, Blacky and Vera, Jovan and Jelena, Marko and
Natalija toast each other and dance. Marko asks his friend for forgive-
ness. Blacky, sipping *šljivovica*, grants it immediately, but adds that he
will never forget the past. Rather than an abstract Vichian perspective
on historical cycles, Kusturica seems to be posing to himself the perpetual problem of the former Yugoslavia, which, as the final intertitle
reads, "has no end." Sooner or later, the director seemingly suggests,
the participants in the war will have to come around to living together
again. It is better to start that process right away and to think about how
to recount the present disasters to future generations. One day, as Ivan
recites, "We will tell our children stories that start like fairy tales: Once
upon a time there was a country." Significantly, the film is dedicated "to
our fathers"—that is, to those figures who, although they were misled

by the lies of the Communist regime, nevertheless contributed to the creation of a nation. The film is also addressed "to their children," their descendants who will know of it only in stories. No message is directed to the generation in the middle.

But the middle generations were not silent, particularly in Sarajevo. Abdulah Sidran passed judgments on *Underground* that were alternatively scathing and moderate, suggesting that the Yugoslav secret service might have blackmailed Kusturica into making public declarations against military intervention in Bosnia. Sidran, however, made important distinctions between artistic work and political naïveté (and attending manipulations). In a late January 1996 interview that appeared in the Italian daily *La Repubblica,* he first declared: "[Kusturica] has a great talent. We made two good films together," before adding: "He made his choice, I made mine. Everyone has his own cross to bear. I think that Kusturica has decided on a sort of suicide. In Bosnia he is considered a renegade, a man who has abandoned his people, his country, and who has said things contrary to the interests of his people." A few days later, in the same paper, Kusturica made a harsh reply, accusing his former friend and collaborator of "needing to shout out his anti-Serbian hatred at the top of his voice," while a few years earlier, the director claimed, Sidran was one of the many Bosnians "praising Milošević."[29]

In subsequent years, the accusations against Kusturica have grown in number and cultural sophistication. While critics from nations other than the former Yugoslavia have felt the need to dutifully summarize the debates and read them in terms of broader discussions about European history and representation,[30] insiders have articulated views that are understandably more opinionated in the interpretation of familiar historical events and cultural dynamics. Pavle Levi, a native of Sarajevo and now an American academic, quoted Cerović in arguing that Kusturica had done too little to condemn the atrocities committed by the Bosnian Serbs, from the destruction of Vukovar to the siege of Sarajevo. In his view, it is thus difficult to believe the director when he says that *Underground* is a cinematic contribution to a humanistic debate: his arguments seem rather selective, and rarely has the filmmaker attempted to address in detail opinions different from his own.[31]

Even after several years, some of the Kusturica's post-Cannes remarks have continued to inspire harsh critiques. In a June 1995 interview published in *Cahiers du Cinéma,* for example, Kusturica compared the war in the Balkans to an earthquake—a natural phenomenon free of any individual blame.[32] In the same period, in describing the condition of being a Slav as being naturally prone to extremisms and tragicomedy,[33] Kusturica, for many, fetishized and orientalized the Balkans in a manner consistent with the worst western stereotypes. His once-charming Balkanist poetics of untimeliness, which had hailed Yugoslavia as a country blessed with an antimodernity in human nature and political affairs, and thus with an unaffected dissention from the grand schemes of cold-war geopolitics, was now turning against him. Balkanism could not justify the new course of history. This, basically, was the accusation leveled at him by the Slovenian academic celebrity Slavoj Žižek, who in several interviews has denounced the exploitation of the western anti-Balkan prejudice for obvious politico-military ends. This is the classic prejudice that interprets the war in Yugoslavia as "the spectacle of a cycle of passions, incomprehensible, mythic, and outside of time, very different from the decadent and anemic life in the West."[34] It is a legitimate accusation, even if Žižek himself, a onetime candidate for the presidency of the Republic of Slovenia in 1990, has never publicly clarified his position with respect to the emergence of Slovenian nationalism during the time that *Underground* was being filmed.[35]

In one of the most informative and balanced assessments of the film, the Bulgarian film scholar Dina Iordanova, who teaches in the United Kingdom, has rejected the charge that "*Underground* contained carefully planned pro-Serbian propaganda," given how "cryptic" that evidence in favor of that is. Instead, she reads the film's dedication to "our fathers" as an invitation to those who experienced Communism and its downfall to consider that "the roots of the present-day war are to be sought in the moral nihilism that prevailed under communism" and that, according to the film, preceded the advent of Tito. The logical result of this stance is, in her view, the attribution of the two main characters' "hypocritical demagogy" to the "omnivorous vigor" and the "impaired moral standards innate in the Balkan social character." One can certainly take issue with this stance. Still, another choice merits consideration. That Kusturica chose not to align himself with the Bosnian Muslim government or with the Muslim intellectuals that operated for an ethnic and religious fundamentalism is understandable. That he decided to move to Belgrade to find a "nurturing atmosphere" when Serbia "was leading a war against his native Bosnia" was a different thing altogether, and it was his choice. Thus, the western moral permissiviseness that pervades critical assessments of Kusturica projects an unaccountibility, romantically reserved for the figure of the artist, onto the all-too-intricate and vital political context of the Balkans.[36]

A different reading has been the postmodern one, less prone to direct negative judgments, at times practiced through a rather flat identification of the film's politics with its aesthetics (see Igor Krstić) or, with more sophistication, by the scholars Kris Ravetto-Biagioli and Tomislav Z. Longinović. In her 2003 essay on Balkanism in film, Ravetto-Biagioli recognized in Kusturica the tradition of Black Wave cinema, evident in the foregrounding of "aesthetic practices that produce pompous forms of political spectacle," for instance, through "juxtapositions and super-impositions of [. . .] cinematic techniques, images, and soundtracks." The end result is the articulation of a new aesthetic form, "one that helps us unthink filmic and mediated forms of 'simple entertainment' that reduce complex relations to basic narratives of good triumphing over evil."[37] Similarly, in his 2005 essay, Longinović argues that "Kusturica engages in 'playing' our sense of the real and involves the viewer in the fundamental deception of the subjects by laughing at human cruelty and gullibility," with the result that *Underground* evokes the hysteria of history as a process of perpetual deception, perpetrated by both domestic myths and imported techno-ideologies."[38]

While not exclusive, a complementary critical narrative would articulate Kusturica's postmodernist approach in light of the consistency of his debts to Yugoslav experimental aesthetics. The identification of the demiurgic character of Kusturica's authorship, one that turns film locations into actual locations (more on this below), has some recognizable dadaist connotations of "live performance," impinging on the familiar convergence of life and art. Indeed, Kusturica's vanguardist connection is not only a critical projection, influenced by some familiarity with western avant-garde practices, but it brings us back to the Sarajevo and Ljubljana of the 1980s. The death of Tito opened a sense of new posthistorical possibilities to the point that, as the critic Miško Suvaković has claimed, "conceptual art in Sarajevo was a late phenomenon within which analytical and political conceptual art was transformed into the eclectic and nomadic art of postmodernism, and urban behavior was treated as a medium of artistic expression."[39] From this environment emerged the aforementioned movement known as the New Primitives, who excelled in experimental narration and in a derisory national self-demystification through music. There was also a darker side, perhaps more visible in the Slovenian capital, the site of the art collective Neue Slowenische Kunst, which radically questioned the representational models, ideology, and artistic epistemology of the socialist regime—and of totalitarian regimes in general. It did so through the familiar strategies of biting irony and political subversion, targeting the ossified language and practices of totalitarian regimes, but without aligning itself with notions of democratic consensus and tolerance for diversity. One of its best-known expressions, the punk-rock band Laibach, staged obsessively repetitive performances that, in terms of military poses and outfits, resembled those of Mussolini. Here, "instead of critical distance and mockery, Laibach performed, one might say, a (hyper)literal repetition of the totalitarian ritual."[40] The band's name embodied the same performative practice: not straightforward rebellion but fanatical identification with the Nazi regime, its language and rituals. The artist and critic Marina Grzinić noted that "[i]nstead of direct subversion, Laibach publicly staged the phantasmatic structure of totalitarian power in all its obscene ambiguity, and with all its un-conscious moments of obscenity, obscenities that the power structure needs constantly to conceal in order to reproduce itself."[41] This kind of avant-garde stance, or "obscene identification," as Zizek might have it, may appear to be disturbingly ambivalent. While being allegorically subversive of totalitarian ideology (the band was banned between 1983 and 1987 for its allegedly destructive terror, which obviously called atten-tion to the state's own language and practices), Laibach's performances were ostensibly authoritarian and undemocratic and thus open to liberal condemnation.

Then Yugoslavia fell. The replacement of the Communist regime by an ultranationalist one did not cause this surrealist inclination to disap-pear; instead, it combined its budding anticonformist subversion with the excesses of ethnic pride and ethno-nationalism. What had emerged in Ljubljana and Sarajevo were avant-garde groups who used to overi-dentify with the language of hegemonic Communist ideology to make fun of it. In his early films, Kusturica had adapted the same strategy through subversive practices associated with music, adolescence, soccer, cinephilia, and sleepwalking caricatures. The troubles began when this surrealist habitus became state music, when allegory and irony got coopted politically.

In this light, the sin of *Underground* may be interpreted as a sarcastic and surreal overidentification with the Balkan antimodern stereotype that crossed the line from being politically allegorical, irreverent, and subversive, as Kusturica wanted it to appear, to literal and sinister, as his detractors maintained, thereby providing a libidinal justification of ethnic cleansing, as the Slovenian Žižek claimed.

Over the years, and since *Underground,* Kusturica has often responded to some of the most negative criticism by vehemently asserting his artistic freedom. In interview after interview and by dint of public appearances and musical concerts, the director has assumed the role of *poète maudit,* wild, often unkempt, and with a (Cuban) cigar in his mouth, above and beyond contingent historical and national issues. As Iordanova had anticipated, his image and his reputation coincide conveniently with a Balkan exoticism defined by a geopolitics of antimodern taste, enriched in his autobiography by references to 1970s rock stars, Johnny Depp, and Ivo Andrić. It is not difficult to hypothesize that the trauma attendant on the reception of his most notorious film has also changed his poetic coordinates and those of his aesthetic self-perception. The once charming untimeliness has become obscene.

From a professional point of view, *Underground* constitutes a *terminus ante quem,* beyond which Kusturica opens a more intimate and sometimes even solipsistic phase of his cinema. After *Underground,* his career was not going to be the same, and whatever he sought to do has induced reconsiderations of what he had done before. Some long-term collaborations broke up; for example, the one with the production designer Miljen "Kreka" Kljaković and the one with the director of photography Vilko Filač, although Filač remained a close friend right up to his untimely death in 2008. The dissolution of the rapport with Bregović was much more publicized because of the fame of the composer. The breakup allegedly occurred because of a dispute over the paternity of the Gypsy music in *Underground,* although in some interviews Kusturica has accused Bregović of believing in Islamization.[42] On the liner notes for the film's soundtrack, Bregović lists himself as the "composer" of the film's music, while Kusturica has maintained that Bregović's role was limited to arranging—very ably, certainly, but without original creativity—traditional musical motifs selected by Kusturica himself and by his co-screenwriter Kovačević. The accusation is perhaps unjust. The respect that the musical world holds for Bregović was (and still is) centered on his ability to assemble a wide range of diverse talents. Some scenes were filmed with the Macedonian band Kočani Orkestar, which mixed Turkish and Arabic rhythms in 7/8 and 9/8 time and with Latin-American influences. The leader of the group, Naat Veliov, had already done trumpet solos in *Time of the Gypsies*. The famous piece that opens the film, "Kalasnjikov," was arranged by Bregović from a Hungarian march. In addition to the frenetic traditional dance tunes from the Čoček region, for the polkas and tangos Bregović had also made use of two Gypsy orchestras directed by Slobodan Salijević and Boban Marković. Among the pieces played at the wedding (without guests) of Blacky and Natalija and also in the reconciliation scene of Blacky, Marko, and Natalija, there is "Mesečina," the text of which was written by Kusturica and then made famous by the five-hour television version that aired in Serbia. As a demonstration of the Hegelian notion of "heterogeneity of effects," these pieces, and "Mesečina" in particular, were adopted as a soundtrack by the opposition to Milošević and sung in the streets during protests against the Serbian dictator: imagination elevated to acts of power and resistence.

After *Underground,* the paths of the two former friends from Sarajevo, Kusturica and Bregović, did not completely separate: in some ways they followed parallel tracks. Bregović has continued to have extraordinary success as a producer, a film composer (even though he has often declared to be done with cinema), and a musician with his new band, Wedding and Funerals Orchestra. Kusturica has invested time and energy in "his" No Smoking Orchestra (where he plays guitar, with his son on drums), which furnishes the accompaniment to his latest films—from *Black Cat, White Cat* and *Life Is a Miracle* on. And, like Bregović, he is often on tour. For some years now, Kusturica and his band have traveled Europe and North and South America, presenting a mixture of "world music" that is often unclassifiable, packed with cinematic references, techno music, and Bosnian (or Yugo-nostalgic) dance tunes. If Bregović is far superior musically, Kusturica has one-upped him in marketing. At concerts he is introduced as "the professor," because of his past teaching experience at Columbia University, or as the "Diego Armando Maradona of the silver screen." In 2001 Kusturica even shot a film dedicated to these concerts, *Super 8 Stories,* thus realizing a perfect and very Balkanist convergence between his cinematic and musical careers. The times of *Underground* may seem long gone, but they are not.

Dissonance

In the post-*Underground* years, Kusturica was besieged by continual questions regarding his identity (A Bosnian director? A Bosnian Serb? What is the Muslim affiliation of that first name?). He resolved his desire for freedom and escape from such interrogations by devoting his time and energy to music and narrative compositions, often with highly symbolic content. Initially, he kept a distance from filmmaking. He could not go home again, literally, since his country was gone, and he was declared there persona non grata. Eventually, he reconnected with his musician friends and resurfaced as a committed and multivalent Balkanist. He made use of music much more than in the past, and even embraced architecture (or urban design) toward a broad intermedial expansion of his poetics of dissidence. The result has been the pursuit of a striking geopolitical dissonance that, with the partial exception of *Super 8 Stories,* has bracketed off recent and past history—as it is typical of Balkanism. When watching his films, we do not understand much about contemporary life in Belgrade, Zagreb, or Sarajevo. Instead, we are transported to a localistic primal scene—in the sense of both ethnographic and unmodern—that feeds western fascination and distantiation. That may be the reason why his popularity as a musician has not matched his success as a filmmaker.

What kind of author has he become? How has his music career and his notoriety as a music performer on world tour informed his filmic poetics? In this final section, I shall examine Kusturica's post-Yugoslav-wars authorial trajectory, which has made him a much bigger public figure, outside Europe and beyond art-film circles. It is a rich scenario, made of films that privilege slapstick and entertainment values while telling

Balkan stories of love, violence, and survival, politically controversial civic initiatives that open old wounds and make new enemies, and music shows that do a bit of both in their combination of surreal humour and polarizing political engagement. In what I refer to as his Balkan drift, Kusturica has positioned his trademark Balkan otherness in the global scene of aesthetic and commercial exchanges. Notwithstanding these expansive ventures, including the identification of an ideal twin brother in the soccer star Diego Armando Maradona, his cinematic path has not intersected with novel narratives, characters, and visions. Instead, it has led to an excess of poetic reiterations, filled with self-references, which in my view reveal a dramatic impasse. The hope is that he will be soon able to realize some the fantastic projects that he has cultivated in the past, and thus change tune.

Cats and Birds

The first images Kusturica shot after the impassioned polemics surrounding *Underground* were those of *Seven Days in the Life of a Bird* (*Sept jours dans la vie d'un oiseau*), a TV film produced for the series Envoyé Spécial by France 2 in collaboration with Komuna Film. The TV film, which is hard to obtain since it was not distributed outside the circuit of French television, is a provocative docu-fiction apparently based on a true story, an event that happened to a certain Slobodan Breneselović. Facing the camera, the protagonist announces that his is a sad story: "To relieve my sadness I learned to whistle. Now I am learning to fly. The difficult part is pretending to be insane. I am afraid that in time I will actually go crazy."

In its almost literal simplicity, this short work presents and allegorizes the drama of the director, who lived variously in Normandy, Paris, and the Balkans (first in Belgrade, then, allegedly, in Montenegro) but was still a stranger everywhere. The work is a first-person account of a Serb who cannot leave his house or return there without crossing his neighbors' properties. In brief, the film tells the story of a man who is denied the right of free access to his home, a situation that in the second half of the 1990s many minorities in the former Yugoslavia, and Kusturica himself, knew only too well. Faced with a regional-planning project that takes no account of his need to come and go from his house—we even see the official map with the lots surrounding his property—the film's protagonist is dumfounded and takes refuge in a bar, in his own office, or in a movie theater. Always wearing a baseball cap bearing the word "Camel" (another ironic reference to Kusturica's musical group?), the poor man grows exhausted. To go back and forth from his house involves crossing, without being seen, the fields, fences, and property lines of his angry neighbors (all six of them, like the number of the former republics of Yugoslavia), who refuse to let him pass. He even tries the land-registry office, but nothing works out. All that is left is hope or, rather, music.

Up to this point, the narration has been accompanied by a sort of Gypsy march played off-screen. When the protagonist tries to relax and goes with his family for a picnic, however, the music becomes diegetic. Slobodan has his little girl turn the tuning knob of the radio until she finds one of the melodies, which he himself calls "traditional music," and which unmistakably bears Kusturica's imprint. At that moment he comes up with a weird idea: he determines to catch birds with a home-made trap. The man falls asleep, however, and dreams of rising above the earth. When he awakes, he falls into his own trap. *Seven Days in the Life of a Bird* ends with the protagonist, completely unable to move, imagining that he is soaring into the air like a bird—exactly like an ideal Kusturician character.

After the airing of the TV film, Kusturica told an interviewer that he liked the reportage format and that, although he had earlier renounced filmmaking, directing the little film was for him a way of saying "yes" again to cinema.[43] This confession anticipated the production of his new full-length feature.

In addition to filming *Seven Days in the Life of a Bird* during the months following the *succès de scandale* of *Underground,* Kusturica also engaged in other activities. In January 1996 the director told *La Repubblica* that he wanted to write a collection of realistic stories and thus put some order to his personal diary—something that later took shape in his autobiography and, more recently, in the collection of short stories *Sto jada* (Hundred of troubles, 2013). As far as the cinema was concerned, he did not commit himself to specific projects, but he mused, ironically, that perhaps he would return with a comedy entitled *How I Did Not Make Crime and Punishment.* In the meantime, on commission from Serbian and German television, he worked on documentaries about the actors he met on the set of *Underground.* Ten years after

Time of the Gypsies, which had been his *Miracle in Milan* (dir. Vittorio De Sica, 1951), and not even three years after his traumatic and most historiographic film, Kusturica returned to his Gypsies, the people most firmly situated "outside of history." The result was *Black Cat, White Cat*. This time, however, he offered a clownish and slapstick version of them, much less lyrical and melodramatic than the film he had made in 1989. He collaborated once more with the screenwriter for *Time of the Gypsies*, Gordan Mihić, who in the past had written wonderful films with Živojin Pavlović, including *The Rats Woke Up* (*Buđenje pacova*, 1967), and who would later be a central figure in the cinema of Goran Paskaljević. To replace "Kreka" and to fill the vacant position of production designer, he chose Milenko Jeremić, who was Kljaković's equal in staging and premodern machinery, calling to mind in a way the Terry Gilliam of *Brazil* (1985), but in open-air locations.

The cinematographers were Thierry Arbogast and, because of production delays, Michel Amathieu. The former had already worked with Luc Besson and André Téchiné, and Kusturica valued highly his stylizing talent, considering it ideal for curbing the coarse and undisciplined garishness of the Gypsy world. The much younger Amathieu, however, was initially hired as a respectable substitute, but within a short time the rapport between him and the director became ideal: Kusturica would call on him for his next three projects, from *Super 8 Stories*, filmed together with a platoon of other photographers, to *Life Is a Miracle* and *All the Invisible Children*. The connection with *Underground*, however, was not completely broken. Over two-thirds of *Black Cat, White Cat* was shot around Taraš (Vojvodina), between Belgrade and Novi Sad, where Kusturica had worked on the final sequences of the controversial 1995 film, although certain scenes make it hard to believe that it was the same site.

Black Cat, White Cat is in some ways an unplanned work. What was supposed to be a television documentary entitled *Musika akrobatika* (Acrobatic music) became a medium-length and finally a full-length feature film. The narrative directions multiplied, and it seems as though a short story by Isaak Babel may also have been a source, especially for the development of the character of the uncontrollable gangster Dadan, splendidly played by Srdjan Todorović.

Along the Danube, and without much effort, the Gypsy Matko De-stanov and his son pass the time as amateur black-market traffickers, buying and selling goods to passing boats. After a deal gone bad, they decide to exploit the past friendship of Matko's distant father, Zarije, with Grga Pitić, the boss of a Gypsy crime family who makes and sells his own Scotch whisky on the black market. Pitić is a cartoonish char-acter who moves around on a motorized wheelchairs, wears shades, and smokes giant cigars. Skeptical and sentimental at once, Grga Pitić supports Matko's plan to steal a gasoline convoy, but he does not offer the necessary manpower. For this, Matko seeks help from the local cocaine-dependent gangster Dadan Karambolo, also a Gypsy, who roams the countryside inside his giant white American-made limousine. Danan accepts, but eventually tricks Matko into agreeing to a condition: the adolescent Zare must marry the criminal's sister, the tiny twenty-five-year-old Afrodita, nicknamed Buba Mara (Ladybird). Zare, however, is in love with young Ida, who works as a waiter in an establishment along

One wrong wedding, two right couples in *Black Cat, White Cat.* Foreground: Ida (Branka Katić) and Zare (Florijan Ajdini); background: Afrodita (Salija Ibraimova) and Grga Veliki (Jašar Destani). Courtesy of Photofest.

the Danube run by her grandmother, Sujka (Ljubica Adzovic, the iconic grandmother in *Time of the Gypsies*). The two swim together, ride her Vespa, and make love in a field of sunflowers reminiscent of a scene in Alexander Dovžhenko's *Earth* (1930). Zare and Afrodita do not intend to marry each other. One of Grga Pitić's grandsons, the giant Grga Veliki, has the opposite problem: he wishes to get married but believes only in love at first sight.

When Zare's grandfather Zarije understands that it will be a loveless wedding, he hypnotizes himself and pretends to be dead, thus counting on the Gypsy custom would require a forty-day suspension of any celebration, but Danan devises a way out: freeze Zarje with a giant sheet of ice to preserve him and reveal his death only after the ceremony.

At the wedding, held along the Danube at Matko's, shots are fired in the air, colorful guests arrive, and a Gypsy band plays incessantly. The celebrant is a neurotic and ineffable character played by Miki Manojlović. During the ceremony, Zare manages to help Afrodita escape. The massive search eventually brings Grga Veliki face to face with her: it is love at first sight. With Grga Pitić's romantic blessing, Danan has to consent to the new wedding plans for his sister, which will be celebrated after and together with the one between Zare and Ida. When Grga Pitić faints and appears to be dead, he too is moved to the attic, under a giant ice sheet, right near his once very close friend Zarije. When the two elders wake up, just in time for the wedding, Dadan is trying to punish Zare for a recent humiliation (he fell into the septic tank of an outside toilet). Zare and Ida, however, manage to escape on a boat with the celebrant and are married in the presence of two feline witnesses, a black and a white cat. The last scene reveals another couple, Zarije and Grga Pitić, toasting each other and the new spouses, before closing with the famous line from Grga Pitić's favorite film: "This is the beginning of a beautiful friendship."

Produced by the French-German-Serbian trio of Marina Girard, Karl Baumgartner, and Maksa Catović, *Black Cat, White Cat* also included the participation of Komuna Film, which distributed the soundtrack album (*Ja Nisam Odavle*) on its label. Full of techno-irreverent pieces, including "Abortion" and "Pitbull," as well as Serbian and Gypsy pieces, the album provokingly credits Kusturica as "supervisor and terrorist." It is here, at the convergence of the audiovisual and musical production, that we must look to understand the innovative nature of the film. *Black Cat, White Cat* is, in fact, both a distinct rupture with the past and also the indicator of a new cinematic direction. I mentioned above the breakup with Bregović: leaving aside the question of their personal relations, his absence is felt in the film's music. Gone are the melodic Balkan medleys, the *sevdah* replete with heartrending sadness that the Sarajevan composer knew how to weave so well. With him, too, a certain strong authoriality disappears, even when (or perhaps especially when) it is masked by ethnographically correct music. In its place there is still a high professional score, but it is now masked with play and irreverence. The film, in effect, marks the debut of the cinematic collaboration with Kusturica's old friend Nele Karajlić, leader of the No Smoking Orchestra, and for Kusturica the beginning of an alternative career as a musician, which he will launch with consummate shrewdness to promote his films and himself.

In spite of everything, the director who is most prominently associated with the Gypsies makes a film whose soundtrack is less Romany-like than one would expect, although traditional Gypsy-sounding tunes pervade the soundtrack, and at times seem much closer to "world music." There are few remnants of authentic Gypsy culture—the scene with the musicians hanging from and tied to a tree is pure invention. What is left is for the most part self-referential, visually as well as musically. Notice how often you hear in the background the leitmotiv of *When Father Was Away on Business,* which serves as a complement to the cameo role of Miki Manojlović as a celebrant.

To speak of the film as a "lightweight" and depoliticized production after the political commitment of *Underground,* as many reviewers did in the heat of the moment, seems justified for the time, but inadequate for the film's long-term poetic implications. Many of Kusturica's later productions, in fact, are much more similar to *Black Cat, White Cat* than they are to *Underground.*

So, who are the Gypsies of this film? They are certainly not the people whose vicissitudes Kusturica set forth ten years earlier. There is no poverty here, no exploitation of and trafficking in minors across the border between Yugoslavia, or the former Yugoslavia, and Italy. For a film about nomads, there are no longer dispersals or migrations, despite the extreme dynamism of the plot and the editing. One has to think of the Gypsies in the film as an invented community-character, highly exoticized and therefore "true" as a caricature. Although he has never been an ethnographer, Kusturica takes us this time into a dimension of extreme fiction that projects intense poetic constraints on the Gypsies: one need only consider the binary obsession in matching pairs of cats, grandfathers, grandchildren, newlyweds, lovers, and sunflowers.

What is Gypsy, then, in the film is much more than the characters and the story. Instead, one must think on the level of pure textual surfaces, evident in the casting—consider the actors impersonating Grga Veliki and Afrodita—the costumes, the makeup, the free editing, the highly colored cinematography, and the histrionic music. We should also consider the paratextual and extratextual levels: note the effect that the "Gypsy" element has on Kusturica's authorship, a true Gypsy of international productions, the celebrated champion of antinaturalism, magic realism (the "Márquez of the Balkans"), and caricatural irreverence. Apparently, the path out of the tragicomic seriousness of *Underground* was a kitschy and carnivalesque sunniness, though not completely lighthearted. Shot over two summers in order to maintain the same photographic light conditions, *Black Cat, White Cat* no longer speaks in historical metaphors. It prefers caricatures: of the location, costumes, cast, and characters. Take Dadan, the schizoid cocaine addict who acts as the entertainer at his little sister's wedding banquet, or the pig who in scene after scene eats away at the rusted-out hulk of a Trabant automobile. It is as though the exaggerations of the preceding film had not been understood and appreciated, or rather, as though they had been taken all too seriously (which did indeed happen).

Shot in the wake of the conflict that destroyed Yugoslavia and in the areas along the Danube and across bridges repeatedly bombed by NATO in 1999, the film raises a question. Is there a relation between the Gypsy caricatures and the world of the war? A possible answer begins by considering that the film is a multigenerational story and, as such, is linked to the preceding work. Recall the end of *Underground*, when a big chunk of land breaks off and floats into the river like a lost island (not far away from where *Black Cat* was shot), and where Slavko Štimac speaks directly to the audience about fathers, children, and national responsibilities. Remember, too, that Kusturica is a director obsessed by

The craziest of them all: Dadan Karambolo
(Srdjan Todorović) in *Black Cat, White Cat*.
Courtesy of Photofest.

the family element even when he seems to be talking about something else. In *Black Cat, White Cat*, the fathers are all either dead or swindlers and scoundrels. It is not that their intentions are evil, but they have no scruples in sacrificing their children to get out of trouble or to pay their debts—like Matko, for example. Dadan is not technically a father, but he acts in that capacity where Afrodita is concerned because their parents are both dead. He is interested in his sister's future not because he wants to make her happy but simply to fulfill a promise made to their dying parents.

Those who seem to have at heart the happiness of their progeny are the grandfathers, the elder Grga and Zarije, the most lovable characters in the film. Zarije, for example, is willing to fake his death to prevent Zare from marrying the wrong person, and he does not hesitate for a moment to give his grandson the proceeds from the sale of his business. The grandfathers are the true heroes; at the end only they can fully understand and repeat the sacred words of friendship from the final scene of *Casablanca*. Their entries and exits are curiously linked to freezing

The beginning of a beautiful friendship: the final toast between Grga Pitić (Sabri Sulejmani) and Zarije (Zabit Memedov) in *Black Cat, White Cat.*

and thawing processes. Beyond any narrative obligations (Kusturica took inspiration from an actual death that occurred before the wedding of a Gypsy couple), the outcome seems to have a broader relevance for the Yugoslav wars; that is, it is necessary to thaw the grandfathers' generation in order to reach a solution that will effectively ensure the happiness of later generations. The future cannot be managed by the fathers, incapable as they are of caring for their children (like Blacky, who rashly wades out of the Danube to take shots at an enemy helicopter and tragically leaves behind his son who cannot swim). The grandfathers are the only hope; they are to be admired, listened to, and perhaps even mythologized with cinematic tributes.

At least superficially, the film shows many points of continuity with Kusturica's preceding work: weddings and Gypsy orchestras are almost necessary ingredients, as is a certain slapstick, even derisive tone. Moreover, it is not surprising that the production seems much richer and more baroque than what it actually cost ($4,500,000): Kusturica likes to stuff his compositions to create dynamic relations between the foreground, the medium ground, and the background. This is why he avoids facile close-ups and, favoring lenses that offer great depth of field, seeks to choreograph several moving figures and actions within the shots. It is no wonder that his films, if first seen on the big screen, seem quite different on a television set.

But in *Black Cat, White Cat* there are also important new developments in tone. If in the past Kusturica filled his screenplays with situations devoid of narrative relevance but rich in visual and spectacular effects, here he goes even further. It is as though the entire film were constructed like a series of out-of-phase and isolated sequences whose connection with or position within the flow of events is not all that important for the story's coherence. The relations between the scenes are not dictated by a desire to dramatize the actions of the characters; for one thing, there are no genuine *characters* in *Black Cat, White Cat*. They are all, to a certain extent, caricatures. The accumulation (and not the interweaving) of scenes leads to the increase in the delirious and carnivalesque effect, with bits of humor worthy of a Spaghetti Western: in one episode, the convalescing grandfather Zarije, in pajamas, gets out of his hospital bed and runs away shouting "Music! Aggression!"; another features the the dead station master strung up on the railroad crossing gate with an umbrella in one hand and Matko's moneybag, obviously empty, in the other. As Jonathan Romney aptly wrote in 1999 in the *New Statesman*, in Kusturica's films "it's never simply a question of several things happening at once [. . .] but of things happening in different directions."[44]

The film also distances itself from the past through its cinematography and music. Aided by a new director of photography, Kusturica abandons his characteristic use of dark and low-key lighting that favored somber tones—especially greens and browns, contrasted with a few points of red and yellow—in preference for a new and brilliant palette that will be seen again in later works. As for the sound, it is surprising to hear pieces of techno music that the director, known for his intensely folkloric accompaniments, uses to define the character of Dadan. It is a very new mixture composed of "two-quarter beat, a combination of rock-and-roll, reggae, and things from the past—a mess, but a nice mess," admitted Kusturica, perhaps aware that he had pronounced the working title (*La bella confusione*) of Fellini's 8 ½.[45] After *Underground*, was this simply an amusement? Srdjan Dragojević, the director of *Pretty Village, Pretty Flame* and *The Wounds* (*Rane*, 1998), told the *New York Times* that, all appearances aside, "at this moment in Yugoslavia, *Black Cat, White Cat* constitutes a deeply political statement."[46]

Asked whether he had an obsession with Gypsies, given that this was his second film on the subject, the director's response pointed to a political affinity of obvious, contemporary relevance: "I grew up among them, loving their view of life and kitsch aesthetic. They taught me that a population can survive even without building fortresses, inventing weapons, or conquering territories."[47] Several critics identified in the film a departure from the political engagement of Kusturica's previous work, but his praise of Gypsy culture as a healthy, perhaps all-too-utopian alternative to militant capitalism, as he often called it, includes a critique of anti-Balkan prejudice and a paean to Yugoslav difference, even though that very country had disappeared a few years earlier. An Italian newspaper's report of his interview at the 1998 Venice Film Festival contradicts the article's title, "Kusturica's Turn: Goodbye Political Cinema." It reads: "In Yugoslavia there are Gypsy professors, engineers, stage directors. [. . .] The world is insensitive towards them. Countless Gypsies were burned alive on the basis of anti-Slav racism."[48] These declarations, like the films to follow, challenged the perception that he had indeed turned the corner on Balkan politics. In many respects, he had not and would not. For instance, his next undertaking with the No Smoking Orchestra, entitled *Super 8 Stories* (2001), sought to project an almost absolute claim of artistic integrity and aesthetic value onto the territories and the populations that western media had condemned as primitively nationalistic, and that western fighter jets had attacked mercilessly. The core of this dissonant phase is, in other words, a rescue operation.

Super 8 Music

Because of its format, genre, and method of production, *Super 8 Stories* was an absolute first. Italian and German companies, including Fandango, Pandora Film, and the Cooperativa Edison (Parma), provided key financial support, while Kusturica was coproducer with his new company, Rasta International, which had replaced Cabiria Films but was still managed with his wife Maja.

Andrea Gambetta of Solares/Fondazione delle Arti (Parma), one of the Italian executive producers, told me in 2009 that the project grew out of the filming of the No Smoking Orchestra engaged first in a few Italian jam sessions, and later in concerts undertaken in 1999 between Berlin,

Paris, Parma, Colorno, Rome, Belgrade, and Novi Sad. The tournée was interrupted in the summer of 1999 by the NATO bombing of Serbia, and then revived under the protest-name of Collateral Damages. The tour became the base for a kind of collective and heterogeneous "home movie"—thus the film's title—that exhibited a more overt emphasis on the trope of individual exile as well as more formal affinities with Kusturica's new intermedial poetics than with the aesthetics of the films that had preceded *Underground.*

The production was a multivalenced choral architecture. Between directors of photography and operators (including Kusturica himself), the filming was the work of about a dozen individuals. The final product, expanded to thirty-five millimeter for theatrical distribution, encompassed diverse formats, including digital video, filmed both amateurishly and professionally; "historical" Super 8, used for home movies shot decades earlier; and regular digital footage "muddied" by coarse-grained black and white, thus appearing to be original Super 8. The "Super 8" in the title refers less to an actual film gauge and more to the film's rhetorical and performance strategy: a home movie among friends on tour, having fun, but also moving in and out of their homeland's terrain of historical devastation.

For some critics, the less-then-dominant presence of Kusturica and the corresponding emphasis on the members of the No Smoking Orchestra made of the final work a sort of documentary myth of the band itself. In reality, the film has an importance that is far from marginal in the directorial trajectory of Kusturica. At times, in fact, it seems like an attempt at a personal and poetic genealogy, a way of partially reinventing oneself as a musician (and not only as a film director) by contextualizing a childhood and a rock vocation inside Tito's Yugoslavia. It is perhaps unlikely that a fictional film could have achieved the same results.

Super 8 Stories begins like a music video, with *contre-jour* images of Kusturica at a Parisian concert of the No Smoking Orchestra. After an opening in color, historical footage shot in Super 8 and the voice-over commentary of the film director and the band leader, Dr. Nele Karajlić, introduce us to the 1970s. It was during that decade that they fell in love with rock-and-roll music, which Tito allowed into the country in order to show that Yugoslavia was not at all like other nations of the Eastern European bloc. The black-and-white register of the original footage pervades the recently shot images of the band members riding in a van from Vojvodina to the West and passing by buldings and bridges damaged by bombing carried out by NATO forces.

As in Wim Wenders's *Buena Vista Social Club* (1999), the various band members are introduced individually, on and off the stage, with a rhetoric of hyperbole—Kusturica is "Sergio Leone at the guitar," while his son Strabor is a drummer faster than Michael Schumacher. There is also a rhetoric of ethnographic authenticity, best represented by a discussion about *kafane,* the local bar-bistro that serves alcoholic beverages and features live Gypsy music ("our blues"). Based on 2/4 time, the music inspires all the members of the group, beginning with their talented percussionist Zoran "Ceda the Guru" Marjanović and Glava the bass player. Nele Karajlić recounts his beginnings in the family's basement, where music meant the oblivion of their daily struggles and, especially, sarcasm, which would later inspire his radio and TV sketches for the program known as the *The Surrealists' Top Chart.* Shot in color, individual profiles are alternated with scenes of slapstick comedy at weddings and funerals shown at a fast pace, filled with black-and-white cinematic references to Fellini (nuns in black) or Kusturica (white brides and geese). A few of the band members lead ordinary lives, earn a living by playing funerals and weddings, and dream of building their own house. That is the case of Balaban, the tuba player, who is from and resides in the Republika Sprska, the part of Bosnia and Herzegovina mostly populated by Bosnian Serbs, as opposed to the Federation of Bosnia and Herzegovina, which has a majority of Muslims and Croats. When the flag of the Republika Sprska appears onscreen at concerts, the band greets it with a miliary salute and plays its anthem. Other band members have either a classical training, like the violinist Leopold, who then undid it by learning music tricks in the *kafane,* or a multicultural one, like Nenad Petrović, the saxophone player, who sees in the improvisation and vitality of American jazz a trait common to the band's ethnic music.

Kuturica's presence is central without being dominant. As the opening images show, the marquee advertising the concert gives him top billing, with his name above that of the band. We see him engaged in juvenile physical confrontations with his son or in affectionate Super 8 films of the two of them playing in the snow. Or, in the company of Karajlić, the band's leader, he answers questions about his work with the

No Smoking Orchestra and the new synergy between cinema and music, evident in *Black Cat, White Cat* and in their concerts. Recalling a style somewhere between the Sex Pistols, Iggy Pop, and Gypsy weddings, Kusturica plays the guitar, tries out a few dance steps, and entertains the audience with references to his films, the works of others, or his own films' multiple cinematic references—including the aforementioned line from *Casablanca*. At times he shares the spotlight with Karajlić, who, attired in tiger-striped shirts or wide and showy jackets, is also the principal narrator. Still, the figure of the director, easily identifiable thanks to his vermilion outfit, straw hat, and perpetual cigar, permeates the production and becomes its key authorial presence.

The most endearing (and serviceable) assessment of their music comes from the late Joe Strummer (1952–2002), the former lead vocalist of the British punk band the Clash, who voices his appreciation of its original combination of melodies from Greek traditions and rhythms from Jewish celebrations. In his view, western music has grown all too monotonous. After their concert tour, it is time to go back home. Black-and-white and Super 8–like images reintroduce us to war-ravaged territories, where—they show us—it is impossible to expect to cross the Danube as if it were a normal thing. The alternative is to play music, to convince oneself that one is leading a good life after all.

Rather than a combination of personalities, both the concert-spectacle and the motion picture present a single stylistic model composed of an eclectic aesthetics that recalls Gene Youngblood's "expanded cinema," in which the music is never simply an accompaniment, and the images are never just illustrations. Kusturica practices his authorship on many levels. Although he is not a professional musician, he has a remarkable knack for show business. He takes care of many aspects of the show, from song lyrics to arrangements, from choreography to costume design. His involvement in the production of the album *Unza Unza Time* (2000), which partially became the film's soundtrack, marked the beginning of this intense film/music convergence. It is worth remembering that the disc jacket was designed by Vojo Stanić (b. 1924), a much older Montenegrin painter from Herceg Novi, personally and aesthetically very close to Kusturica. In a 2007 volume dedicated the painter, the director calls him an "acrobatic artist" and praises his stylistic affinities with Chagall and thus with his own cinema.[49]

Because of its apparent status as nonfiction, *Super 8 Stories* is interesting as a series of often straightforwardly political statements. After an evening that turned out badly because one member could not get his guitar in tune and another had a stomach ache, Kusturica makes a significant remark backstage: "It is important to begin well [because] we are an unstable people." What is the meaning of that "we" coming from the mouth of a film director very much aware of cameras and microphones? In the geopolitical space of the film, the sentence seems to refer to Yugoslavia, whose emotional vulnerability (even when expressed in violent forms) has obsessed Kusturica throughout his film career, as is evident in his predilection for adolescent naïfs.

Although in *Super 8 Stories* one may not hear explicit comments about the war between the former republics of Yugoslavia—reference to NATO bombings are a different thing—the film's paean to Balkan folklore, Gypsy and Serbian, mainly, furthers the kind of Bakhtinian derision that pervades *Black Cat, White Cat* and, as such, amounts to a political statement. Without mentioning familiar interethnic conflicts, the music and the backstage comic happenings speak of the continuous need for pride and emotional survival in the face of recent and perpetual Balkan tragedies, as well as a rebellion against the West's condemnation of the Serbs and, consequently, of their cultural exile.

The idea that Gypsy music is apolitical because it affords direct and immediate satisfaction (when compared to the cinema, for example) is false, just as the supposed apolitical nature of the Mexican songs is false in *When Father Was Away on Business*. Their easy-listening quality and their exoticism speak eloquently of basic impulses, which, in the context of Balkanist discourse, have a political connotation: by harkening back to Gypsy culture, these songs foster the identification between musical vitality and Balkan stereotypes. The representation of a resilient, instinctive, and Dionysian impetus is displayed with pride and romanticism but also with cunning; it is imbedded in both the individual spirits of the musicians and in the nature of their male conviviality, at times a bit vulgar and macho. We see it when Stribor, who pretends to play the anti-intellectual and yet is anything but naïve, concludes his self-introduction by proffering a convenient and spontaneous poetic idea that should cancel any political ambiguities and that his father has often made his own: "What counts in art is to express one's own emotions." Similarly, in a brief exchange between Karajlić and Kusturica on the emotional dynamics of the audience's reception at their concerts, the former lets escape the expression "in the heart of the Balkans," as if to indicate the vector of primal involvements and direct and authentic performances.

Despite these postures of transparency and artistic spontaneity, the particular marriage of images and music maintains a keen political quality all its own. For example, at the beginning of the film Karajlić sings of the retirement from soccer of Asim Ferhatović, the celebrated Bosnian forward of the FK Sarajevo team (the municipal stadium now bears his name). But it is not simply a question of nostalgia for the acclaimed national soccer player. In the 1980s, Karajlić's band, the Zabranjeno Pušenje, had dedicated a song to the same player, "Nedelja Kad Je Otišo Hase" ("The Sunday When Hase Left"). In appearance a tribute to Ferhatović, the piece was in reality dedicated to Tito, who had died on the first Sunday in May 1980. In the film, the stanzas and refrains of the song, not only those that refer to Ferhatović ("Hase is unique" and "Attack!") but also the more general ones ("Yugoslavia!"), are intercut with the famous archival images, already seen in *Underground,* of the funeral processions after the death of Tito, with children laying flowers on the railroad tracks before the arrival of the train bearing the body of the nation's leader. Kusturica thus made it hard to separate soccer from a controversial national nostalgia.

In several places, the political dimension seems more straightforward. These moments occur when there are shots of destroyed Yugoslav bridges, when there are domestic images from prewar Sarajevo, or when it is easy to relate the band members' peregrinations across Europe to their exile from Sarajevo at a time when they were forced to leave their homes in Bosnia and reestablish themselves in Serbia. In several interviews, Kusturica has stated that the originality of *Super 8 Stories* was in its lack of conscious and meticulous planning, even if in his previous films such planning had been subject to radical changes. Without many predesigned stylistic solutions, attempted nonetheless amidst the the contingencies of the tour, Kusturica could not make a film like his others. And in effect, the result is less a film than a long video clip—with a final running time of seventy-five minutes extracted from the seventy-five hours of total footage.

In an interview that appeared in the French journal *Repérages,* Kusturica called the film "a life documentary."[50] And it is indeed ironic that many of the film's sketches feature death: white coffins, corpses that return to life, the destruction of bridges and buildings. Its political dimension, however, connects it eloquently to past and future productions. At its center is a nostalgia for a spatial, physical, and even emotional fullness—a compendium of a childhood and youth passed inside Tito's Yugoslavia—which variously links Kusturica's cinema before and after *Underground.* As if communicating from a condition of exile, the members of the No Smoking Orchestra do not speak of the present but solely of a past that will never return and that can be recaptured only in the dimension of Gypsy music, ancient and eternal, and of the gloriously retro format of Super 8 images. As Kusturica recounted in that same *Repérages* interview, Tito's Yugoslavia—from a political and social point of view—is dead, and disintegration ensued. But from a cultural and artistic perspective, that unity can still be maintained and perhaps even originate new efforts for political reunification. It is a hope that the director does not seem to have much faith in but that does persist, as a poetic utopia, represented on the stage or envisioned on screen, as the next projects reveal, beginning with *Life Is a Miracle* (2004).

Life Is a Miracle—He Promises

Filmed under the working title of *Hungry Heart* and coproduced by Alain Sarde, France 2, Canal+, as well as by Maja and Emir Kusturica, *Life Is a Miracle* is a tragic fable of the war in Bosnia. The comparison with *Underground* is inescapable but also problematic: the film does not offer a macropolitical interpretation of the nation's history; instead, it deals with what happened or could have happened to a group of ordinary individuals living in a remote area of Bosnia not far from the Serbian border. The focal point of the action is a family of three and some of their friends, stationed an isolated railroad station that serves no passengers but through which passes a mail carrier's handcar and the trains of history.

Set in Bosnia in 1992, the story centers on Luka, an idealistic engineer by nature melancholic and naïve, who left Belgrade with his family to complete a narrow-gauge railroad, began by the Austrians a century earlier. It lies in an isolated area between Bosnia and Serbia, and the hope is that it will link the two regions and develop local tourism. Both his task and the actor playing him—Slavko Štimac, the hero of *Do You Remember Dolly Bell?* and later the good brother in *Underground*—suggest an obvious comparison with the figure of the director. Luka is married to the melodramatic and paranoid Jadranka, a former opera singer, with whom he has a talented teenage son, Miloš. Nearby friends are Veljo, the mailman, who like a silent-film comedian gets around on handcars and speeders, and Vujan Perić, the local undertaker, whose suicidal mule—in one of the film's many proleptic instances of a death wish—seeks her own demise by standing on the railroad tracks.

Life in this part of the world is anything but tranquil. Wild bears, rumored to be Croatian, kill a neighbor. When local politicians who use black-market dealings to finance their party visit with great fanfare the nearby village and go hunting for bears, they find instead their own death. There is also an active local orchestra, for which Luka plays, whose members include a few familiar faces from the No Smoking Orchestra: the violinist Dejan Sparavalo plays the orchestra director, while Nele Karajlić plays a Hungarian musician.

One night, when Luka is at home playing with a scale model of the railway tracks crossing the local countryside, the television broadcasts images of early, violent, and ethnically motivated conflicts in Yugoslavia. Luka ignores the news that soon will bring disaster to his family. Jadranka immediately understands what is happening: their son will have to go to war instead of joining his beloved soccer team, Belgrade's Partizan. At the ceremony for the inauguration of the railway, history is beyond Luka's misogynist comprehension ("Nothing will happen, woman. Here we have reasonable people"), but not beyond Jadranka's, whose songs mock the incompetence of local patriarchal power.

At the farewell party for Miloš's departure for military service, Jadranka falls in love with the Hungarian musician (played by Karajlić) and leaves her husband. The next day, Luka can no longer ignore news of the war: the army commandeers his railway station. When Luka later receives the news that Miloš has become a war prisoner, he thinks he can exchange his son for Sabaha, a Muslim nurse, whom he had met earlier and who has found refuge in his house. The problem, though, is that he is falling in love with her. As their affection blossoms, the war surrounds them, with its violence, lies, and misunderstandings. At a certain point,

An unlikely love story: Luka (Slavko Štimac)
and Sabaha (Nataša Solak) in *Life is a Miracle*.
Courtesy of Photofest.

Sabaha could be free but wishes to remain close to him. Months go by, and when Jadranka returns, Luka has to chase after a fleeing Sabaha and promise her that he won't go back to his wife. But their love is doomed, or so it appears: she must be returned to the Muslim camp because she is on the lists of the UNPROFOR (United Nations Protection Force). On a bridge, as Sabaha moves toward her homeland, the exchange of prisoners returns Miloš to his father's arms. With the family reunited at the station, Jadranka would like to have her husband back, but he wants to reconnect with Sabaha. Seeing a handcar moving toward the Bosnian border, Luka jumps on it. Thanks to the romantic and suicidal mule, he narrowly avoids a collision with an oncoming train and meets Sabaha, who was on the train and was coming to him. The final shot reveals Luka, Sabaha, and the mule happily exiting a tunnel.

Even with this ending, it would be wrong to assume that *Life Is a Miracle* is just a fable. On the one hand, the film continues Kusturica's aesthetic strategy that the critic Lodovico Stefanoni once described as "the cohesion of the sound space and the fragmentation of the visual space."[51] On the other hand, even amid an explosion of disconnected segments and narrative episodes, it develops a general historical picture that is precise and easily recognizable. One of the principal threads, though not the only one, is the attempt to avoid concentrating on guilt and derision: in many scenes, possibly fraught with dangerous controversies, the director avoids laying blame solely at the feet of the Muslims or exalting the Dionysian and warlike spirit of the Serbs, as he had been accused of doing in *Underground*. If, in one sequence, the film shows a television newscast describing an ethnically based attack on a Serbian victim (by a Muslim attacker, allegedly), in another one, during the dialogue between Luka and Veljo after a neighbor has been savagely killed, he has Veljo tell Luka that it was "Croatian" bears, and not "Persian" ones, that were responsible for the slaughter. Still, one may argue, different enemies, but the same victims.

Elsewhere, the barbs of Kusturica's derision are directed at no one except himself, thus perhaps disarming any possible attacks—as he had already done with his cameo role as an arms dealer in *Underground*. For example, faced with the incredulity of Luka, who seems more interested in rehearsing with the orchestra than in joining the bear hunt—i.e., becoming involved in politics—Veljo tells him that one cannot devote oneself to music while people are being killed. Moreover, following his usual pattern, Kusturica elaborates on and creatively complicates his references. When Veljo declares that "the bears are slaughtering everybody," the film casts bears as the objective correlative of a pressing menace coming from the West—from Croatia and from the West in general. The allegory continues when Luka refutes Veljo's statement by quoting the Communist line, according to which Tito killed the last bear—that is, he managed to subdue every threat of interethnic conflict between the republics of Yugoslavia. He did so even by illegal means, including corruption and smuggling, and he could do it because "Tito was Tito, after all," as Kusturica has the mayor tell the party secretary. But Tito's times are gone, and what's left of him are statues: Luka's line about Tito's extermination of threatening bears is uttered as a member of the orchestra lays his lit cigarette on the head of a bust of the famous Marshal. And with Tito dead, everything is possible.

To avoid controversy and confuse his opponents, Kusturica also presents the war not as a military or a political *fact* but as a hyperbolic subject worthy of cultural and even anthropological *interpretation*. In so doing he mixes Balkanisms and misogyny, ridiculing himself as well as his critics. Music and gender play a major role in his universe. In many of the film's scenes, the music and the musicians become an integral part of the narration, saturating the diegesis—as Stefanoni has argued. At the same time, the relation between war and unrestrained masculinity reaches a level of mocking self-consciousness, sufficiently reprehensible to preclude any facile suspicion of ethnic sympathy. It is not by chance that in the film's complicated ethnic ordeal, Slavko Štimac is the film's Serbian protagonist; his very presence, his young and tragic face, and his love for animals help coomplicate the film's moral compass. Further, in *Life Is a Miracle* the defense from accusations of Balkanism relies on a new relevance granted to female characters, particularly in terms of perspective and agency. Perhaps the most symptomatic scene in this regard is the inauguration of the railroad, with its presentation of the locomotive draped in a Yugoslav flag. Although Luka participates in the celebration by playing his clarinet, Jadranka, who had immediately understood the winds of war, is its star. She sings and dances wildly, throwing in slapstick buffoonery, operatic arias, and mimed scenes amid banners, Yugoslav flags, and the bemused reactions of the authorities. The lyrics are as important as the music: her duet with the orchestra conductor (Dejan Sparavalo) is superb.

He sings about the importance of leaders being male, whether they are called "pope," "king," "sultan," "professional," or "intellectual," for only a man is able to "change mud into gold, turn a stone into a flower." "Honey," he concludes, "it's a man's world." Undeterred by these slogans, Jadranka fiercely replies, first by poking fun at his dreams of vainglory and patriarchal omnipotence, including waging war or ratifying a NATO pact. Then, she sarcastically adds: "You men can write history, constitutions, and poetry, but you do all of this just because of me." In the end, she concludes: "To conquer a woman's heart is the hardest victory." As the male audience members present at the inuguration appear somewhat skeptical of this view, a phallic locomotive descends from above completely swathed in a Yugoslav flag. In their patriarchal vanity, the spectacular rituals of political celebrations will prove her right. Symbolized by this enormous mechanical cylinder, the alleged victory of nationalized masculinity will soon produce unpleasant results.

Similarly, most male figures in the film do not fare particularly well. Many of them cannot keep their promises or are simply ridiculous. At the farewell party for Miloš, who is leaving for military service, Aleksić

(Stribor Kusturica) assures Luka that there will be no war, "if everything goes according to plan." Obviously, this is either a gross mistake or a lie, which Jadranka detects immediately. The prize for the ridiculous, however, goes to the new mayor, Filipović, who plays the saxophone at the ceremony and flirts with Miloš's aunt, played by another Kusturician actress, Mirjana Karanović. Although she usually plays the faithful mother and spouse, here she is Nada, Radovan's coarse and bewigged wife. Once alone in a room, their sexual relation becomes a perverse game, not uncommon in Kusturica's films. From his saxophone case, Filipović extracts a pair of boxing gloves, which he uses to pummel Nada's buttocks to sexual and musical rhythms with an underlying nationalist basis: it is not by chance that he ends the match with a hard right dedicated to Momčilo, who would appear to be none other than Momčilo Krajišnik, the Bosnian Serb politician whom the Hague Tribunal sentenced to twenty years for war crimes. The musical and nationalist delirium quickly reaches its collective climax when, at Aleksić's suggestion, the melancholy Hungarian melodies give way to a sort of snappy Gypsy rap. The lyrics of the song speak of protecting one's home and Red Riding Hood from the Big Bad Wolf, and they proudly refer to Tuzla as the place they call home. With alcohol, geese, obese children, Dionysian dancing, and shots fired into the air, the atmosphere is pure revelry. In contrast to all that is the lonely and sad smile of Jadranka, modern-day Cassandra.

Several irreverent, ironic episodes ridicule the military forces. Immediately after the forced mobilization of the Bosnian Serbs, a sergeant as arrogant as he is absent-minded demonstrates the use of a bazooka to the new recruits. One of them places the weapon on his shoulder, but he confuses its direction and destroys an occupied privy behind him. A few scenes later, Kusturica ridicules the armed forces in an even more grotesque manner. These are not regular soldiers but smugglers captained by Filipović. Thanks to their profits from oil and cigarette trafficking, they travel about with enormous amounts of cocaine and an entourage of women in skimpy outfits. One of the women's tasks is to dribble cocaine along the railroad tracks so that certain officers, with Filipović in the lead, can sniff it without inconveniencing themselves: they simply stretch out on their bellies at the front of the locomotive and, with their heads down, inhale the powder as the train crawls slowly along. Their actions are accompanied by music from the ever-present Gypsy orchestra. Filipović is probably, for Kusturica, the emblem of human vice and corruption. Power-hungry, the former party secretary is incapable of hiding his sexual narcissism. He roams about the front with a ridiculous telephone that works by means of a satellite dish attached to a large case carried in his arms; with it, he rings up erotic hotlines in Germany, identifying himself as the "Serbian stallion." In one scene, at the height of an ecstatic conversation, Filipović goes into a railroad tunnel to masturbate out of sight of his men. Kusturica kills him off, having the former party secretary's death from a bazooka shell coincide with his final *petite mort,* which recalls the beginning of *Underground,* when Marko achieves orgasm in rhythm with the Nazi bombardments.

As a counterbalance to these figures who are, unfortunately, not just caricatural, the director establishes a series of characters who are the bearers of idealism and hope. Luka, the director's oldest cinematic alter ego, is the first of a group that even includes the love-sick mule. At the beginning of the film, the naïve Luka does not recognize any of the signs of the imminent war: he is interested only in toys and animals like his scale-model railroad and his cats. This does not stop him from experiencing some daring adventures. After forgiving Sabaha and deciding to stay with her for good, he runs along the path leading to his birthplace and, as he nears the house, begins stripping off his clothes until he is practically naked. It is clearly a moment of personal rebirth, this time in the arms of Sabaha, with a love that is revealed in their tender conversations, their embraces as they roll down the hill, and even the couple's dreams of flying. For the kind of rebirth and reconciliation that Kusturica has in mind, it is significant that Sabaha is Muslim. The fact that she embodies only the apolitical traits of love and generosity—she is a nurse (of all things) and indifferent to the fact that Luka is *not* Muslim—makes the idea of reconciliation slightly problematic, however. It is as though women in Kusturica do not hold a spontaneous and articulated political consciousness but are for the most part devoted only to love.

Captain Aleksić is another idealistic character and one who, all in all, is honest. Because he is a military figure, he is certainly not an alter ego of Kusturica, but he is nonetheless linked to him since it is his son who plays the role. It is Aleksić who orders the smugglers' tunnel to be sealed up and who initiates the fatal attack on Filipović. Straightforward and generous, the captain is a sensitive figure, similar in many ways to the figure of Blacky in *Underground*. One scene in particular reveals this aspect. After learning that Miloš is a prisoner, Luka goes to Aleksić and asks to be assigned a mission that will help free his son; he threatens to kill himself if he cannot do something about it. At first, Aleksić nearly explodes in anger, but he calms down and tells Luka about his brother Stevan, who disappeared two years earlier and for whom he has never ceased looking. When he had requested a transfer to be able to look for him, headquarters told him quite simply that they were not fighting a private war. Aleksić's philosophy of life—"Death doesn't hurt, my friend. It's living that hurts"—summarizes the emotional climate of many of Kusturica's films; superficially, they are about celebration of life, but ultimately we find them imbued with depression and melancholy.

As we have seen, Kusturica does not hold back his severe judgment on the cynicism of war, nationalist insanities, and murders committed for business reasons. He does it in a humorous tone, though, giving space to the Balkan excesses of music and drink, as in the scene of the cocaine-sniffing mercenaries. He also presents his own *pars costruens* when he uses subdued and comparatively more effective tones. In one scene, Veljo and Luka prepare a dinner while they wait for Miloš's return. Veljo has brought a great variety of vegetables to Luka's house, because, as the pair says: "What goes into a Bosnian stew?" "Everything." It is an eloquent, if unsubtle, reference to the country's ethnic diversity, as well an homage to Kusturica's own father, who, in the director's fond memories, used to prepare it for his friends.[52]

Like many of his films, this one teems with favorite cinematic references that range from tribute to ridicule. The ancient, bearded, and surly carpenter Vujan is reminiscent of the old, bearded, and ridiculous gravedigger in Sergio Leone's *A Fistful of Dollars* (1964). Veljo's white horse nods to Fellini's *The White Sheik* (1952). Similarly, the often arbitrary appearance of so many solitary horses seems to recall *La Strada* (1954). The flying bed imagined by Luka in his delirium as he convalesces in his birthplace can be connected to the multitude of levitations in Kusturica's works, but it is also, for film buffs at least, a tribute to a whole series of films beginning with Edwin S. Porter's *Dream of a Rarebit Fiend* (1906)

A Kusturician village on wheels: Luka (Slavko
Štimac), Nada (Mirjana Karanović), Veljo
(Aleksandar Berček), and Jadranka (Vesna
Trivalić) in *Life is a Miracle*. Courtesy of Photofest.

and *The Thief of Bagdad* (1924), starring Douglas Fairbanks. Kusturica
does not spare himself when it comes to references to his own cinema.
The cat that mesmerizes the pigeon is one of the many examples of
hypnotism that have marked his films since *Do You Remember Dolly
Bell?* When Sabaha returns to Luka's house after helping a neighbor's
wife give birth, an accordionist plays a muted rendition of the leitmotif
from *When Father Was Away on Business*.

On the technical level, Kusturica continues to fill his films with musical rhythms and to fine-tune the cadence of diegetic or extradiegetic
sounds through editing. For example, the mixing of singing and slapstick, already present in *Underground,* was taken up again in *Black
Cat, White Cat* with comic results: consider the episode in which the
obese soprano, using only her buttocks, pulls a nail out of a board. In
Life Is a Miracle, this combination of music and comedy structures
the railroad-inauguration scene, in which Jadranka sings, dances, and
repeatedly falls down. Elsewhere in the film, every time Luka plays the
flute his melodies are always those heard for the first time at the inau-

guration, and which have become the leitmotif of the film, forming an interweaving of diegetic tunes and extradiegetic accompaniments. In an unusual scene, as Luka plays his instrument on the swing in front of his house, the camera reproduces his point of view, visually and musically, with a vertical rocking motion to the beat of a musical accompaniment more complex than the sound of Luka's flute; the result is a blending of the diegetic and subjective track with the extradiegetic and objective one. Characteristically, Kusturica fills the frame space with details and dynamic actions, as in the scene when Veljo enters the hall where Luka is rehearsing with the orchestra. We see him enter the room through a door in the background; framed in a medium shot, a trombone slide goes in and out, while in the foreground cymbals are played with an obviously comic intent. Kusturica likes to add dynamic effects even to what might be simple shots. It is not by chance that his tableaux are always paradoxically mobile, like the touching image of a white dove on the tip of a cannon barrel as the military convoy heads for the front.

In *Life Is a Miracle*, however, there are some innovations and new emphases. Kusturica has always been conscious of outside spaces, but in *Life Is a Miracle* he shows a particular interest in the natural environment—an interest that was dominant in *The Brides Are Coming*. When father and son argue or have dinner, or when the wife swings and talks on the telephone, it is impossible not to take notice of the countryside: it is visible from every window in the house, including the oxeye aperture on the upper floor, which permits the characters to watch the world through a kind of natural lens. The director uses the hills themselves as a setting for the soccer exchanges between father and son, the rolling of Radovan's dead body, and the amorous capers of Luka and Sabaha— once more, love and death. Fundamental elements in representing the landscape are the tunnels (it may be always the same one), the railroad tracks, and the various railroad handcars and speeders, which, together with trains in general, have played a major role in cinematic history. In particular, Kusturica uses tunnels to mark emotional transitions in his characters, to emphasize their darkest moments but also to suggest positive transformations or rebirths. Moreover, they are subterranean places, horizontal and not vertical as in *Underground*, that easily lend themselves to the revelation of dramas and epiphanies. It is no accident that the final scene of the film, suspended in a freeze frame, shows Luka and Sabaha finally emerging, physically and metaphorically, from a tunnel to enter into the more open spaces of their future. The film's shooting location—near the village of Mokra Gora in southwestern Serbia, about 120 miles from Belgrade and near the border with Bosnia—inspired the generous use of the countryside. As Kusturica was shooting the film and having railroads and cottages built there, he developed the idea of planning and building a traditional village, which he called Küstendorf. As I mentioned above, the word in German literally means "coastal village" (though Kusturica's town is on top of a mountain), but it is also a play on words: *kustu-dorf*, i.e., the village of Kustu (Kusturica), with a touch of czarist-Soviet narcissism. The place also has other names: Drvengrad ("the wooden village," because of its construction material) and Sharingrad ("multicolored village," from its style of decoration). Far from mere vanity, the erection of the village has a personal justification that tells us a great deal about the director's poetic obsessions. "This is my Utopia," he said in an interview with *The Guardian's* Fiachra Gibbons. "I lost my city [Sarajevo] during the war, now this is my home. I am finished with cities. I spent four years in New York, ten in Paris, and I was in Belgrade for a while. To me now they are just airports."[53] Thus, Küstendorf represents a significant demiurgic realization of Kusturica's latest authorial profile: one that turned a filmmaker into city founder, city planner, and all-around city ruler—a continuation of his filmmaking career by other means.

Even when describing his efforts with some irony, Kusturica has been quite serious about his cultural ambitions for Küstendorf, as he described them in Marie-Christine Malbert's documentary, *Emir Kusturica, tendre barbare* (2004), which is included in the British DVD edition of *Life Is a Miracle*. Küstendorf has its own Eastern Orthodox church, a library, workshops for the preservation of Serbian artisanal, culinary, and musical traditions, a film school, for which Kusturica serves as instructor and animator, an international festival, and a hotel. Against domestic and international efforts to move away from traditional Serbian life and values and to succumb uncritically to western lifestyles, with his village Kusturica has not only sought to revive traditional cultural practices; he has found a home as well as a vivid reification of his poetic Balkanist untimeliness. For this effort, which promised to contribute to effective reconciliations between the Serbian and Bosnian peoples,

Kusturica received in 2005 the Philippe Rotthier European Prize for Architecture (Brussels).

The village was officially inaugurated in September 2004 on the occasion of the world premiere of *Life Is a Miracle* and in the presence of the Serbian prime minister, Vojislav Koštunica. An admirer of the director's work, Koštunica in the early 2000s had made Kusturica the master keeper of the Mokra Gora Nature Park, consisting of about forty-two square miles of land, twenty-four of which were private property, inhabited by about 4,500 individuals who were not asked about the erection of the village and the ensuing media attention around it. As of late, his association with regional authorities and the Mokra Gora Nature Park has witnessed some controversy in conjunction with the accusation of misspent state funds, a charge that Kusturica has rejected.[54]

Küstendorf has come to play a critical role in the cinematic (and personal) life of Kusturica. Besides functioning as a second home, the village annually hosts an International Film and Music Festival, where the director presents the works of others as well as his own, including his recent *Promise Me This* and *Maradona by Kusturica*. During the festival, he also fosters relations with producers and distributors and creates publicity for the films he wished to make, such as the epic *Pancho Villa* with Johnny Depp, and the ones he appears to have started, such as *Love and War*, starring Monica Bellucci.

Life Is a Miracle had a longer life in other ways. As was the case for *Time of the Gypsies* and *Underground*, the income from the film allowed for a television version broadcast in Serbia. Aired in 2006, the series consisted of six fifty-minute episodes. The film's title was also used as the name of a world tour by the No Smoking Orchestra and the DVD of their concert in Buenos Aires. After several lean years for an auteur accustomed to extensive appreciation, the film received a number of prestigious recognitions, including the César as best film of the European Union and the Prix de l'Education Nationale at the 2004 Cannes Festival. That year, it was nominated for even more important awards, and it is ironic that the winner for best direction was the French film director of Romani ethnicity Tony Gatlif, for *Exiles* (*Exils*). Still, the following year Kusturica was selected to preside over the Cannes jury.

Also in 2005, Kusturica managed to offer his contribution to a worthy cause, the compilation film *All the Invisible Children*, whose seven episodes depict the tragic phenomenon of child abuse in places as disparate as Africa, Serbia, the United States, Italy, England, Brazil, and China. Once again, however, his approach for his segment, entitled *Blue Gypsy*, did not stray away from his familiar poetic palette. Produced by MK Film Productions and RAI Cinema for the Italian Development Cooperation of the Ministry for Foreign Affairs, on behalf of the World Food Program of the United Nations and UNICEF, *All the Invisible Children* benefited from the collaboration of seven directors besides Kusturica: Spike Lee, Jordan and Ridley Scott, John Woo, Mehdi Charef, Kátia Lund, and the virtually unknown filmmaker Stefano Veneruso, who was also a coproducer along with Maria Grazia Cucinotta and the project's originator, Chiara Tilesi. Even if all the directors were not successful in avoiding sentimentality and predictable outcomes, the compilation film was warmly received when it was shown at the Venice Film Festival in 2005.

The plight of juveniles was a theme that Kusturica had already treated with great sensitivity in *Time of the Gypsies*. Here, however, neither the originality of the story nor its visual qualities are particularly noteworthy, although *Blue Gypsy* does possess a significant pedagogical force. Written by his son Stribor, the segment is unfortunately overburdened with self-referencing elements that appear from the first slapstick images, showing the crash between a Gypsy wedding party, featuring the ever-present musical band here riding on a cart pulled by a tractor, and a funeral procession.

Blue Gypsy is the story of a Gypsy boy, Uroš (played by Uroš Milovanović, who would two years later be the protagonist of *Promise Me This*), who has just been admitted to a juvenile prison. Instead of a tragedy, the event is a relief: within the prison's walls he finds the peace and friends he does not have "outside." In real life, in fact, his father violently forces him to keep stealing from cars and houses—since he is quite good at it—which leads to his imprisonment. After serving his time, he is affectionately welcomed back by his family of young musicians and pickpockets. Although Uroš is a changed man, his father is relentless. Eventually pursued by the police after a burglary gone bad, he starts running away across fields of wheat and eventually catapults himself back into prison, where he returns to being master of his destiny.

In *Blue Gypsy*, the Romany universe is not glorified as a Dionysian liberation, an antibourgeois subversion, or a young person's utopia. Quite the contrary. It is represented as an environment in which the exploitation of juvenile criminality is, unfortunately, a common condition that robs youngsters of their freedom by condemning them to a life of abuse made of forced thievery, continuous danger, and inevitable incarceration. Paradoxically, the jail becomes a safe haven. At least in prison the rules are clear, and a boy can act somewhat freely, while on the outside there is the nightmare of exploitation. The "blue" of the title seems to refer both to the bruises from the blows that Uroš endures and to the melancholy and sadness of family abuse.

The short film manifests much of the director's poetic temperament. The initial encounter between the two rituals of a wedding and a funeral—i.e., of love and death—embodies the emotional and moral synthesis dear to Kusturica, the meeting of joy and sadness. The beginning sequence of the wedding seems to come from the outtakes of *Black Cat, White Cat*. The rehearsals of the prison chorus and the presence of a hypnotic turkey, distracting Uroš from his soccer duties during a prison match, recall *Do You Remember Dolly Bell?*, with the amateurs bordering on the grotesque, even in their physiognomies. Resembling sailors' uniforms from a century ago, the costumes worn by the young members of the prison chorus are similar to Mento Papo's way of dressing in *Buffet Titanic*. Together, these references to Kusturica's own work—perhaps too frequent in such a short film—make one suspect that it may be difficult for the director to transcend his own cinematic universe.

A new stylistic element, briefly touched upon, is the chorality of close-ups, possibly adopted for the film's expected televisual distribution. For a director who never leaves off crowding and layering compositions, *Blue Gypsy* devotes special attention to the faces of the young prisoners. The shaven heads of the incarcerated boys offer a visual pretext for repeated close-ups showing the physiognomies of these extremely young inmates; as they stare into the camera, they solicit from the audience a solidarity that is made more of affection than moralistic appeal. This is true of everyone, beginning with the protagonist himself. After all, these are individuals who beg for understanding even when—or especially when—their irresponsible and manipulative parents force them to commit crimes.

Again effective is Kusturica's familiar spatial play of ups and downs, which recalls the title of a short story ("Down and Up, Up and Down"), which the director published in a Sarajevan periodical in 1982. Uroš is rather short but has the upper bunk in the prison cell. He often looks up, throws flaming matches on the ceiling, steals from cars by hoisting himself up, and, with a magical and surreal leap, escapes his pursuers by pole vaulting over a fence and back into prison. Spatial metaphors aside, in spite of the crimes that he is forced to commit by his father, who surrounds himself with a band of cunning and thieving children, Uroš is able to look ahead, or at least he tries to imagine an alternative to his world of abuse. Too young to make it on his own or to go elsewhere—and here the film is quite moving—he has no other alternative except to "fly" and to land once more in prison, the safest place he knows.

This short film's feeling of hope carried over in the director's next production, *Promise Me This* (2007). Coproduced by Rasta International, Fidélité Films, and France 2 Cinéma in association with Studio Canal, Canal+, and TPS Star, *Promise Me This* combines the bucolic and primitive Balkan environment of *Life Is a Miracle* with the fragmented narration and slapstick stylizations of *Black Cat, White Cat*. There are, however, some important differences. Unlike the first film, there is no imminent war and no shadow of looming human tragedy. *Black Cat, White Cat*'s references to Gypsies are replaced by the introduction of Serbian and Russian characters who are just as farcical and caricaturized. What remains is the pure inventive joy of the mise-en-scène, numerous Rube Goldberg–like contraptions, and many other attractions halfway between burlesque and childlike wonder.

A rotating spiral wheel serves as the background for the opening credits and then reappears at intervals throughout the film. With an effect on the characters that is sometimes hypnotic, sometimes soporific, it foreshadows the magico-illusionist dimension of the work. One wonders about the poetic motivations of a film that seems stubbornly devoted to the pristine and beloved hills and forests between Serbia and Bosnia as well as to nature in general. Although the film is filled, much more than in the past, with religious buildings, figures, and practices (churches, Eastern Orthodox popes or priests, ceremonies) and presents an extraordinary richness of visual solutions, it still shows the signs of a worrisome narrative and visual impasse.

When three inspectors from the Ministry of Education approach a small, semi-abandoned village in the Serbian hills, their Trabant repeatedly falls into the open-field trap doors that the old Živojin Marković, with help from of his grandson Tsane, has prepared for unannounced visitors. They are the sole inhabitants, except for Bosa (Ljiljana Blagojević from *Dolly Bell*), the middle-aged Russian language teacher who dresses in tight clothes (like her counterpart in *Amarcord*) and loves to bathe naked outside in the summer. The order from Belgrade is clear: one student cannot justify the expense of the school; Tsane must go to the city school. The boy, however, is still a boy: while Živojin spends his days repairing the local church, Tsane plays with a bull named Cvetka and with periscopes and other optical devices that permit him to scan the countryside and Bosa's body. Still, Tsane has to leave the village and become an adult, as a concerned Živojin tells his grandson; the old man asks of the boy only three things: sell the bull, buy a Russian icon of St. Nicholas, and get himself a wife.

After a poignant farewell, Tsane arrives in the city, where he experiences an unwelcoming reception and many surprises. First, he passes by a circus attraction consisting of a human cannonball, which will provide the film with a humorous refrain. He then meets a group of violent and insulting criminals headed by the delirious Bajo (Miki Manojlović), who sports a black-and-white moustache and who has a peculiar erotic attraction to turkeys. Transfixed by the sight of skyscrapers, Tsane is also mesmerized by the city girls, especially Jasna, with whom he falls in love. The story then follows three intersecting tracks. First, the violent negotiations between the criminals and a couple of colorful Russian brothers, the Krivokapićs (one of whom is played by Kusturica's tall son Stribor), experts in explosives. The two bands plan to destroy a number of old downtown buildings and replace them with a new World Trade Center. The second track is the long courtship and eventual love story between Tsane and Jasna, who attend the same school, and the third is the finally blossoming romance between Živojin and Bosa, after she successfully rejets the overtures of the school inspector (played by Ivica Maksimović of the No Smoking Orchestra).

The three narratives continuously intersect. The Krivokapić brothers are the grandsons of Živojin's best drinking buddy, the late Trifun, and once they realize it, they help Tsane liberate Jasna from Bajo's plans of turning her into a dancer and prostitute in his club. Jasna's mother, in fact, used to work for Bajo and owes him money, and the criminal boss is used to turning debts into opportunities. The two love stories between Tsane and Jasna and between Živojin and Bosa share similar acrobatic climaxes: it is only when one or two of the potential lovers find themselves dangling from higher places, whether a scaffolding or a bell tower, that they muster the courage to declare their love.

When Tsane and Jasna escape from the city and return to the village, making love while hidden in the trunk of a car, all the film's characters join up. The church bell, which Živojin has repaired, announces his wedding to Bosa. It won't be the only one, and it won't happen without a fight. After Živojin reunites with his beloved Tsane and meets his old buddy's grandsons, they all have to repulse the assault of the irrepressible Bajo. He has shown up at the village with paramilitary vehicles and a small army all dressed in black. During the fight, the two couples find themselves in the church, ready to take their wedding vows and surrounded by an orchestra of musicians. As Bajo ends up in one of Živojin's trapdoors, the priests celebrate the two weddings, interrupted only by the human cannonball, who falls into the church and asks for the latest soccer results. The final image is of a window in Živojin's house, framing a solitary tree set in the surrounding countryside. All the promises have been kept. "Happy End," the film's final title announces.

Everybody's getting married in *Promise Me This*: Živojin (Aleksandar Berček), Bosa (Ljiljana Blagojević), Jasna (Marija Petronijević), and Tsane (Uroš Milovanović). Courtesy of Photofest.

Filmed in Serbia between Užice and Küstendorf in 2006, *Promise Me This* is a carnivalesque and circus-like celebration of cinema, life, and their liberating rituals. There are no Gypsies, but it is as though the entire production were situated and narrated in the surreal atmosphere that we have come to associate with Kusturica's Romany. Still, the film also pushes in other directions. The connections with *Life Is a Miracle* are many, beginning unfortunately with their disappointing critical and commercial reception, which in the case of *Promise Me This* was quite dramatic. Let's begin with its goliardic aspect. Some more and some less, all the characters are out of a cartoon strip or a bizarre fable. The grandfather (played by Aleksandar Berček, who was the postman in *Life Is a Miracle*) looks and behaves like the typically good-natured but slightly crazy inventor. The half-deserted village is his experimental territory: there is no area that he has not probed or excavated, installing trapdoors controlled remotely from his fort-like house with its primitive control panels and chimney-periscopes that allow him to see everything in the neighborhood. Tsane himself is a surreal figure: a twelve-year-old boy who has grown up as an orphan in the heart of Serbia, he plays with bulls and has never been to a city, yet he agrees to go there for the first time to find a wife. The character of Jasna is equally unrealistic: still an adolescent, she marries a much younger (and shorter) boy with whom she seems to have nothing in common and follows him to a far-off village in the country. The criminals are comic-strip characters, as are the colorful Krivokapić brothers; their humor is nearly as violent as their weapons, although we almost never see blood or real suffering. Even the castration of Bajo is more likely to bring on a smile rather than any sense of sympathy for the character's obvious pain.

Much of the criticism of *Promise Me This* has emphasized the obscurity of its cultural references and the obviousness of its cinematic ones. Fellini is frequently recalled, beginning with the character of the seductive schoolteacher in a clinging pink sweater and continuing with the sex-based slapstick humor. There are also references to American silent-film stars—Keaton in the lead—especially for the role that premodern technology plays in the construction of the sets or for the use of hidden trapdoors. The Jean Vigo of *Zéro de conduite* (1933) is present in the scene of the folding bed, with the difference that in this film no one is tied to it. Just the opposite happens: Tsane and his grandfather are catapulted from it vertically to speed their awakening. Self-references abound. There is the familiar and nostalgic presence of the actors playing Bosa and Bajo, the beautiful Dolly Bell and the father figure in *When Father Was Away on Business,* as well as Marko in *Underground,* among others. The audience hears some of the melodies from Kusturica's most famous films, particularly *Time of the Gypsies.* Plus, the ubiquitous turkeys reappear once again: Bajo interacts with one as though it were a person—or more accurately, a lover to use and then abandon. There are the obsessive characters who for one reason or another rise above the earth and may even find themselves dangling. This characteristic is most evident in Tsane and the grandfather, pigheaded dreamers whose innocence—attributed either to age or to temperament—leads them constantly to defy life's gravity. Some of Kusturica's self-referencing selects more recent items. The small orchestras that follow weddings and funerals also play in *Underground, Black Cat, White Cat,* and *Blue Gypsy.* The isolated village and its surroundings are reminiscent of *Life Is a Miracle* (which was filmed in the same area), and *Promise Me This* also inherits some of its actors, from Stribor Kusturica (one of the Krivokapićs) and Aleksandar Berček (Živojin) to Obrad Djurović (old Vujan).

In this surreal bildungsroman and picaresque fantasy that results in a sort of harmless yet not always entertaining Balkanism, there are nevertheless elements of a politico-religious nature that are in many ways new, even if not fully developed. A fair amount of the film is shot

Love as world upside down: Tsane in *Promise Me This.* Courtesy of Photofest

around sacred places or images: the grandfather repairs the roof of the village church and even replaces its bell; at the end of the film two weddings are celebrated there; Tsane visits a church in the city to light a candle for Trifun, and he goes about the city for hours holding the icon of St. Nicholas. Kusturica did not become a Tarkovsky or a Bresson, but his sometime irreverent attitude toward priests has not made of him a Buñuel.

It should be remembered, however, that in 2005, on St. George's Day, Kusturica was baptized at the Savina Monastery in Montenegro according to the Serbian Orthodox rite, and with the name Nemanja Kusturica. To the accusation that this gesture was the final betrayal of his Muslim and Bosnian roots, Kusturica has replied somewhat incoherently. For example, when Fiachra Gibbons from *The Guardian* asked him in March 2005 how his family, which had been Muslim for generations, reacted to the news that he had had an Orthodox church built in the middle of Küstendorf, the director responded: "My father was an atheist and he always described himself as a Serb. OK, maybe we were Muslim for 250 years, but we were orthodox before that and deep down we were always Serbs, religion cannot change that. We only became Muslims to survive the Turks." Ideologically, the increased space accorded to religious settings and symbols accentuates a growing anti-western tendency consisting of sarcastic attacks and comments, often associated with a romanticism for Balkanic (Serbian, actually) stories featuring young, often innocent, individuals.

Promise Me This is Kusturica's most openly anti-American work—at least until the Maradonian home movie of a few years later. But in that film, it would be the Argentine champion doing the talking. Here, Bajo is often the spokesperson. For example, commenting on how Jasna's mother, Gica, can liquidate her debt with him, Bajo describes his conditions as though they were those of an "international bank." "I don't cancel debts," he explains to her, "but if you cooperate you will get a credit. Otherwise I will screw you to death." The reference to the financial politics of the International Monetary Fund (IMF) is obvious if we take into account what Kusturica has said explicitly in many interviews. His criticism of the IMF is in line with his denunciation of NATO and the United States for the bombardments in Serbia, undertaken with "good intentions," perhaps, but in reality the cause of poverty and suffering for a large part of the population. Ironically, Bajo is the most explicit in spouting anti-American phrases or slogans, not because he hates the United States but because he admires it. In fact, he is the character who seems to harbor a perverse admiration for everything that smacks of America, from the World Trade Center (which he wants to reconstruct in Serbia, as evidenced by the scale model with the twin towers from which he is hardly ever separated) to military public relations. "Everything that obstructs the road to democracy will be destroyed!" he says proudly, before comparing Hitler to what seems unequivocally to be the Atlantic alliance. The Nazi dictator, says Bajo, was motivated by hatred when he attacked Poland, while the powers today are motivated by pity: they "kill through compassion."

This attitude, implicit in the past, seems to go arm in arm not only with the space accorded to the Eastern Orthodox religion, but also with that reserved for Serbian pride or for Russian characters and references. Like *Life Is a Miracle*, *Promise Me This* flies many Serbian flags, but their use seems more gratuitous than motivated by the plot. Serbian pride is also obvious in Bajo's words when he jokingly (though not completely in jest) asserts that "America needs protection, and it can get it from Serbia." Kusturica is astute: he does not assume an exalted tone, but he is always tendentiously irreverent. When Bajo begins to shoot at the wedding procession near the end of the film, in the general stampede the grandfather asks who opened fire; as an old Communist, he assumes that it is fascists, and he is afraid that the attack signals the beginning of the Third World War. He corrects himself immediately, and adds that in their part of the world the Second World War has not yet ended—a conclusion that obviously refers to the internal tensions of the former Yugoslavia.

As for the Russian references, the usually irreverent tone is transformed at times into its opposite. For example, during the broadcast of an Olympic award ceremony, the grandfather rises to his feet for the Soviet anthem (which, since 2000, has also been the Russian one); Tsane, however, is adjusting the two metal eyepieces of the periscope to focus on Bosa's breasts as she bathes in the outdoor pool. The young boy's amusement during that patriotic celebration, which could be seen as excessively irreverent, if not blasphemous, does not last long. When he sees the tears of one of the female Russian athletes on the television screen and then his grandfather's tears, Tsane immediately becomes serious. That is not the moment to be playing around with voyeuristic pleasures.

The affinity between Kusturica and Russian culture is not completely new. As mentioned earlier, at the beginning of their concerts, the No Smoking Orchestra comes onstage to the strains of the Soviet anthem. Besides this musical aspect, Kusturica's tributes to Russian and Soviet cinema are well known. Recent press conferences have also publicized cultural and not only religious affiliations between Serbia and Russia that confirm his new, dissonant, and antiwestern poetic inclination. In June 2007, upon the invitation of its director Nikita Mikhalkov, *Promise Me This* opened the Moscow International Film Festival (it had been presented in competition at Cannes the month before). To journalists, Kusturica spoke of the film as a tribute to Dovženko (in his rendering of the countryside, perhaps), but above all, he added, what had brought him to the Russian capital was his conviction that Russian cinema and Serbian cinema share common roots.

This declaration won the sympathies of Russian film culture, which for years had shown its appreciation of the Bosnian director's style. After *Underground*, for example, the Moscow periodical *Iskusstvo Kino* published a list of the most important directors of the century. Kusturica and Quentin Tarantino shared first place. The periodical recognized Kusturica for his talent in having synthesized the imagination of Dostoevsky's 1864 novella *Notes from Underground* with the cinemas of Fellini and Tarkovsky. Some Russian filmmakers supposedly even tried to re-create his burlesque inventions. Perhaps ironically, one of Kusturica's most highly regarded roles as an actor is that of a KGB agent in the French thriller *Farewell* (2009), directed by Christian Carion. Less ironic is the fact that in January 2010 the Moscow-based International Foundation for the Unity of Orthodox Christian Nations awarded Kusturica its 2009 prize. This recognition of a religious nature was conferred upon him by the Moscow Patriarch Alexy II, "For the outstanding activity on strengthening unity of Orthodox Christian Nations. For consolidation and promotion of Christian values in the life of society." In the same edition, one of the other prizewinners was the Russian President Dmitry Medvedev.

As the declarations of affinities between Russian and Serbian cinema (and taste) required some explanations, the film that Kusturica presented in Moscow in 2007—*Promise Me This*—contained cultural references that were mostly foreign to western critics, whose many negative reviews betrayed their difficulty in appreciating its humor. Even when it is performing slapstick routines, the film is not really funny. Apparently, it was not even very successful in Serbia: the director's bucolic, Balkanist emphasis was viewed as conservative, and by some as downright reactionary—and this at a time when the country was drawing closer culturally and commercially to the West.

What *Promise Me This* does confirm is the presence of an enormously talented director, albeit, unfortunately, one who has increasingly sought thematic (and commercial) encouragement outside the confines of Serbia. He has found it, for instance, in one of his soccer idols, Maradona, whom he viewed as a soulmate, as if Balkanism could be a category of the spirit, not just the result of a distinct national and cultural affiliation. In the end, the documentary film on the Argentine champion was not only about Maradona but about his and Kusturica's shared spiritual and political sympathies. This curious pairing, desired more by the director than by the *pibe de oro,* gave many the impression that Kusturica used it to cement his status as an international celebrity whose fame is no longer defined solely by his activities in cinematic or musical circles.

Kindred Spirits

In May 2005, with his presidency of the Cannes jury as a pulpit, Kusturica announced his next project, *Maradona by Kusturica.* He did so during a press conference in the company of the film's key subject, Diego Armando Maradona, who seemed slightly out of place in the public-relations arena of the Promenade de la Croisette. During press conferences Kusturica promised that his film would ferret out the real Maradona. As it turned out, the elusiveness of the soccer player forced numerous interruptions and difficulties and prevented the film from becoming the revealing biopic that Kusturica had announced. Instead, it turned out to be a sort of home movie about Kusturica's efforts to capture Maradona and place him within his own frame of reference. The final title of the film is therefore most appropriate, much more so than its working title, *Don't Forget Fiorito,* although that, too, seemed to promise a dialogue between the two celebrities.

Two rebels and a camera: Kusturica with
Maradona in *Maradona by Kusturica*.
Courtesy of Photofest.

Filmed for the most part in Buenos Aires, Naples, and Belgrade
with money from France (Fidélité) and Spain (Pentagrama Films, Telecinco Cinema), the film begins well but proceeds by fits and starts.
It is evident that the production schedule was often beyond the director's control: Maradona is either not available, or he has forgotten the
appointment, and it is no easy task to coordinate the production with
the soccer champion's habits and multiple engagements. Ultimately,
Maradona by Kusturica proves to be a false documentary, as the title
itself alerts us. At the structural and rhetorical level, Kusturica wears
two hats in his relation with Maradona, that of interviewer and that of
director, and in both roles he eventually splits off into an unabashed
admirer and a sympathetic critic.

The identification is obvious from the beginning of the film. After a
quotation from Baudelaire ("God is the only being who, in order to reign,
does not even need to exist"), the film opens with the 2005 Buenos Aires
concert of the No Smoking Orchestra. Against a background of the music
from Sergio Leone's *The Good, the Bad, and the Ugly*, the lead singer
Nele presents the director as the "Mr. Diego Armando Maradona of
the film world." Kusturica then introduces his soccer idol by modifying
a quotation from Jorge Luis Borges: far from being a boat tied to the
docks, Maradona has always been free from ties and strings. As such,
he could have been, in the words of the director, the unfaithful father

of *When Father Was Away on Business* or the masochistic protagonist of *Black Cat, White Cat.*

The film continues by weaving four main strands: sport, cult, politics, and family. Through historical footage, Kusturica retells the storied career of the champion as he passes from the shabby little soccer fields of Villa Fiorito, where Maradona grew up, and the spectacular stadium-cathedrals of his renowned teams, Boca Juniors, Barcelona, and Naples, to the world-televised glories of the World Cup. He gives special attention not only to Maradona's world-famous goals against England in 1986 but also to his lesser-known yet remarkable goal against Belgrade's Red Star, which the Argentinian restages on the same playing field with the director. Soccer brought more than fame: it brought a church of cult members, armed with rosaries, who celebrate Maradona's achievements as if they were the stations of the cross or the rituals of a holy mass. As in Catholic culture, glory and pain are mixed: if the goals against England were divine gifts (with the first one Maradona was famously baptized the "Hand of God"), the church acknowledges that Diego-Jesus sacrificed his life to soccer.

Politically, Maradona is quite vocal in his criticism of U.S. foreign policy, which at the Summit of the Americas held in Mar del Plata in 2005 he polemically described as "imperialist." He also makes much of his friendship with Venezuela's late President Hugo Chavez and with Fidel Castro as well as of his fondness for the writings and spirit of the Argentinian Che Guevara. The most poignant dimension, however, regards his family, particularly his former wife, Claudia, who gave him two daughters and stuck by him in good times and bad, from his drug dependency through his various escapades. The film's most confessional moments occur when Maradona displays self-consciousness and regret—when, for instance, he sincerely wonders what kind of player he would have been had he not become cocaine-dependent. Linked to these personal moments of tragedy and eventual redemption are two moving songs that celebrate his life and also invite sympathy for it. Maradona himself sings "Maradò, Maradò" in public, while "La vita tombola," performed in the street by Manu Chao, is intercut with images, including footage from home movies, of his darkest years on and off the field.

In the end, as the many animated sketches reveal, he has been not only a soccer player but also an influential political figure, consistently dribbling and contrasting what he considers detestable leaders, including Margaret Thatcher, Tony Blair, Queen Elizabeth, Prince Charles, Ronald Reagan, and George W. Bush. Still, deep down, Maradona has remained a mystery, an actor reading from well-rehearsed scripts even in his most authentically confessional performances, including those on display in this film.

Maradona by Kusturica shows that the director needed the ball-player (and not vice versa) both as a subject different from himself and as a comparable figure in terms of biography, creativity, independence, and political affinity. We are often witness to fanciful and significant authorial projections; at other times, the film's subject emerges with an inherent power to fascinate and to move. Kusturica the interviewer does not conceal his dependence on Maradona, even when he shows some distance from him. He landed first in Buenos Aires in 2005, and then again in 2006 for a trip that turned out to be almost useless. The film shows Kusturica and his troupe waiting for the champion outside his house and coming away almost totally ignored, following him during political speeches in public and in private, seducing him with a thousand courtesies and compliments. At least initially, Kusturica hesitates to disturb Maradona's privacy: he is afraid of becoming a paparazzo, even though he wants very much to tell the story of the soccer star. But he never hesitates to display his admiration: he calls Maradona the "Sex Pistol of the international [soccer] scene" and highlights the role of the Almighty in the famous "Hand of God" goal that evened the geopolitical score between a nation that was deeply in debt with the IMF and that had lost a war, and its wealthy, winning opponent. He emphasizes the player's iconic value through a comparison with of the most iconoclastic artists and most experimental filmmakers of all time: "If Andy Warhol were alive," says Kusturica in voice-over at the beginning of the film, "I am sure he'd put Maradona in his [serigraphs] alongside Marilyn Monroe and Mao Zedong." For Kusturica Maradona possesses a charisma that paradoxically transcends the soccer field: "If he had not been a footballer, he could have become a revolutionary." The director also gives ample space to the fans, the cult, and the simple devotion that Maradona arouses in people, both for his resounding victories and also for his terrible personal setbacks, mostly related to drugs.

Every so often, in fact, Kusturica brings Maradona down from the heights of Olympus and back to earth, though he never goes so far as to equate him with an ordinary human being. The best soccer player of all time seems to him more like a good-natured Mexican revolutionary—a foreshadowing of the long-planned project on Pancho Villa?—or, to return to the cinema, like the protagonist of a film by Sergio Leone or Sam Peckinpah. Kusturica has his own ideas about Maradona's personal troubles; commenting on archival film clips showing the arrests, the antidoping trials, and even the stark-staring eyes of the champion obviously under the influence of drugs, the director maintains that if Maradona had lived only on the playing field he would have been happy: his troubles began when the referee's whistle signaled the end of the game.

The trip to Villa Fiorito provides another opportunity to celebrate the champion's history and myth, as well as his origin from a marginal geography and culture not at all aligned with the rhythms, conveniences, and traps of the modern world. Against the backdrop of mountains of smoking garbage where children walk about in search of food or something they might sell, Kusturica the interviewer talks to his own daughter (Maradona is absent) and wonders what it means to return among poor people. Would it really be a meeting, an authentic rapport, or would that even be possible? What do the poor mean to Maradona? Perhaps recalling his own similar relations with Gypsies, Kusturica wonders if it may not be better or even inevitable to retain the poor as an idea, a symbol for which to wage political battles. The real poor unfortunately are less idealistic: they would immediately think of their idol's money, and their ideal "goodness" would vanish in an instant.

I referred earlier to a split in Kusturica's roles. As an interviewer, the director often appears as a subject or as an equal presence in the film. We see him in a mirror off to the side of the interviewee or doing battle with journalists in scenes that cause us to remember that there are two names—not only one—in the film's title. From the beginning, in fact, Kusturica does not conceal his aesthetic desire to show Maradona as a Kusturician (and even Balkanist) character *ante* and *post litteram,* naïve and seductive at the same time. "Diego could easily have been the hero from [of] my first film," he states proudly, comparing the shanty neighborhood in Sarajevo where he set *Do You Remember Dolly Bell?* with Maradona's childhood environment. The comparison is weak: the poor section of Sarajevo is not exactly analogous to one of the most depressed areas of Buenos Aires. But it does not matter: the Kusturician music strengthens the identification and carries it forward. The director imagines Maradona in the role of the adulterous father in prison in *When Father Was Away on Business,* but he also adds that nothing would be easier than "to see [Diego] acting in *Black Cat, White Cat* as the man who is his own worst enemy."

What seems to interest Kusturica in these parallels is not only the personal closeness of his film characters with Maradona but also the celebration of their comparable greatness *as characters* within contexts that are geographically distant, but culturally and morally quite close to one another. It is in this sense that the director insists on the similarity between the nobility of spirit of Villa Fiorito's underclass (which Maradona still embodies) and that of the destitute population of Sarajevo. In his view, this nobility, which no longer exists in the wealthy West, consists of a sense of individual dignity attached to a collective one, and of personal sacrifices undertaken together for the common good. Kusturica is adept at using every detail to support his comparisons. When Maradona tells about his mother, who would use suction cups to relieve the back pain of her husband, a porter, when he came home exhausted, the director immediately inserts the scene from *When Father Was Away on Business* in which Meša asks his two sons to massage his back by walking on it. In places like Villa Fiorito or the Balkans, insists the director, poverty is not an embarrassment as it is in the West. It is transformed, instead, into an "expression of suffering," an experience that enriches the spirit when faced with extreme material deprivation. This same nobility, explains the director, prompted Maradona to prefer the Boca Juniors to the wealthier River Plate team, because that was what he had dreamed of as a child and what he had promised his father. Money had nothing to do with it.

It is in this convergence that Kusturica reveals his true motives. Aside from his love for soccer and his admiration for Maradona's incredible talents, one of the apparent reasons he decided to make the film was the ideological kinship that he felt with Maradona and with his (geo) political vision—one, for instance, manifested publicly at Mar del Plata. Naturally, in this projection of closeness between marginalized nations, there is also gratification and even narcissism. "Argentina and Serbia have been crushed by the western power of the IMF, but they continue to fight, and this makes me feel close to Maradona," the director states at one point. In addition to this economic diagnosis, Kusturica immediately makes room for soccer and the cinema: "Above all, in Serbia Diego is quite popular, and our soccer is very much like Argentina's. And then, someone even called me the Maradona of the cinema."

It is through this underdog view that Kusturica shows the goals from the World Cup match with England at least half a dozen times to elevate the significance of the event from one of soccer performance to one of geopolitics. After the military defeat of Argentina in the Falkland Islands War, that match provided the South American nation with an exquisite revenge: it was obtained not with the power of money or superior military might but through the artfulness of the goal, *and* it was broadcast live on worldwide television. "It was like stealing an Englishman's wallet," said Maradona, with a sly and mocking smile. In this sense, one of Kusturica's most explicit editorial intrusions is represented by the cartoon inserts, strikingly retro experimental interruptions. Accompanied by the irreverent lyrics of the Sex Pistols' "God Save the Queen," these animated sequences are always derisory, but also quite aggressive, and thus more than humorous fillers.

In the end, Maradona appears as a kind of divinity who, with his talent, has struck a fundamental chord in the human being, one that easily overpowers the allegedly hegemony of the sex drive. The proof? Every night the customers of the Cocodrilo, a Buenos Aires strip bar, cannot stop watching the TV sets if they are showing Maradona's goals, even though they are surrounded by scantily dressed dancing girls vying for their attention. For this reason, Maradona has enjoyed the luck that is the prerogative of all the gods who are respected. In the end, all is forgiven him. It is a dynamic shared by many other superstars of contemporary popular culture. This license to make mistakes, however, has not been granted to Kusturica in equal measure. He has not been permitted to leave the playing field, to withdraw and to enjoy the glories of his past efforts and successes. Perhaps too demanding, critics have persisted in expecting from him masterpieces, even thirty years after that first, extraordinary *Do You Remember Dolly Bell?*—masterpieces that perhaps lie among the thousand plans tucked away in drawers and that all too rarely see the light of the film camera.

Bridges on the Balkans

Laughter only unites; it cannot divide.

—Mikhail Bakhtin, "From Notes Made in 1970–1971"

In 1995, the controversies surrounding *Underground* compelled many critics to separate the director's latest film from his previous work. Against this temptation, in my 1996 monograph I invited readers to reject the timeworn schizophrenia centered on the division between the film's form (beautiful and fascinating) and its content (criminal and sacrilegious) in favor of a simpler approach. I sought to situate *Underground* in relation to Kusturica's other films and the most corrosive and iconoclastic segment of Yugoslav cinema, the Novi Film of Makavejev, Pavlović, and Djordević, with one significant caveat: the Yugoslav avant-garde of the early 1960s emerged during a cold-war regime, not a civil war.

The Balkan wars and their aftermath, which involved everyone either directly or through the medium of television, have made the average spectator particularly sensitive (and responsive) to discursive and formal strategies, either in their narrative articulations (*who* does *what* and *why*?) or in those that are purely cinematic (special effects, diegetic use of documentary material, music, acting methods, dialogue). Following the perhaps inevitable question about the power of cinema (significantly propagated by television) "in time of war" and of heated ideological polarization during and after the war, here I have asked an old question and a new one: Where did the derisive historical representation of *Underground* come from, especially one that was downright Pantagruelian in its radical sarcasm? What can the later Balkanist drift, coinciding with an expansion of Kusturica's presence in the national and international public sphere, tell us about his authorship as a whole, as well as about its own geneaology? While keeping *Underground* at the chronological and symbolic center of Kusturica's filmography, I have thus asked: If we compare the director's film poetics with the historical and ideological universe of early-to-mid-1990s Yugoslavia, which of the two "worlds" underwent the greatest rotation? Did, perhaps, a critical eclipse occur? Has another rotation occurred since the mid-1990s, one that has defanged his once-biting and sarcastic humor?

In this study I have sought to show that, all in all, before and after *Underground,* Kusturica has not changed his ideas about cinematic expression very much. He has never intended it to be a faithful and *natural* representation of reality (indeed, which reality—the one imposed by the language of propaganda?) but as an ironic, inventive, and at times bitter exploration of historico-cultural conflicts. Like a kind of ophthalmologist, the director has focused on some original figure/ground articulations, where by *articulation* I mean the controversial relation of certain unmodern characters or peoples (Bosnian, Yugoslav, or Gypsy) with history, understood variously as politics and national propaganda, modern civilization (from capitalism to rock-and-roll), or in the form of civil wars. When examined closely, such articulations are not only between an individual (or a collective) and an external environment, but also between an individual and himself (more rarely herself), between an intimacy difficult to preserve and an identity to be assumed. Kusturica, in fact, is obsessed by situations of (non)adaptive behavior, personal or ethnic, in which a character, physically or generationally in transition (from the very young Malik to the adolescents Dino, Perhan, Uroš, and Tsane, all the way to the restless Axel), entertains a conflictual, dissonant, and untimely relationship with an extraneous social and cultural context that is hostile and mystifying, and that forces dramatic changes. His narratives of disfunctional behavior subsume a Bakhtinian anthropology, filled with Hieronymus Bosch–like physiognomies, and asynchronous with western modernity, where magic events like levitation and telekinesis or the most absurd deceits and manipulations are all and always possible. As a result, there are few special effects in his films because the real attractions are the characters, including the animals (turkeys, turtles, fish, geese, and monkeys). The Kusturician universe often appears to be pagan and premodern, passionately linked to ceremonies and collective rites such as weddings and banquets; it is obsessed by the reality value of dreams and by direct contact with death—sought after in the numerous attempts at suicide (Ankica, Perhan, Ivan); and it is extraordinarily prone to commingle opposing emotions, with the result that one actually laughs at almost everything.

Kusturica is able to create cinema with his farcical stories and to visualize the "unreal" actions of his characters because he does not appear to believe in modern psychology. To cause brides to fly through the air (Azra and Jelena), or to swim beneath the water, or to move spoons with only one's eyes are not only a film buff's pagan passion. Such moments are also a discourse on human beings, our bodies, and on the cultural unity of our being. From the regionalist microstory of *Do You Remember Dolly Bell?* and *Promise Me This* to the politicized one of *When Father Was Away on Business, Super 8 Stories,* and *Life Is a Miracle,* from the ethnology of *Time of the Gypsies* to the cartoon figures of *Arizona Dream* and *Maradona by Kusturica,* all the way to the cruel ethology of *Underground,* Kusturica seems to have chosen characters who think or who cinematically reveal everything about themselves through a shocking and instinctive corporeality. In time of war, such a human—all too human—position became ideologically obsolete, tactically indefensible, and even perverse. With *Underground,* his poetic primitivism or unmodernity became obscene.

To many, *Underground* represented a watershed that poetically separated the Sarajevo-born Kusturica from his homeland (another rotating universe?) and that in the process turned him into a Balkanist auteur-musician who entertains fans on world stages as well as journalists and filmmakers from the hills of his Küstendorf. Kusturica himself has consciously treated the film as a key divider of his life and career. As I mentioned earlier, his autobiography significantly ends right before the start of the filming of *Underground.*

As far as the rewriting of history is concerned, Kusturica has recently continued in his demiurgic phase with the controversial planning and initial construction of Andrićgrad, a village dedicated to the memory of Ivo Andrić, his favorite writer and often the only Yugoslav one known in the West. With works under way near Višegrad, Andrićgrad will sit at the mouth of the Drina River, the setting of Andrić's most famous the novel, *The Bridge on the Drina.* The press has emphasized that the plan, allegedly marred by violations of public procurement laws, has reignited Bosnia's divisions. A Catholic Croat, Andrić favored the (Serbian) Cyrillic alphabet in his writing, praised the Habsburg Empire as a more "civilized" occupier than the Ottomans, and often denigrated the Balkans' Muslim heritage. Furthermore, the plan was designed in and sanctioned by the Serbian Republic of Bosnia and Herzegovina, whose president, Milorad Dobik, has appeared to deny that Srebrenica was a genocide. The gesture was also meant to please western media. The scholar Marina Antić has written on how Andrić's elevation as the most celebrated Balkan writer is part of a quasi-colonial Western European viewing of the region. If the Balkans are lazily positioned as a "bridge" between East and West, Andrić's book itself acts, for Western Europeans, as a "bridge" linking "us" and "them."[55]

When described as such, his career appears markedly divided between the pre-*Underground* period and the Balkanist drift, which in Küstendorf (and more recently in Andrićgrad) gains—literally—territorial referentiality. The idea of a split filmography, no matter how justifiable, postulates the primacy of history over poetics. The former Yugoslavia, this argument would suggest, has changed so much that its authors have changed too, undergoing a process of Balkanization. While sensible, this position runs the risk of ignoring the aesthetic imprint that marked his emergence as filmmaker, as if that somehow disappeared. Once there was a good Artist, the cantor of tolerance for Gypsy difference, and after the war, he became a Bad Artist who aspires to exercise a sort of godlike sovereignty not only over his films' meaning but also over the sites and territories of his Balkanist narratives—very much in Marko's footsteps.

Instead, as I have sought to argue, Kusturica has not radically changed his aesthetic toolbox in time of war. To approach what happened after 1995, it may be helpful to return briefly to one of his early shorts, the 1978 *Guernica*. When Kusturica has the film's Jewish protagonist, under the duress of Nazi occupation, cut out all the noses from the family's photo albums before reassembling them in a *Guernica*-like collage, he is revealing a key and most resilient cipher of his cinema—namely, the internalization of foreign prejudices and identity markers. This is not far away from the ways in which Kusturica has operated throughout his career by absorbing the Balkanist stereotypes before reassembling them, playfully, tragically, and nostalgically, for the western viewer. "Once there was a country," is how the subtitle of *Underground* reads.

Of couse, this is where the problem lies. While seeking full sovereignty over his poetic untimeliness, including territorial sovereignty after the loss of his country, his authorship got stuck on the tracks of a surrealist dream of rebellion and obedience. It is a utopia that has Bosnian avant-garde traits of obscene overidentification but remains codependent on western prejudice and recognition and that, like his first film's protagonist, is leading him by the nose.

Without trying to psychoanalyze the director, it seems that two of the visual and narrative obsessions of his films—being reborn and dying— may be useful in explaining what happened more recently to the poetics of an auteur personally and aesthetically traumatized by the Balkan war. Kusturica has often repeated that he was (re)born at Cannes—i.e., he acquired his personal identity as an international director after the Palme d'Or in 1985. A (re)birth can also be identified with the period spent in the United States. There he learned (and rejected) the dramaturgic rules of Hollywood, he established relationships that were fundamental for his career (with Miloš Forman, for example, whose link with Cannes was so important, and with Johnny Depp), and he learned to speak English well enough to be able to work and to communicate with technicians, producers, and critics all over the world.

During these glorious baptisms and learning experiences, Sarajevo persisted as a concrete, familiar place to which Kusturica could actually return. His homecoming from the set of *Arizona Dream,* filled with bitterness at the death of his father and the emergence of violent local polemics, was difficult but not impracticable. The success of *Underground* made such a return impossible. The result was that a particular Kusturica-effect died in Sarajevo, namely the satirical gravitas and the bittersweet sarcasm that had characterized his early works and that even survived—in the epic qualities of the mise-en-scène and the historiographical tone—in his most controversial film. After *Underground,* however, that extraordinary capacity to grasp the sense of history in the behavior of important individuals and of marginal characters became all too rare. In this writer's opinion, nowithstanding the formal continuities, the director who for years produced charming Balkanic effects for audiences worldwide and who enriched himself with rebirths at Cannes and in New York has not existed for some time. And this is said without nostalgia. As all emigrants know, one can't go home again. What we have today is an artist who in one way appears to be a perennially displaced person, and in another way is increasingly obsessed with re-creating

Balkan symbols, colors, and melodies by amping up the familiar strategies of stylization, caricature, and self-reference. In sum, we have an artist-architect so driven to feel rooted in his native Yugoslav soil that he has created *ex novo* a traditional village.

After the void, fulfillment. When Kusturica makes such statements as "culture is my country," he tells us clearly in what dimension he now operates. Without the old Sarajevan "center of the world," but with a reference geography enormously internationalized, the Kusturica of recent years is an entertainer, sarcastic and irreverent to be sure, but often more tempted by slapstick than by drama, often on "world tour," and surprisingly solipsistic. He represents, in short, the lighter and more humorous side of that "Balkan spirit" that Larry Wolff and Maria Todorova, among others, have defined as untamed temperament, creative vitalism, and shopworn spontaneity.

Onto the stages of theaters and stadiums scattered throughout the world has leaped the Balkan guitarist and auteur par excellence, creator of absurd lyrics and inventive syncretisms ("Unza Unza Time"), arranger and reviver of beloved melodies and rhythms from Russia, Romania, Macedonia, and Bulgaria, as well as a filmmaker readily given to (self-)referencing. Unfortunately, the effect is a somewhat artificial anthropological exoticism, a "Made in the Balkans" product that exploits the global market in popular culture (even if Kusturica pretends not to do it), but which has lost the capacity to sting, especially on the big screen.

But there is hope. It resides in the projects hidden away in a drawer—always numerous and fascinating, in spite of the periodic renunciations. There exists, in fact, an symptomatic *projectural* Kusturica. The most important of these uncompleted works are adaptations of Ivo Andrić's *The Bridge on the Drina* and *Bosnian Chronicle,* Fyodor Dostoevsky's *Crime and Punishment,* set in Brighton Beach with Johnny Depp as a Raskolnikov who plays bass in a punk band, and an adaptation of the D. M. Thomas novel *The White Hotel,* for which Nicole Kidman was eager to have the lead role. These projects are classical, ambitious, and somewhat impossible to produce. Still, with or without them, one hopes that such a talented director, obsessed with railroads and bridges, will jump the dead-end track of Balkanism and move toward new creative shores.

Notes

1. Recent works on Balkanism by cultural historians and media critics such as Maria Todorova, Dušan I. Bjelić, Obrad Savić, Sabrina Petra Ramet, and Sabina Mihelj have highlighted the emergence of Balkanist value judgments in Western Europe, but also their convenient usage within Balkan nations, particularly since the wars of the 1990s. Pervasive around European borders, this form of "nesting Orientalism," as Milica Bakić-Hayden has defined it, has been taken up by filmmakers and film critics.

2. In the meantime, to raise funds for his projects but probably also on a bet and for enjoyment, Kusturica furthered a third career as an actor, working with such established directors as Neil Jordan and Patrice Leconte or young ones like Giovanni Robbiano and Roberto Andó. There was another change of direction as his involvement at the production level increased, partly due to his collaboration with his wife Maja, with whom he has formed a series of production companies (Cabiria, Rasta International, Komuna) that specialize in promoting the films of emerging directors (Dušan Milić, Miloš Jovanović, Edoardo De Angelis) or in producing musical CDs and DVDs (soundtracks, concerts, etc.).

3. Halpern, "(Mis)Directions of Emir Kusturica."

4. Gadamer articulated this notion in his *Truth and Method*.

5. Levi, *Disintegration in Frames*, 67.

6. Gocić, *Notes from the Underground*; and Iordanova, *Emir Kusturica*.

7. Iordanova, *Emir Kusturica*, 97.

8. Kusturica, *Dove sono in questa storia*, 321.

9. Karahasan, *Sarajevo*, 96–97.

10. Kusturica, "Do You Remember Dolly Bell?," 166.

11. Pavlović was the one who influenced Kusturica the most. See Ceretto, "Conversazione con Emir Kusturica," 26.

12. Even Uncle Šiba played a role. While on the committee of the Bosnian television network, Krvavac pushed for the production of *Dolly Bell* and even completed the end credits that Kusturica, having begun his required military service, could not finish. See Kusturica, *Dove sono in questa storia*, 171, and "Do You Remember Dolly Bell?," 174.

13. The film's credits identify Sidran as the sole screenwriter, while Kusturica is indicated separately as "assistant screenwriter." Sidran went on to win the 1981 Best Script Award at the Film Festival of Pola for the film, a recognition that he received again in 1985 for *When Father Was Away on Business*.

14. Kusturica, *Dove sono in questa storia*, 181–89 and 180–81.

15. Vecchi, *Emir Kusturica*, 36.

16. See Thompson, *Forging War*; and Ramet, *Balkan Babel*.

17. Crespi, "Intervista," 22.

18. Ibid.

19. De Gaetano, "Una musica per matrimoni e funerali di Goran Bregović," 68–69.

20. A French translation of the song's Gypsy lyrics is in Bouinea, *Le petit livre de Emir Kusturica,* 89.

21. See Iordanova, *Cinema of the Other Europe,* "Mimicry and Plagiarism," and "Welcome Pictures, Unwanted Bodies."

22. Gourgouris, "Hypnosis and Critique," 336–37.

23. Grünberg and Kusturica, *Il était une fois. . . . . Underground,* 74.

24. Finkielkraut, "La propagande onirique de Emir Kusturica," 7.

25. Almaric, "La croisade des bedeaux."

26. Regourd, "Alain Finkielkraut et Jdanov," 16; Mr. Busy, "The Business," 51.

27. Gopnik, "Cinéma disputé," 32–37.

28. Handke, *Eine winterliche Reise zu den Flüssen Donau.*

29. Bianchin, "La mia guerra di poeta a Sarajevo," 29; Fusco, "Niente da farmi perdonare," 33.

30. Bertellini, *Emir Kusturica* (1996) 5–12; (2011), 19–25, 113–14; Galt, *Redrawing the Map,* 123–74; Ziegler, *Debating Serbia.*

31. Levi, *Disintegration in Frames,* 98.

32. Jousse and Grünberg, "Propos de Emir Kusturica," 69–71.

33. Pflaum, "In der Falle der Geschichte," 16.

34. Žižek, "*Underground,*" *Plague of Fantasies,* and "Multiculturalism."

35. Homer, "Nationalism, Ideology, and Balkan Cinema."

36. Iordanova, "Kusturica's *Underground* (1995)," 73, 74, and 76–77.

37. Ravetto-Biagioli, "Laughing into an Abyss," 93–94.

38. Longinović, "Playing the Western Eye," 41–42.

39. Suvaković, "Conceptual Art," 243.

40. Grzinić, "Neue Slowenische Kunst," 252.

41. Ibid., 253.

42. Ceretto, "Conversazione con Emir Kusturica," 26.

43. Ciment, "Emir Kusturica," 20.

44. Romney, "Slav Labour," 34–35.

45. Feinstein, "Enough Retirement!" 20.

46. Ibid.

47. Robiony, "La mia vita?" 25.

48. Manin, "La svolta di Kusturica," 37.

49. Kusturica, "Vojo Stanić," 42.

50. Chauville, "*Super 8 Stories,*" 32–33.

51. Stefanoni, "Papà e' in viaggio d'affari," 60.

52. Kusturica, *Dove sono in questa storia,* 78.

53. Gibbons, "He Duels, He Brawls."

54. "Kusturica Quits after Featuring on Auditors' Black List"; Andrić, "Kusturica Quits Nature Park Post in Acrimony."

55. Antić, "Living in the Shadow of the Bridge," 7–9.

Interviews with Emir Kusturica

A Montage

What follows is a series of excerpts, organized by theme, from selected published interviews with Emir Kusturica. Unless otherwise noted, all translations are my own.

The Discovery of Cinema

On weekends [while growing up] I used to work to make some money. The job consisted in bringing coal to heat up the cinematheque. Often, when the job was done, the director would allow us in for free. One of the first films I saw was Visconti's *Senso*. I did not understand a thing about it, but I realized that something important and unusual was happening onscreen. Some time later, another film shocked me: Fellini's *La strada*. With that film I entered the magic world of cinema. [. . .] Those films were very close to my most intimate emotions: a strong, Mediterranean pulse. [. . .] That kind of new realism had everything a film needs:

emotions and the power to make you travel inside a narrative. Then, of course, I started making amateurish films. I came to cinema through coal, isn't that amazing?

—From Serge Kagansky, "*Arizona Dream*: Intervista e Emir Kusturica," *Il Mucchio Selvaggio* 17.181 (February 1993): 56.

Prague

At FAMU they instituted a very good practice: make students learn all the sides of filmmaking. You would start as assistant operator and end up as director. [. . .] That period at FAMU taught me to absorb the Czech view of the world: a way to approach human dramas without pretensions, which is quite compatible with my Slavic sensibility.

—From Lorenzo Codelli, "Entretien avec Emir Kusturica," *Positif* 296 (October 1985): 19.

Sidran and the Adolescence of a Nation

Sidran's novel depicted an epoch and a series of situations that were quite familiar to me: the character of the father who truly believed that communism would have surely found full realization by the end of the century; the group of youngsters who desired nothing else but to play and sing; those neighborhoods filled with primary emotions, of direct affection. Everything was close to me. . . .

—From Lorenzo Codelli, "Entretien avec Emir Kusturica," *Positif* 296 (October 1985): 20.

Filming Gypsies' Bodies and Colors

In *Time of the Gypsies,* the issue was thermal, so to speak. I needed to balance the performance of both professional actors and local Gypsies, who were largely illiterate and needed to memorize their lines. We could not film the scenes in a traditional way, from different points of view, that is, protecting ourselves and then creating the film at the editing table. We needed more fluidity. The actors' replies had to be filmed without cuts; otherwise the alchemy among all the actors would have been lost. It was not easy. Gypsies lead a life and think at

a pace that is different from ours. Their body temperature is usually around 100 to 102 degrees Fahrenheit. Music, which is quite present in the film, drives them crazy, and makes them very aggressive. I had to provoke the professional actors and bring them to the same body and emotional temperature.
—From Alberto Crespi, "Intervista: Emir Kusturica," *Cineforum* 285 (June 1989): 21–22.

My film resembles their typical outfit. Underneath their shirt they wear three shirts of different colors. Their pants look like they come from another planet. In my film about them everything is mixed, because that's the way life is.
—From Iannis Katsahnias, "*Le temps des gitans*: Entre ciel et terre. Propos de Emir Kusturica," *Cahiers du Cinéma* 425 (November 1989): 38.

Cinema and Nation

This story developed out of my own personal experience. I have been a victim of Communism, and I know that the only good things about Communism were its mistakes. They were numerous: from soccer to cinema. Living with these mistakes, I have been deceived because I did not understand the course of history—a history without logic, because there is no logic when a European country destroys itself right as Europe is marching toward integration. The political markers of this film are stamped on my skin, and now it is part of my dignity. I myself have been a victim of propaganda. When I got out of the tunnel to make my first film, I did not die, but I realized that the world had to be viewed from a perspective that was different from the one I had been taught.
—From Michel Ciment, "Entretien avec Emir Kusturica," *Positif* 417 (November 1995): 25.

Black Cats, White Cats

The initial plan was to make a documentary about Gypsy music. Then I discovered that the music, with its own eclectic way of asserting itself, corresponded to my idea of making films. As my friend Peter Handke has often put it, my films are between Shakespeare and the Marx Brothers. This confirms the fact that music is for me a central theme.

—From Luisa Ceretto, "Conversazione con Emir Kusturica," in *Emir Kusturica: Visioni gitane di un acrobata*, special issue, ed. Luisa Ceretto, *Quaderni del Lumière* 28 (1998): 22.

Maradona

I wished to come back to the mythology of my childhood, and at this time, football was a central point of interest. Suburbs were the places where tough guys prepared their future. This film shows my faith on the parallel lives that Maradona and I have had. We have many things in common. My chance is that I haven't had as many problems as he did, but I've got strong feelings on world justice and unfair situations of poverty, like him. Maradona is not representative of the football establishment [. . .] on the contrary, he has a strong political vision of the world, freedom, and autonomy that very few people have. I concentrated on certain parts of his life, and I played with my previous works using fiction.

—From Goran Čvorović, "Maradona's Dribbling with Stars," *Vecernje Novosti* (Belgrade), April 23, 2008. Trans. Nina Novaković and Matthieu Dhennin from kustu.com.

Music

I believe cinema and music to be very similar forms of expression. I took this very seriously after the success of *Dolly Bell* at the Venice Film Festival. Right when in Sarajevo they thought that it was time to canonize me, I took them by surprise by becoming punk, and one of the angriest at that. I had been following the No Smoking [Orchestra] for quite a while: they were of the New Primitives group, solid types. I heard that they were looking for a bass player, and I showed up. They hired me, but then I had to study: one year spent in my basement to work hard for the rehearsals. [My favorite genres are] reggae and Bulgarian jazz, which is unheard stuff in the West, but it is a fascinating thing, filled with Slavic flavors. [. . .] I believe that the trumpets of the Serbian Gypsies produce today the most energy-filled sound one could listen to in Europe.

—From Egle Santolini, "Kusturica: Pirata del rock," *La Stampa*, February 4, 1999, 24.

For me, film has to be close to music. If you're not close to music, it's very difficult to believe you could structure a whole film. I don't know any good director who does not have a good ear. If I had a film school, I would always choose people based on whether they at least know how to whistle, how to fit their vision into a certain musical frame.

—From John Wrathall, "Gypsy Time," *Sight and Sound* 7.12 (1997): 11.

Part of the Truth (*Dio Istine*; 1971)
Director: Emir Kusturica
Black and white

Fall (*Jesen,* 1972)
Director: Emir Kusturica
Black and white

Guernica (1978)
Czechoslovakia
Production: Karel Fiala; graduation film, FAMU (Prague)
Director: Emir Kusturica
Writers: Emir Kusturica and Pavel Sykora, from a novella by Antonije Isaković
Editors: Borek Lipský and Peter Beovský
Cast: Miroslav Vydlák, Bozik Prochazka, Hana Smrčková, Karel Augusta, Jirí
    Menzel
Language: Czech, German
Black and white
25 min.
Preserved at the Narodni Filmovy Archiv (Prague)
Availability: *Le Court des Grands* (Fox Pathé Europa, France)

The Brides Are Coming (*Nevjeste Dolaze*; 1978)
Yugoslavia
Production: Televizija Sarajevo
Director: Emir Kusturica
Writer: Ivica Matić
Cinematographer: Vilko Filač
Music: Zoran Simjanović
Art Director and Costume Designer: Karlo Klemenčić
Cast: Milka Kokotović-Podrug (Jelena), Miodrag Krstović (Martin), Bogdan

Diklić (Jacov), Tatjana Poberznik (Kata), Adnan Palangić (Drvoseča), Zaim Muzaferjia (Nikola), Zoran Simonović (Gost I)
Language: Serbo-Croatian, Bosnian
Color
73 min.
Availability: Karmen Video (Russia)

Buffet Titanic (*Bife "Titanic"*; 1979)
Yugoslavia
Production: Televizija Sarajevo
Producer: Senad Zvizdić
Director: Emir Kusturica
Writers: Emir Kusturica and Jan Beran, from the eponymous novella by Ivo Andrić
Cinematographer: Vilko Filač
Music: Zoran Simjanović
Editor: Ruža Cvingl
Art Director: Kemal Hrustanović
Costume Designer: Orenka Mujezinović
Cast: Boro Stjepanović (Mento Papo), Bogdan Diklić (Stjepan), Nada Durenska (Agata), Zaim Muzaferija (Nail), Ante Vican (Augustin), Zijah Sokolović (Zike), Fadil Karup (Faćo), Bahra Šapović (Gošća), Seša Vukosavljević (Majka), Ranko Gučevac (Ustasha), Muris Oručević (Ustasha), Zlatko Martinčević (Ustasha), Vasja Stanković (Starac), Miro Matović (Gost)
Language: Serbo-Croatian
Color
64 min.
Availability: Karmen Video (Russia)

Do You Remember Dolly Bell? (*Sjećas li se Dolly Bell?* 1981)
Yugoslavia
Production: Sutjeska Film Sarajevo, Televizija Sarajevo
Producer: Olja Varagić
Distributor: Academy
Director: Emir Kusturica
Writers: Emir Kusturica and Abdulah Sidran, from a story by Abdulah Sidran
Cinematographer: Vilko Filač
Music: Zoran Simjanović
Editor: Senija Tičić
Art Director: Kemal Hrustanović
Costume Designer: Ljiljana Pejčinović
Sound: Vahid Hamidović and Ljubomir Petek
Cast: Slavko Štimac (Dino), Slobodan Aligrudić (Mustafà), Mira Banjac (Sena),

Ljiljana Blagojević (Dolly Bell), Pavle Vujisić (the uncle), Nada Pani (the aunt), Boro Stjepanović (the young official, Cvikeraš), Zika Ristić (the older official), Mirsad Zulić (Braco Šintor, a.k.a. Pog)
Language: Bosnian, Serbo-Croatian
Color
108 min.
Availability: Koch Lorber Films

When Father Was Away on Business (Otac na službenom putu; 1985)
Yugoslavia
Production: Forum Sarajevo
Executive Producer: Mirza Pašić
Distributor: Academy
Director: Emir Kusturica
Writer: Abdulah Sidran
Cinematographer: Vilko Filač
Music: Zoran Simjanović
Editor: Andrija Zafranović
Art Director: Pedrag Lukovac
Costume Designer: Divna Jovanović
Sound: Ljubomir Petek and Hasan Vejzagić
Cast: Miki Manojlović (Meša), Moreno Debartoli (Malik), Mirjana Karanović (Sena), Mustafa Nadarević (Zijo), Mira Furlan (Ankica), Pavle Vujisić (Muzafer), Davor Dujmović (Mirza), Slobodan Aligrudić (Cekić), Amer Kapetanović (Joza), Silvija Puharić (Maša), Aleksandar Dorčev (Dr. Ljahov), Predrag-Pepi Laković (Franjo), Emir Hadžihafisbegović (Fahro)
Language: Bosnian, Serbo-Croatian
Color
135 min.
Availability: Koch Lorber Films

Time of the Gypsies (Dom za vešanje; 1989)
Yugoslavia
Production: Forum Sarajevo/Televizija Sarajevo
Producers: Mirza Pašić and Milan Martinović
Distributor: RCA/Columbia Pictures
Director: Emir Kusturica
Writers: Emir Kusturica and Gordan Mihić
Cinematographer: Vilko Filač
Music: Goran Bregović
Editor: Andrija Zafranović
Art Director: Miljen "Kreka" Kljaković
Costume Designer: Mirjana Ostojić

Sound: Ivan Zakić and Srdjan Popović
Visual Effects: Vlatko Milcević and Srdjan Marković
Language Consultant: Rajko Djurić
Cast: Davor Dujmović (Perhan), Bora Todorović (Ahmed Dzida), Ljubica
  Adžović (Baba), Husnija Hašimović (Merdzan), Sinolička Trpkova (Azra),
  Zabit Memedov (Zabit), Elvira Sali (Danira, a.k.a. Daca), Suada Karišik (Dza-
  mila), Ajnur Redžepi (Perhan's son)
Language: Romany, Serbo-Croatian, Italian, English
Color
138 min.
Availability: Sony Pictures, Ace Film (South Korea)

Arizona Dream (1993)
France
Production: Constellation/UGC/Hachette/Première with Canal+ and CNC
Producers: Claudie Ossard and Paul R. Gurian
Executive Producers: Yves Marmion and Richard Brick
Director: Emir Kusturica
Writers: David Atkins and Emir Kusturica
Script: David Atkins
Cinematographer: Vilko Filač
Music: Goran Bregović, with Iggy Pop
Editor: Andrija Zafranović
Art Director: Miljen "Kreka" Kljaković
Costume Designer: Jill M. Ohanneson
Sound: Vincent Arnadi
Visual Effects: Max W. Anderson, Peerless Camera Co. Ltd
Cast: Johnny Depp (Axel), Jerry Lewis (Leo Sweetie), Faye Dunaway (Elaine),
  Lili Taylor (Grace), Vincent Gallo (Paul Léger), Paulina Porizkova (Millie),
  Candyce Mason (Blanche), Alexia Rane (Angie), Polly Noonan (Betty), Ann
  Schulman (Carla), Michael J. Pollard (Fabian)
Language: English
Color
136 min.
Availability: Warner Bros.

Underground (*Podzemlje / Bila Jednom Jedna Zemlja*; 1995)
France
Production: Ciby 2000 (Parigi), Pandora Film (Francoforte), and Novo Film
  (Budapest), with Komuna/PTC (Belgrade), Mediarex/Etic (Praga), and Tchap-
  line Films (Sofia), and the support of Film Fonds Hamburg and Euroimages
Executive Producer: Pierre Spengler
Associate Producers: Karl Baumgartner and Maksa Catović

Director: Emir Kusturica
Writers: Dušan Kovačević and Emir Kusturica, from a story by Dušan Kovačević
Cinematographer: Vilko Filač
Music: Goran Bregović
Editor: Branka Ceperac
Production Designer: Miljen "Kreka" Kljaković
Art Director: Branimir Babić, Vlastimir Gavrik, and Vladislav Lasić
Costume Designer: Nebojša Lipanović
Visual Effects: Alison O'Brien, Petar Živković, Paddy Eason, Roman Tudžaroff, and Martin Kulhánek
Sound: Marko Rodić
Cast: Miki Manojlović (Marko), Lazar Ristovski (Petar Popara, a.k.a. Blacky), Mirjana Joković (Natalija), Slavko Štimac (Ivan), Ernst Stötzner (Franz), Srdan Todorović (Jovan), Mirjana Karanović (Vera), Milena Pavlović (Jelena), Bora Todorović (Golub), Bata Stojković (Deda), Davor Dujmović (Bata), Branislav Lečić (Mustafa), Dragan Nikolić (film director), Erol Kadić (Janez), Predrag Zagorac (Tomislav), Hark Bohm (Dr. Strasse), Emir Kusturica (arms dealer), Charlie (Soni), Slobodan Salijević Orchestra (Gypsy orchestra), Boban Marković Orchestra (Gypsy orchestra)
Language: Serbian, German, English
Color
167 min.
Availability: New Yorker Video

Seven Days in the Life of a Bird (*Sept Jours dans le vie d'un Ouseau*; 1996)
France
Production: France 2, segment of the program *Envoyé Spécial* (broadcast on June 13, 1996)
Director: Emir Kusturica
Writer: Emir Kusturica
Music: Slobodan Salijević Orchestra
Cinematographer: Ratko Kusić
Language: Serbian
Color
30 min.

Black Cat, White Cat (*Crna Mačka, Beli Mačor*; 1998)
France/Germany/Yugoslavia
Production: Ciby 2000 and France 2 Cinema (Paris), Pandora Film (Frankfurt), Komuna (Belgrade)
Producers: Karl Baumgartner, Maksa Catović, and Marina Girard
Director: Emir Kusturica
Writers: Emir Kusturica and Gordan Mihić

Cinematographers: Thierry Arbogast and Michel Amathieu
Music: Dr. Nelle Karajlić, Dejan Sparavalo, and Vojislav Aralica
Editor and Sound Designer: Svetolik-Mića Zajć
Art Director: Milenko Jeremić
Costume Designer: Mirjana Ostojić
Visual Effects: Brynley Cadman
Sound: François Groult, Nenad Vukadinović, and Svetolik-Mića Zajc
Cast: Bajram Severdžan (Matko Destanov), Srđjan Todorović (Dadan Karambolo), Branka Katić (Ida), Florijan Ajdini (Zare Destanov), Ljubica Adžović (Sujka), Zabit Memedov (Zarije Destanov), Sabri Sulejmani (Grga Pitić), Jašar Destani (Grga Veliki), Stojan Sotirov (officer at the Bulgarian border), Predrag "Pepi" Laković (priest), Predrag "Miki" Manojlović (state officer)
Language: Romany, Serbian, Bulgarian, and German
Color
130 min.
Availability: Artificial Eye (U.K.)

Super 8 Stories (*Super 8 Priče*; 2001)
Italy, France, Germany, Federal Republic of Yugoslavia
Production: Pandora Film, Orfeo Films, Fandango
Producers: Raimond Goebel and Carlo Cresto-Dina
Executive Producers: Karl Baumgartner, Christoph Friedel, Andrea Gambetta, Emir Kusturica, and Domenico Procacci
Director: Emir Kusturica
Writer: Emir Kusturica
Cinematographers: Michel Amathieu, Chico de Luigi, Petar Popović, Gian Enrico "Gogo" Bianchi, Ged Breiter, Frédéric Burque, Pascal Caubère, Raimond Goebel, Thorsten Königs, Ratko Kušić, Emir Kusturica, and others
Music: No Smoking Orchestra
Editor and Sound Designer: Svetolik-Mića Zajć
Costume Designer: Aleksandra Keskinov
Production Designer: Aleksandar Denić and Darija Stefanović
Art Director: Radovan Marković
Sound: Didier Burel, Marton Jankov, Maricetta Lombardo, Nenad Vukadinović, and Frank Zinter
Cast: Aleksandar Balaban (tuba), Nenad Gajin Coce (guitar), Goran Markovski Glava (bass), Dražen Janković (keyboards), Dr. Nele Karajlić (lead singer), Emir Kusturica (guitar), Stribor Kusturica (drums), Zoran Ceda Marjanović (percussion), Zoran Milošević (accordion), Nenad Petrović (saxophone), Dejan Sparavalo (violin), Dragan Radivogević (sound technician), Joe Strummer (himself)
Formats: Digital video, 8mm, and 16mm, black-and-white and color
Language: Serbian, English

90 min.
Availability: Fandango (Italy)

Life Is a Miracle (Život je čudo; 2004)
France, Serbia, and Montenegro
Production: Les Films Alain Sarde, Cabiria Films, France 2 Cinema, Canal+,
   Rasta Film Productions
Producers: Mari-Kristin Malber, Alain Sarde, Emir Kusturica, and Maja Kus-
   turica
Director: Emir Kusturica
Writers: Ranko Bozić and Emir Kusturica, from an idea by Gordan Mihić
Cinematographer: Michel Amathieu
Music: Emir Kusturica and Dejan Sparavalo, with the No Smoking Orchestra
Editor and Sound Designer: Svetolik-Mića Zajć
Production Designer: Olivera Varagić
Art Director: Milenko Jeremić
Visual Effects: Miloš Paleček
Digital Visual Effects: Leticja Jung
Cast: Slavko Štimac (Luka Djukić), Vesna Trivalić (Jadranka Djukić), Nataša
   Solak (Sabaha), Vuk Kostić (Miloš Djukić), Aleksandar Berček (Veljo), Nikola
   Kojo (Filipović), Mirjana Karanović (Nada), Davor Janjić (Tomo), Stribor Kus-
   turica (Captain Aleksić), Dr. Nele Karajlić (Cuhaj, the Hungarian cymbalist),
   Dejan Sparavalo (orchestra conductor)
Language: Serbian
152 min.
Availability: Artificial Eye (U.K.)
TV series: *Life Is a Miracle* consisted of six fifty-minute episodes. It was broadcast
   on Serbian television in 2006.

Blue Gypsy (2005), one of the seven segments of the TV film *All the Invisible
   Children*
Italy, France, and Serbia
Production: MK Film Productions and Rai Cinema
Producers: Chiara Tilesi, Maria Grazia Cucinotta, Stefano Veneruso, and Maja
   Kusturica
Directors: Mehdi Charef, Emir Kusturica, Spike Lee, Kàtia Lund, Jordan Scott,
   Ridley Scott, Stefano Veneruso, and John Woo
Blue Gypsy segment
Producers: Mari-Kristin Malber, Alain Sarde, Emir Kusturica, and Maja Kus-
   turica
Director: Emir Kusturica
Writer: Stribor Kusturica
Cinematographer: Milorad Glušica

Editor: Svetolik-Mića Zajć
Music: Stribor Kusturica, Zoran Marijanović, Dejan Sparavalo, and Nenad
Janković
Art Director: Radovan Marković
Costume Designer: Vesna Avramović
Cast: Uroš Milovanović (Uroš), Dragan Zurovac (Warder), Vladan Milojević
(music conductor), Advokat Goran R. Vračar (Uroš's father), Mihona Vasić
(Uroš's mother), Mia Belić (Mita), Dalibor Milenković (Samir), Miroslav
Cveković (Sima)
Language: Serbian
108 min.
Availability: Rai Cinema (Italy)

Promise Me This (*Zavet*; 2007)
France and Serbia
Production: Rasta International/Fidélité Films and France 2 Cinema, with Stu-
dio Canal, Canal+, and TPS Star
Director: Emir Kusturica
Writers: Ranko Bozić and Emir Kusturica, based on a short story by Rade
Marković
Cinematographer: Milorad Glušica
Editor: Svetolik-Mića Zajć
Music: Stribor Kusturica and the Poisoners
Sound: Jean-Luc Audy
Art Director: Radovan Marković
Costume Designer: Nebojša Lipanović
Cast: Uroš Milovanović (Tsane), Aleksandar Berček (Živojin Marković, the grand-
father), Marija Petronijević (Jasna), Miki Manojlović (the criminal leader),
Ljiljana Blagojević (Bosa), Stribor Kusturica (Topuz), Kosanka Djekić (Gica,
Jasna's mother), Vladan Milojević (Runjo)
Language: Serbian
126 min.
Availability: O1 Distribution (Italy)

Maradona by Kusturica (2008)
France and Spain
Production: Pentagrama Films, Telecinco Cinema, Wild Bunch, Fidélité Pro-
ductions, in association with Rasta Films
Producers: José Ibañez, with Belen Atienza, Alvaro Augustin, Olivier Delbosc,
Marc Missionnier, Gaël Nouaille, and Vincent Maraval
Director: Emir Kusturica
Cinematographer: Rodrigo Pulpeiro Vega
Editor: Svetolik-Mića Zajć

Production Designer: Paula Álvarez Vaccaro
Music: Stribor Kusturica
Sound: Raul Martínez Avila
Cast: Diego Maradona, Emir Kusturica, Manu Chao, Stribor Kusturica
Language: English, Spanish, Italian, and Serbian
90 min.
Availability: Optimum Home Releasing (U.K.)

Music Videos

"Unza Unza Time" (No Smoking Orchestra, 2000)
"Rainin' in Paradize" (Manu Chao, 2007)

* * *

For a complete list of the awards received by Emir Kusturica, his acting roles, and the films and television programs about his work and persona, see the filmography in Giorgio Bertellini, *Emir Kusturica* (Milan: Il Castoro, 2011), 181–88.

Almaric, Jacques. "La croisade des bedeaux." *Libération*, October 25, 1995; accessed June 13, 2014. http://www.liberation.fr/evenement/1995/10/25/la-croisade-des-bedeaux_146085.

Andrić, Gordana. "Kusturica Quits Nature Park Post in Acrimony," *Balkan Insight*, March 11, 2013.

Antić, Marina. "Living in the Shadow of the Bridge: Ivo Andrić's *The Bridge on the Drina* and Western Imaginings of Bosnia." *Spaces of Identity* 3.3 (August 2003): 7–17.

Baecque, Antoine de. "Dans les entrailles du communisme." *Cahiers du Cinéma* 496 (November 1995): 38–42.

Bakhtin, Mikhail. "From Notes Made in 1970–1971." In *Speech Genres and Other Late Essays*, ed. Caryl Emerson and Michael Holquist, trans. Vern W. McGee, 132–58 Austin: University of Texas Press, 1986.

Bakić-Hayden, Milica. "Nesting Orientalisms: The Case of Former Yugoslavia." *Slavic Review* 54.4 (1995): 917–31.

Bertellini, Giorgio. *Emir Kusturica*. 2d revised and expanded ed. Milan: Il Castoro, 2011 [1996].

———, ed. *Emir Kusturica*. Rome: Dino Audino Editore, 1995.

Bianchin, Roberto. "La mia guerra di poeta a Sarajevo." *La Repubblica*, January 21, 1996, 29.

Bianchini, Stefano. *La questione jugoslava*. Florence: Giunti, 1996.

Binetruy, Pascal. "L'Ouest, du nouveau? Cinq Cinéastes européens face au desert Américain." *Positif* 588 (2010): 69–72.

Bjelić, Dušan I. "Global Aesthetics and Serbian Cinema in the 1990s." In *East European Cinemas*, ed. Anikó Imre, 103–19. London: Routledge, 2005.

Bjelić, Dušan I., and Obrad Savić, eds. *Balkan as Metaphor between Globalization and Fragmentation*. Cambridge: Massachusetts Institute of Technology Press, 2002.

Boni, Stefano, ed. "Emir Kusturica" (Special Issue). *Garage* 14 (1999).

Bouineau, Jean-Marc, ed. *Le Petit Livre de Emir Kusturica*. Garches: Spartorange, 1993.

Bourguignon, Thomas. "*Arizona Dream*: L'étoffe des rêves." *Positif* 383 (January 1993): 18–19.

Ceretto, Luisa, ed. "Conversazione con Emir Kusturica [Paris, October 6, 1998]." In "Emir Kusturica: Visioni gitane di un acrobata" (Special Issue), ed. Luisa Ceretto. *Quaderni del Lumière* 28 (December 1998): 17–27.

Cerović, Stanko. "Kusturica's Lies Awarded the Golden Palm in Cannes." *Monitor* (Podgorica), June 12, 1995, republished and expanded in *Bosnia Report* (London) 1 (1995): 10.

Chauville, Christophe. "*Super 8 Stories*, le magicien d'unza: rencontre avec Emir Kusturica." *Repérages* 23 (October 2001): 32–33.

Chevrie, Marc. "Un rêve éveillé: *Papa est en voyage d'affaires.*" *Cahiers du Cinéma* 376 (October 1985): 59–60.

Chiesi, Roberto. "*All the Invisible Children.*" *Cineforum* 46.453 (2006): 44–45.

Chion, Michel. "*Papa est en voyage d'affaires*, d'Emir Kusturica." *Cahiers du Cinéma* 373 (June 1985): 24.

Ciment, Michel. "Emir Kusturica: Les couleurs, la texture, l'espace, les sentiments." *Positif* 452 (October 1998): 19–23.

Codelli, Lorenzo. "De la colline de Kusturica. Le cinéma yougoslave aujourd'hui." *Positif* 296 (October 1985): 12.

———. "La capitulation du cinéma yougoslave (sur le 28e festival de Pula)." *Positif* 247 (October 1981): 57–59.

Comuzio, Ermanno. "*Underground.*" *Cineforum* 36.351 (January–February 1996): 52–55.

Cuadernos de filmoteca canaria. *Claroscuro balcánico: El cine de Emir Kusturica.* Las Palmas de Gran Canaria: Gobierno de Canarias, 2001.

Daković, Nevena. "Mother, Myth, and Cinema: Recent Yugoslav Cinema." *Film Criticism* 21.2 (Winter 1996–97): 40–49.

Daney, Serge. "*Papa est en voyage d'affaires.*" In *Ciné Journal 1981–1986*, ed. Serge Daney, 295–97. Paris: Cahiers du Cinéma, 1986.

De Bruyn, Olivier. "*Arizona Dream*: Emir au pays d'oncle Sam." *Positif* 383 (January 1993): 16–17.

De Gaetano, Domenico. "Una musica per matrimoni e funerali di Goran Bregović." In "Emir Kusturica" (Special Issue), ed. Stefano Boni *Garage* 14 (1999): 67–73.

Delgado, Jérôme. "Maradona par Kusturica." *Séquences* 268 (September–October 2010): 59.

De Marinis, Gualtiero. "*Otac na sluzbenom putu/Papa' e' in viaggio d'affari.*" *Cineforum* 245 (June–July 1985): 9–10.

De Vincenti, Giorgio, ed. *Iugoslavia: il Cinema dell'autogestione.* Venice: Marsilio/Quaderno no.12 of the Mostra Internazionale del Nuovo Cinema, 1982.

Dhennin, Matthieu. *Le lexique subjectif d'Emir Kusturica: Portrait d'un réalisateur.* Lausanne: Editions L'Age d'Homme, 2006.

Finkielkraut, Alain. "La propagande onirique de Emir Kusturica." *Liberation*, October 30, 1995, 7.

———. "L'imposture Kusturica." *Le Monde*, June 2, 1995, 28.

Forbes, Jill. "*When Father Was Away on Business.*" *Monthly Film Bulletin* 52.623 (December 1985): 383–84.

Fusco, Maria Pia. "Niente da farmi perdonare." *La Repubblica*, January 24, 1996, 33.

Gadamer, Hans Georg. *Truth and Method.* Ed. and trans. Garrett Barden and John Cumming. New York: Continuum, 1975.

Galt, Rosalind. *Redrawing the Map: The New European Cinema.* New York: Columbia University Press, 2005.

Garbarz, Franck. "Underground." *Positif* 417 (November 1995): 15–17.

Gili, Jean A. "Emir Kusturica: L'homme n'est pas un oiseau (*Le temps des gitans*)." *Positif* 345 (November 1989): 2–8.

———. "Promets-moi: la vache, l'Icône et la fiancée." *Positif* 564 (2008): 42.

———. "*Te souviens-tu de Dolly Bell?*" *Positif* 267 (May 1983): 75.

Glenny, Misha. "If You Are Not for Us." *Sight and Sound* 6.11 (November 1996): 10–13.

Gocić, Goran. *Notes from the Underground: The Cinema of Emir Kusturica.* London: Wallflower Press, 2001.

Gopnik, Adam. "Cinéma disputé." *New Yorker*, February 5, 1996, 32–37.

Gottardi, Michele. "Emir il giovane." *Segnocinema* 96 (1999): 7–8.

Goulding, Daniel J. *Liberated Cinema: The Yugoslav Experience.* 2d ed. Bloomington: Indiana University Press, 2009.

———, ed. *Post New Wave Cinema in the Soviet Union and Eastern Europe.* Bloomington: Indiana University Press, 1989.

Gourgouris, Stathis. "Hypnosis and Critique." In *Balkan as Metaphor between Globalization and Fragmentation,* ed. Dušan I. Bjelić and Obrad Savić, 323–50. Cambridge: Massachusetts Institute of Technology Press, 2002.

Graffy, Julian. "*Life Is a Miracle.*" *Sight and Sound* 15.4 (April 2005): 66.

Grmek Germani, Sergio, ed. *Onda Nera.* Trieste: Alpe Adria Cinema, 1998.

———, ed. *La meticcia di fuoco: Oltre il continente Balcani.* Venice: Biennale di Venezia, 2000.

Grünberg, Serge, and Emir Kusturica, eds. *Il était une fois. . . . Underground.* Paris: Cahiers du Cinéma, 1995.

Grzinić, Marina. "Neue Slowenische Kunst." In *Impossible Histories: Historical Avant-Gardes, Neo-Avant-Gardes, and Post-Avant-Gardes in Yugoslavia, 1918–1991,* ed. Dubravka Djurić and Miško Suvaković, 246–69. Cambridge: Massachusetts Institute of Technology Press, 2003.

Halpern, Dan. "The (Mis)Directions of Emir Kusturica." *New York Times Magazine,* May 8, 2005; accessed June 13, 2014, http://www.nytimes.com/2005/05/08/magazine/08EMIR.html?pagewanted=all&_r=0.

Handke, Peter. *A Journey to the Rivers: Justice for Serbia*. Trans. Scott Abbott. New York: Viking, 1997.

Hansen-Love, Mia. "Kusturica et son arche: Le vie est un miracle d'Emir Kusturica." *Cahiers du Cinéma* 590 (May 2004): 67–68.

Homer, Sean. "Nationalism, Ideology, and Balkan Cinema: Re-reading Kusturica's *Underground*." In *Did Somebody Say Ideology? Slavoj Žižek and Consequences*, ed. Fabio Vighi and Heiko Feldner, 237–48. Cambridge: Cambridge Scholars Press, 2007.

———. "Retrieving Emir Kusturica's *Underground* as a Critique of Ethnic Nationalism." *Jump Cut: A Review of Contemporary Media* 51 (Fall 2009); accessed April 28, 2014, http://www.ejumpcut.org/archive/jc51.2009/Kusterica/.

Horton, Andrew. "Cinematic Makeovers and Cultural Border Crossings: Kusturica's *Time of the Gypsies* and Coppola's *Godfather* and *Godfather II*." In *Play It Again, Sam: Retakes on Remakes*, ed. Andrew Horton and Stuart V. McDougal, 172–91. Berkeley: University of California Press, 1998.

———. "Filmmaking in the Middle: From Belgrade to Beverly Hills, a Cautionary Tale." In *Before the Wall Came Down: Soviet and East European Filmmakers Working in the West*, ed. Graham Petrie and Ruth Dwyer, 157–67. Lanham, Md.: University Press of America, 1990.

———. "From Satire to Sympathy in Yugoslav Film Comedy." *East European Quarterly* 20.1 (Spring 1986): 91–99.

———. "The New Serbo-Creationism." *American Film* 11.4 (January–February 1986): 24–30.

———. "Oedipus Unresolved: Covert and Overt Narrative Discourse in Emir Kusturica's *When Father Was Away on Business*." *Cinema Journal* 27.4 (Summer 1988): 64–81.

Horton, Andrew James. *The Celluloid Tinderbox: Yugoslav Screen Reflections of a Turbulent Decade*. Shropshire, U.K.: Central Europe Review, 2000; reprint, *Kino-Eye* 3.10 (September 2003); accessed April 28, 2014, http://www.kinoeye.org/03/10/celluloidtinderbox.php.

Imre, Anikó, ed. *East European Cinemas*. London: Routledge, 2005.

Iordanova, Dina. *Cinema of Flames: Balkan Film, Culture and the Media*. London: British Film Institute, 2002.

———. *Cinema of the Other Europe: The Industry and Artistry of East Central European Film*. London: Wallflower, 2003.

———. *Emir Kusturica*. London: British Film Institute, 2002.

———. "Kusturica's *Underground* (1995): Historical Allegory or Propaganda?" *Historical Journal of Film, Radio, and Television* 19.1 (1999): 69–86.

———. "Mimicry and Plagiarism." *Third Text* 22.3 (May 2008): 305–10.

———. "Welcome Pictures, Unwanted Bodies: Gypsy Representations in New Europe's Cinema." In *"Gypsies" in European Literature and Culture*, ed. Valentina Glajar and Domnica Radulescu, 235–40. London: Palgrave Macmillan, 2008.

———, ed. "Romanies and Cinematic Representation." Special Issue of *Framework: The Journal of Cinema and Media* 44.2 (Fall 2003).

Iordanova, Dina, Richard Taylor, Julian Graffy, and Nancy Wood, eds. *BFI Companion to Eastern European and Russian Cinema.* London: British Film Institute, 2000.

Janigro, Nicole. *L'esplosione delle Nazioni. Il caso jugoslavo.* Milan: Feltrinelli, 1993.

Jousse, Thierry. "Kusturica sur terre." *Cahiers du Cinéma* 493 (July–August 1995): 28–29.

Karahasan, Dževad. *Sarajevo: Exodus of a City.* Trans. Slobodan Drakulić. New York: Kodansha International, 1994.

Katsahnias, Iannis. "Freaks, Freaks. . . ." *Cahiers du Cinéma* 425 (November 1989): 34–37.

Krstić, Igor. "Representing Yugoslavia? Emir Kusturica's *Underground* and the Politics of Postmodern Cinematic Historiography." *Tijdschrift voor Mediageshiedens: Media en Orlog* (Amsterdam) 2.2 (December 1999): 138–59.

"Kusturica Quits after Featuring on Auditors' Black List." *Balkan Insight,* February 28, 2013.

Laura, Ernesto G., and Ljupka Lazić. *Il film Jugoslavo.* Lecce: Elle Edizioni, 1982.

Levi, Pavle. *Disintegration in Frames: Aesthetics and Ideology in the Yugoslav and Post-Yugoslav Cinema.* Stanford, Calif.: Stanford University Press, 2007.

Liehm, Antonín J., and Mira Liehm. *The Most Important Art: Soviet and Eastern European Film after 1945.* Berkeley: University of California Press, 1977.

Longinović, Tomislav Z. "Playing the Western Eye: Balkan Masculinity and Post-Yugoslav War Cinema." In *East European Cinemas,* ed. Anikó Imre, 35–47. New York: Routledge, 2005.

Lounas, Thierry. "Les dangers du traffic." *Cahiers du Cinéma* 528 (October 1998): 73–74.

Manchot, Pierre. "Emir Kusturica, compositeur et librettiste: Caractéristiques opératiques du film *La vie est un miracle.*" In *Musicologie et Cinéma,* ed. Pascal Pistone, 79–87. Paris: Universitè de Paris-Sorbonne/Observatoire Musical Français, 2006.

Manin, Giuseppina. "La svolta di Kusturica: addio cinema politico." *Corriere della Sera,* September 12, 1998, 37.

Maraldi, Antonio, ed. *Il cinema di Emir Kusturica.* Quaderno 26 of the Centro Cinema Citta' di Cesena, 1993.

Méjean, Jean-Max. *Emir Kusturica.* Rome: Gremese, 2007.

———. "Promets-moi." *Jeune Cinéma* 314 (2007): 66–67.

Mihelj, Sabina. "The Media and the Symbolic Geographies of Europe: The Case of Yugoslavia." In *We Europeans? Media, Representations, Identities,* ed. William Uricchio, 159–76. Bristol: Intellect Books, 2008.

Mr. Busy. "The Business." *Sight and Sound* 6.2 (February 1996): 51.

Muratović, Amir. "*Nevjeste dolaze*/Matić's Project Achieved by Kusturica." In *Alpe Adria Cinema: Incontri con il cinema dell'Europa Centro-Orientale, Catalogo X Edizione 1998–1999*, 423–26. Trieste: Alpe Adria Cinema, 1999.

Nave, Bernard. "Maradona par Kusturica." *Jeune Cinéma* 317–18 (2008): 128.

Nick, James. "A Royal Rumpus." *Sight and Sound* 18.7 (2008): 16–18.

Petrie, Graham, and Ruth Dwyer, ed. *Before the Wall Came Down: Soviet and East European Filmmakers Working in the West.* Lanham, Md.: University Press of America, 1990.

Petrović, Aleksandar. *Novi film.* Belgrade: Institut za film, 1971.

Ramet, Sabrina Petra. *Balkan Babel: The Disintegration of Yugoslavia from the Death of Tito to the Fall of Milosevic.* Boulder, Colo.: Westview Press, 2002.

Ravetto-Biagioli, Kriss. "Laughing into an Abyss: Cinema and Balkanization." In *A Companion to Eastern European Cinemas*, ed. Anikó Imre, 77–100. Malden, Mass.: Wiley-Blackwell, 2012.

———— (as Kriss Ravetto). "Mytho-Poetic Cinema: Cinemas of Disappearance." *ThirdText* 43 (Summer 1998): 43–57.

Rayns, Tony. "*Underground*: Il était une fois un pays." *Sight and Sound* 6.3 (March 1996): 53–54.

Regourd, Serge. "Alain Finkielkraut et Jdanov." *Le Monde*, June 9, 1995, 16.

Robiony, Simonetta. "La mia vita? Un azzardo." *La Stampa*, September 12, 1998, 25.

Rollet, Sylvie. "Filmer le désordre," *Positif* 417 (November 1995): 18–22.

————, ed. "*Papa Est en Voyage d'Affaires*: Emir Kusturica." *Avant-Scène Cinéma* (Special Issue) 447 (December 1995): 1–84.

Romney, Jonathan. "Slav Labour." *New Statesman* 12.554 (May 10, 1999): 34–35.

Roth-Bettoni, Didier, and Bernard Bénoliel. "Emir Kusturica" ["L'exil intérieur" and *Arizona Dream*: Sous le signe du poisson."]. *Le Mensuel du Cinéma* 2 (January 1993): 52–61.

Rouyer, Philippe. "*Chat noir, Chat blanc*—Le bon temps des gitans." *Positif* 452 (October 1998): 17–19.

Sidran, Adulah. *Romanzo Balcanico: il cinema, il teatro, la poesia, la Storia*, ed. Piero del Giudice. Reggio Emilia: Aliberti Editore, 2009.

Stoil, Michael J. *Balkan Cinema: Evolution after the Revolution.* Ann Arbor, Mich.: UMI Research Press, 1982.

————. *Cinema beyond the Danube: The Camera and Politics.* Metuchen, N.J.: Scarecrow Press, 1974.

Stefanoni, Lodovico. "Papà e' in viaggio d'affari." *Cineforum* 254 (May 1986): 59–62.

————. "*Ti ricordi di Dolly Bell?*" *Cineforum* 22.220 (December 1982): 67–72.

Stojanović, Dušan. *Velika avantura filma.* Belgrade, 1970.

Strazzari, Francesco. *Notte balcanica: Guerre, crimine, stati falliti alle soglie d'Europa.* Bologna: Il Mulino, 2008.

Sudar, Vlastimir. *A Portrait of the Artist as a Political Dissident: The Life and Work of Aleksandar Petrović.* Chicago: Intellect/University of Chicago Press, 2013.

Suvaković, Miško. "Conceptual Art." In *Impossible Histories: Historical Avant-Gardes, Neo-Avant-Gardes, and Post-Avant-Gardes in Yugoslavia, 1918–1991*, ed. Dubravka Djurić and Miško Suvaković, 210–45. Cambridge: Massachusetts Institute of Technology Press, 2003.

Teodorović, Dragan. *Emir Kusturica and the No Smoking Orchestra: 10 Godina*. Banja Luka: Radio-televizija Republike Srpske, 2011.

Thompson, Mark. *Forging War: The Media in Serbia, Croatia, and Bosnia-Hercegovina*. 2d ed. Bloomington: Indiana University Press, 1999.

Todorova, Maria. *Imagining the Balkans*. Oxford: Oxford University Press, 1997.

Tornabuoni, Lietta. "Non l'ho visto: Quant'è brutto." *La Stampa*, June 8, 1995, 2.

———. "Un'allegoria barocca per la ex-Jugoslavia." *La Stampa*, May 27, 1995, 17.

Toubiana, Serge. "Exclusion intrinsèque/L'effet 'Itinéris.'" *Cahiers du Cinéma* 493 (July–August 1995): 30–33.

Turan, Kenneth. "Sarajevan's Journey from Cinema Hero to 'Traitor.'" *Los Angeles Times*, October 6, 1997, F1.

Vecchi, Paolo. *Emir Kusturica*. Rome: Gremese, 1999.

Wolff, Larry. *Inventing Eastern Europe: The Map of Civilization on the Mind of the Enlightenment*. Stanford, Calif.: Stanford University Press, 1994.

Wrathall, John. "Chat noir, chat blanc." *Sight and Sound* 9.5 (May 1999): 41–42.

———. "Gypsy Time." *Sight and Sound* 7.12 (1997): 10–13.

Yarovskaya, Marianna. *"Underground." Film Quarterly* 51.2 (Winter 1997–98): 50–54.

Young, Deborah. *"All the Invisible Children." Variety* 150.4 (2005): 67.

Zeppenfeld, Axel. "Promets-moi." *Cahiers du Cinéma* 631 (February 2008): 44–45.

Ziegler, Fiona. *Debating Serbia: The Controversy over Emir Kusturica's film* Underground *and the Image of Serbia*. Geneva: Graduate Institute of International and Development Studies, 2009.

Žižek, Slavoj. "Multiculturalism, or, the Cultural Logic of Multinational Capitalism." *New Left Review* 225 (September–October 1997): 28–51.

———. *"Underground,* or Ethnic Cleansing as a Continuation of Poetry by Other Means." *InterCommunication* 18 (1996); accessed April 28, 2014, www.ntticc.or.jp/pub/ic_mag/ic018/intercity/zizek_E.html.

———. *The Plague of Fantasies*. London: Verso, 1997.

Zorzoli, Barbara. "Emir Kusturica e la No Smoking Orchestra." *Colonne Sonore* 3.15 (November–December 2005): 27–28.

Selected Writings by Emir Kusturica (in chronological order)

"L'acacia de Sarajevo." *Libération*, October 21, 1991, 5.

"Europe, ma ville flambe!" *Le Monde*, April 24, 1992, 4.

"Une profession de foi." In *Le petit livre de Emir Kusturica*, ed. Jean-Marc Bouineau, trans. Svetlana Novak, 16–38. Garches: Spartorange, 1993.

"L'incendie des feux nationalistes." *Positif* 384 (February 1993): 50–51.

"Sguardo dai tetti di Sarajevo." *Il Manifesto*, October 1, 1993.

"Bosnia, non vincera' nessuno." *Il Manifesto*, December 30, 1993.

"Mon imposture." *Le Monde*, October 26, 1995, 13.

"*Underground*: Souvenirs de bord." *Cahiers du Cinéma* 496 (November 1995): 42–44; republished as "Souvenirs de bord" in *Il était une fois . . . Underground*, ed. Serge Grünberg and Emir Kusturica, 11–17. Paris: Cahiers du Cinéma/ CiBY 2000, 1995.

"En bas et en haut, en haut et en bas—Coup de foudre en deuxième coup d'oeil." Trans. Svetlana Novak. *Positif* 417 (November 1995): 29–30 (originally appeared in *Svijet* (Sarajevo) in 1982).

"Vojo Stanić: An Acrobatic Artist." In *Vojo Stanić: Sailing on Dreams*, ed. Robert Boyers, 42–51. New York: Palgrave Macmillan, 2007.

Smrt je neprovjerena glasina (Death is an unverified rumor). Belgrade: Novosti, 2010; French trans., Vladimir André Céjovic and Anne Renoue: *Où suis-je dans cette histoire?* (Where am I in this story?) Paris: Jean-Claude Lattès, 2011; Italian trans., Alice Parmeggiani: *Dove sono in questa storia*. Milan: Feltrinelli, 2011.

Sto jada (Hundred of troubles). Belgrade: Novosti, 2013.

Selected Interviews (in chronological order)

"Povogar x Emirjen Kusturico, režiserjem filma 'Se spominiaš Dolly Bell?'" *Ekran* (Ljubljana) 6.6–7 (1981). Italian trans. from the Slovenian: Aleš Doktarić amd Igor Prinčić, "Intervista con Emir Kusturica." In *Iugoslavia: Il Cinema dell'Autogestione*, ed. Giorgio De Vincenti, 353–59. Venice: Marsilio, 1982.

Laura, Ernesto G., and Ljupka Lazić. "Emir Kusturica." In *Il film jugoslavo*, ed. Laura-Lazić, 100–101. Lecce: Elle edizioni, 1982.

Parra, Daniéle, and Robert Grélier. "Extrait d'un entretien avec Emir Kusturica." *Revue du Cinéma* 407 (July–August 1985): 38–39.

Codelli, Lorenzo. "Entretien avec Emir Kusturica." *Positif* 296 (October 1985): 12–22.

Jouando, Martine, and Desan Bogdanović. "Interview with Emir Kusturica." Pressbook for *When Father Was Away on Business* (1986).

Crespi, Alberto. "Intervista. Emir Kusturica." *Cineforum* 285 (June 1989): 20–22.

Ciment, Michel, and Lorenzo Codelli. "Entretien avec Emir Kusturica." *Positif* 345 (November 1989): 18–22.

Katsahnias, Iannis. "*Le temps des gitans*: Entre ciel et terre. Propos de Emir Kusturica," *Cahiers du Cinéma* 425 (November 1989): 38.

Beauchamp, Michel, and Gérard Grugeau. "La Quête du pays incertain: En-tretien avec Emir Kusturica." *24 Images* (Canada) 49 (Summer 1990): 56–61.

Ostria, Vincent, and Thierry Jousse. "Entretien avec Emir Kusturica." *Cahiers du Cinéma* 455–456 (May 1992): 60–63, 65.

Binder, David. "A Bosnian Movie-Maker Laments the Death of the Yugoslav Nation." *New York Times*, October 25, 1992, S4, 7.

Ciment, Michel. "Entretien avec Emir Kusturica: Comment 'voler' le film." *Positif* 383 (January 1993): 20–25.

Elhem, Philippe. "Entretien avec Emir Kusturica/Le vol du flétan." *24 Images* (Canada) 66 (April–May 1993): 19–23.

Martiradonna, Sabino, and Stefano Ottaviano. "L'esilio interiore: Intervista con Emir Kusturica." *Ti ricordi di Sarajevo?* Exhibition Catalog. Rome: n.p., 1993.

Grünberg, Serge. "Comment Kusturica déplaça les montagnes." *Cahiers du Cinéma* 492 (June 1995): 66–68.

Jousse, Thierry, and Serge Grünberg. "Propos de Emir Kusturica." *Cahiers du Cinéma* 492 (June 1995): 69–71.

Grünberg, Serge. "A propos d'*Underground*, 36 questions à Emir Kusturica." In *Il était une fois. . . . Underground*, ed. Serge Grünberg and Emir Kusturica. Paris: Cahiers du Cinéma, 1995. 19–39.

Jousse, Thierry. "Kusturica sur terre." *Cahiers du Cinéma* 493 (July–August 1995): 28–29.

Nepoti, Roberto. "Emir Kusturica: 'Da Milošević non ho preso soldi.'" *La Repubblica*, October 1, 1995, 30.

Autera, Leonardo. "Kusturica: 'I serbi sono delle vittime.'" *Corriere della Sera*, October 1, 1995, 9.

Ciment, Michel. "Entretien avec Kusturica." *Positif* 417 (November 1995): 22–30.

Pflaum, H. G. "In der Falle der Geschichte." *Süddeutsche Zeitung*, November 23, 1995, 16.

Ciment, Michel. "Les couleurs, la texture, l'espace, les sentiments profonds. . . ." *Positif* 452 (August 1998): 19–23.

Gibbons, Fiachra. "He Duels, He Brawls, He Helps Cows to Give Birth . . . and He Makes Films." *The Guardian*, April 23, 1999; accessed June 13, 2014, http://www.theguardian.com/film/1999/apr/23/features2.

Rumiz, Paolo. "Né con voi, né con Milosevic." *La Repubblica*, June 22, 1999, 28.

Fuller, Graham. "The Director They Couldn't Quash: Emir Kusturica." *Interview* 29.9 (September 1, 1999): 68–71.

Feinstein, Howard. "Enough Retirement! Kusturica Returns to Gypsy Life." *New York Times*, September 5, 1999, S2, 7, 20.

Kaufman, Anthony. "Momentum and Emotion, Emir Kusturica's *Black Cat, White Cat*." *IndieWire*, September 9, 1999; accessed June 13, 2014, http://www.indiewire.com/article/interview_momentum_and_emotion_emir_kusturicas_black_cat_white_cat.

Favetto, Gian Luca. "L'occhio gitano. Tutti gli sguardi di Emir Kusturica." *La Repubblica*, February 2, 2001, 10.

"Emir Kusturica en son village." *L'Humanitè*, September 9, 2005.

Halpern, Dan. "The Shows: The Many Lives of Emir Kusturica." *New York Times*, May 12, 2005; accessed June 13, 2014, http://www.nytimes.com/2005/05/11/arts/11iht-kustu.html?pagewanted=all.

"Kusturica célèbre l'amour et l'air pur." *Le Figaro*, January 29, 2008; accessed June 13, 2014, http://www.lefigaro.fr/cinema/2008/01/29/03002-20080129 ARTFIG00519-kusturica-celebre-l-amour-et-l-air-pur.php.

"Maradona dribla zvezde [Maradona's Dribbling with Stars]." *Večernje Novosti*, April 23, 2008.

"Do You Remember Dolly Bell?" In *My First Movie/Take Two: Ten Celebrated Directors Talk about Their First Film*, ed. Stephen Lowenstein, 162–81. New York: Pantheon, 2008.

"Naši geni na Ćupriji [Our Genes on the Bridge]." *Večernje Novosti*, March 21, 2009.

"Johnny Believed in My Madness." *Večernje Novosti*, July 26, 2009.

Adeline Fleury. "Kusturica: 'Mon village est un laboratoire culturel.'" *Le Journal du Dimanche* April 17, 2011.

Adžović, Ljubica, 49, 52, 55, 102
All the Invisible Children. See *Blue Gypsy*
American cinema. *See* Hollywood
Andrić, Ivo, 15, 21–22, 39, 95, 145–48
Angelopoulos, Theo, 63–79
Arizona Dream, 5, 21, 58, 63–72, 145, 147
auteur, 10–13, 18, 20, 33, 60, 125, 145
awards, 6, 22–23, 36, 48, 63, 78, 125, 134–35, 149n13. *See also* festivals

Babaja, Ante, 17–18
Balkanism (vedi anche Balkan excess), 4–5, 10–11, 62, 92–93, 97, 112, 117–18, 124, 132, 136, 140, 143, 146–48, 149n1. *See also* primitivism
Belgrade, 7, 9, 18, 23, 36, 38, 52, 74–77, 81–83, 89, 93, 97, 98, 100, 109, 114, 115, 124, 129, 137, 138
Bijelo Dugme (White Button), 7, 61–62. *See also* Bregović, Goran
bildungsroman, 25, 28, 132
Bjelić, Dušan I., 149n1
Black Cat, White Cat, 22, 36, 52, 96, 100–107, 111
Black or Novi cinema, 3, 12, 17–18
Blagojević, Ljiljana, 25, 129
Blue Gypsy (segment of *All the Invisible Children*), 126–27, 132
Bosch, Hieronymous, 60, 144
Bosnia and Bosnian: characters, 8, 14, 24–25, 76, 113, 121, 144; cinema and television, 3, 12, 17, 20, 25, 80, 149n12;

geography and culture, 3, 6–9, 13, 32, 34, 40, 91, 110, 114, 116, 119, 124, 128; Kusturica as Bosnian, 19, 23, 79, 92–93, 97, 133; music, 7, 8, 40–41, 61, 96, 110, 147; wars, 3–4, 9, 40, 81, 91, 113–14, 145. *See also* New Primitives; Sidran, Abdulah
Bregović, Goran, 7, 61–62, 70, 95–97, 103. *See also* Bijelo Dugme
Bresson, Robert, 133
Brides Are Coming, The, 20–22, 123
Brouwer, Adriaen, 58
Bruegel the Elder, Pieter, 60
Buffet Titanic, 21–22, 24, 127
Bulajić, Veljko, 17, 85
Buñuel, Luis, 133

Cannes film festival, 4, 17, 36, 48, 63, 78, 79, 81, 82, 91, 125, 135, 136, 147
Cerović, Stanko, 81–82, 91
Chagall, Marc, 13, 47, 77, 88, 111
Chaplin, Charlie, 10, 14, 50–51, 59, 88
communism, 10, 28, 29–31, 79, 82, 83, 92, 152, 153
Czech cinema, 1, 12, 19, 32, 39, 48, 152

death: as filmic event, 26, 29, 40, 51, 60, 64–65, 69, 86, 102, 105–6, 113, 115, 120; as poetic recurrence, 13, 54, 60, 64–65, 67, 72, 89, 93, 113–15, 120–21, 123, 127, 144, 147. *See also* suicide
Death is an unverified rumor (Smrt je neprovjerena glasina), 13–15, 95, 99, 145

De Sica, Vittorio, 85, 100
Djordjević, Mladomir "Purisa," 17–18
documentary film, 18, 25, 5, 100, 109,
  114, 124, 136, 137, 143, 153
Do You Remember Dolly Bell?, 5, 8–9,
  19, 21, 23, 25–30, 32–33, 40, 45, 47,
  56, 89, 115, 122, 127, 129, 132, 140,
  142, 145
Dragojević, Srdjan, 79, 107
dreams, 5, 13, 15, 22–25, 28, 29, 33, 47,
  50, 54–58, 60, 64–69, 71–73, 99, 110,
  118, 120, 132, 141, 144, 147
Drvengrad (Wooden Village). *See* Küstendorf

Ederlezi (St. George's Day), 61–62
editing, 103, 104, 122, 152

FAMU (Filmová a televizní fakulta Akad-
  emie múzických umění; Film and TV
  School, Prague), 3, 11, 16–19, 21, 48,
  79, 152
Fellini, Federico, 88, 107, 110, 121, 131,
  135, 151
festivals, 4, 6, 14, 15–16, 19, 22, 36, 48,
  63–64, 79, 108, 124–26, 135, 149, 154.
  See also awards
Filač, Vilko, 11, 21, 33, 95
financing, 16, 23, 52, 73, 74, 108, 114,
  126, 128
Finkielkraut, Alain, 79–80, 82
Ford, John, 59
Forman, Miloš, 16, 33, 36, 39, 44, 53, 147

Gatlif, Tony, 63, 125
Gocić, Goran, 10–11
Gorica, 13–14, 48, 52. *See also* Sarajevo
Guernica, 19, 22, 146
Gypsies, 49, 51–54 61, 63, 103–4, 144;
  culture and perceptions of, 57, 59, 63,
  100, 102, 103–4, 107, 112, 126, 146; as
  film characters, 56–57, 62–63, 89–90,
  95–96, 101, 103–4, 107, 144; music,
  7, 9, 22–23, 61–62, 75–76, 78, 83, 87,
  89–90, 95–96, 99, 100, 102–3, 106–7,
  110–12, 114, 119–20, 150n20, 153. See
  also *Blue Gypsy*; Gatlif, Tony

Handke, Peter, 82, 150n28, 153
Hitchcock, Alfred, 14
Hladnik, Bostjian, 17–18
Hollywood, 3, 63, 64, 66, 71, 147
humor, 1, 3, 6, 12, 13, 36–38, 72, 107,
  121, 129, 131, 136, 141, 143, 148

Iordanova, Dina, 10–11, 92, 95. 149n6,
  149n7, 150n21, 150n36

Karajlić, Dr. Nele, 9, 103, 109–13, 115
Karanović, Mirjana, 34, 33, 43–44, 75,
  119, 122
Karanović, Srđan, 16
Keaton, Buster, 131
Kenović, Ademir, 21
Kljaković, Miljen "Kreka, 74, 95, 100
Komuna Film, 98, 102, 149n2
Kovačević, Dušan, 20, 36, 73–74, 96
Krvavac, Hajrudin "Šiba," 9, 14–16, 21,
  149n12
Küstendorf (Coastal Village), 6, 12, 124–
  25, 131, 133, 145–46
Kusturica, Maja, 108, 114, 149n2
Kusturica, Stribor, 112, 119, 126, 129,
  132

Laibach, 10, 94
Lang, Fritz, 84
Leone, Sergio, 110, 121, 137, 140
Levi, Pavle, 8, 91, 149n5, 150n31
levitation, 54, 58–60, 67, 89, 121, 144
Lévy, Bernard-Henri, 79
Life Is a Miracle, 96, 100, 114–25, 128,
  131–32, 134, 145

Makavejev, Dušan, 18, 32, 39, 143
Manojlović, Miki, 34, 44, 49, 75, 77, 102,
  103, 129
Maradona, Diego Armando, 97–98,
  136–42, 154
Maradona by Kusturica, 6, 125, 136–42,
  145, 154. *See also* Maradona, Diego
  Armando
Marković, Boban, 96
Marković, Goran, 16, 18
Mayakovsky, Vladimir, 66

Mihić, Gordan, 36, 52, 100
Milosević, Slobodan, 4, 19, 74, 82, 91, 96
Mimica, Vatroslav, 18
music, 3, 11, 21, 27, 29–30, 32, 53, 69,
    78, 83, 87, 89, 94, 111, 120–22, 126,
    137, 141, 143, 154; as authorship, 6–10,
    12–13, 22–23, 95–97, 102–3, 108–10,
    117–18, 124–25, 136, 145, 154; from
    the Balkans, 3, 6–7, 9, 12–13, 25, 40,
    60–63, 80, 96–97, 99, 102–3, 145; Bul-
    garia, 62, 70, 154; Hungary, 7, 96, 115,
    119; Macedonia, 7, 61, 70, 96; Mexico,
    34, 40, 70, 112; Romania, 62. *See also*
    Bregović, Goran; Gypsies; music; New
    Primitives; *sevdah*

Negulescu, Jean, 14
Neue Slowenische Kunst, 9–10, 94,
    150n40
New Primitives, 7–9, 12, 94, 154. *See also*
    surrealists
No Smoking Orchestra (Zabranjeno
    Pušenje) 7–9, 48, 53, 96, 103, 108–9,
    111, 113–15, 125, 129, 135, 137
Novi cinema, 3, 12, 17–18

Paskaljević, Goran, 16, 18, 49, 52, 57,
    62, 100
Peckinpah, Sam, 140
Penn, Arthur, 72
Petrović, Aleksandar, 17–19, 49, 62
Polanski, Roman, 72
Popov, Stole, 36
Prague, 3, 11–13, 16–17, 25, 74, 152
Prague Group, 17–19, 49
primitivism, 4–5, 8, 25, 145. *See also*
    Balkanism
Promise Me This, 6, 25, 125–26, 128–36,
    145

Rasta International Film Production, 108,
    128, 149n2

Sarajevo: as biographical reference, 4,
    7–8, 11, 13, 15–16, 20, 23, 25–26, 28,
    48, 53, 66–67, 73–74, 82, 91, 96, 124,
    140–41, 145, 154; as critical reference,

32–33, 41, 47–48, 91; as film setting
    and poetic influence, 7–9, 11–13, 20,
    23–28, 29–35, 47–48, 66–67, 80, 91,
    93–94, 97, 113, 140–41, 147; music and
    culture from, 7–9, 11, 13, 26–28, 61,
    70, 93–94, 113
self-references, 3, 10, 88–89, 98, 103, 148
sevdah and *sevdalinka*, 7, 40, 48, 62, 103.
    See also music
Seven Days in the Life of a Bird, 98–99
Sidran, Abdulah, 26–27, 33–34, 36, 91,
    149, 156
slapstick, 3, 6, 50, 97, 100, 106, 110, 118,
    122, 126, 128, 131, 136, 148. *See also*
    Chaplin, Charlie; Keaton, Buster
šljivovica, 37, 90
soccer, 7, 14, 27, 35, 37, 40–42, 52, 61,
    95, 98, 113, 115, 123, 127, 130, 136–39,
    141–42, 153
South American Literature, 60, 66, 104,
    137, 142
spaghetti western film, 9, 107. *See also*
    Leone, Sergio
Štimac, Slavko, 19, 23–24, 104, 115–16,
    118, 122
suicide, 35, 50, 57–58, 64, 72–73, 78, 89,
    91, 115, 116, 144
Super 8 Stories, 6, 7, 97, 100, 108–13, 145
surrealists, 8–10, 110. *See also* New
    Primitives

Tarkovsky, Andrey, 47, 59, 60, 72, 88,
    133, 135
television, 3, 8, 20, 22–23, 52–53, 73, 82,
    86, 96, 99, 100, 115, 117, 125, 142, 143,
    149n12
This Is Walter (*Das ist Walter*), 9. *See
    also* Krvavac, Hajrudin
Time of the Gypsies, 5, 7, 34, 36, 48,
    50–59, 61, 71, 72, 74, 78, 89, 98, 100,
    102, 125, 126, 132, 145, 152
Tito (Marshall Josip Broz): death of, 8,
    35, 38, 93, 109, 113; as film reference,
    28, 34–35, 39, 42, 44, 45, 83, 85–86,
    117; as historical figure, 13, 14, 18, 28,
    34, 35–39, 42, 47, 74, 77, 86–87, 92–93,
    109, 114

Todorova, Maria, 148, 149n1
turkeys, 49–53, 56–58, 60, 69, 71, 127,
129, 132, 144

Underground, 5, 7, 10, 12, 20–22, 24, 33,
43, 46, 58, 73–91, 100, 103–4, 107, 109,
114, 120, 121–23, 135, 143–47; controversy over, 4, 61, 91–97, 117
unmodernity and untimeliness, 3–5, 7, 9,
28, 47, 53, 63, 92, 95, 124, 145–46. *See
also* Balkanism

Vigo, Jean, 14, 77, 88, 131
Vukotić, Dušan, 18

Wajda, Andrzej, 39, 89
Walter Defends Sarajevo (Valter brani
Sarajevo), 9, 14
When Father Was Away on Business, 5,

32, 34, 36, 39, 44–48, 56, 70, 72, 75,
103, 112, 149n13

Yugoslavia: as film and poetic reference,
5, 8, 23, 32, 35, 41, 49, 86, 89–90,
98–99, 103–4, 107–8, 109, 112–15, 117,
134, 143, 146; film culture in, 7, 16, 22,
32, 49, 52–53, 61–62, 75–78, 107–8; as
nation, 4–5, 7–8, 12, 15–17, 22–23, 27,
31–32, 34–35, 38–39, 51–53, 66, 77–78,
94, 112, 143, 146; as seen from abroad,
27, 32, 34–35, 75, 92, 109; Yugoslav
press and media, 17, 34, 38–39, 61, 108

Zabranjeno Pušenje. *See* No Smoking
Orchestra
Zafranović, Lordan, 17, 18
Zagreb School, 18, 43
Zizek, Slavoj, 92, 94–95, 150n34

Giorgio Bertellini is an associate professor in the departments of Screen Arts and Cultures, and Romance Languages and Literatures, at the University of Michigan. He is the author of the award-winning *Italy in Early American Cinema: Race, Landscape, and the Picturesque*.

Books in the series Contemporary
Film Directors

Nelson Pereira dos Santos
Darlene J. Sadlier

Abbas Kiarostami
Mehrnaz Saeed-Vafa and Jonathan
Rosenbaum

Joel and Ethan Coen
R. Barton Palmer

Claire Denis
Judith Mayne

Wong Kar-wai
Peter Brunette

Edward Yang
John Anderson

Pedro Almodóvar
Marvin D'Lugo

Chris Marker
Nora Alter

Abel Ferrara
Nicole Brenez, translated by
Adrian Martin

Jane Campion
Kathleen McHugh

Jim Jarmusch
Juan Suárez

Roman Polanski
James Morrison

Manoel de Oliveira
John Randal Johnson

Neil Jordan
Maria Pramaggiore

Paul Schrader
George Kouvaros

Jean-Pierre Jeunet
Elizabeth Ezra

Terrence Malick
Lloyd Michaels

Sally Potter
Catherine Fowler

Atom Egoyan
Emma Wilson

Albert Maysles
Joe McElhaney

Jerry Lewis
Chris Fujiwara

Jean-Pierre and Luc Dardenne
Joseph Mai

Michael Haneke
Peter Brunette

Alejandro González Iñárritu
Celestino Deleyto and Maria del
Mar Azcona

Lars von Trier
Linda Badley

Hal Hartley
Mark L. Berrettini

François Ozon
Thibaut Schilt

Steven Soderbergh
Aaron Baker

Mike Leigh
Sean O'Sullivan

D.A. Pennebaker
Keith Beattie

Jacques Rivette
Mary M. Wiles

Kim Ki-duk
Hye Seung Chung

Philip Kaufman
Annette Insdorf

Richard Linklater
David T. Johnson

David Lynch
Justus Nieland

John Sayles
David R. Shumway

Dario Argento
L. Andrew Cooper

Todd Haynes
Rob White

Christian Petzold
Jaimey Fisher

Spike Lee
Todd McGowan

Terence Davies
Michael Koresky

Francis Ford Coppola
Jeff Menne

Emir Kusturica
Giorgio Bertellini

The University of Illinois Press
is a founding member of the
Association of American University Presses.

———————————————————

Composed in 10/13 New Caledonia
with Helvetica Neue display
by Lisa Connery
at the University of Illinois Press
Manufactured by Sheridan Books, Inc.

University of Illinois Press
1325 South Oak Street
Champaign, IL 61820-6903
www.press.uillinois.edu